BOWER

Also by Dan Robson

Killer: My Life in Hockey

(with Doug Gilmour)

Change Up: How to Make the Great Game of Baseball Even Better

(with Buck Martinez)

Quinn: The Life of a Hockey Legend

The Crazy Game: How I Survived in the Crease and Beyond

(with Clint Malarchuk)

BOWER

A LEGENDARY LIFE

DAN ROBSON

HarperCollins*PublishersLtd*

Bower

Copyright © 2018 by Dan Robson.
All rights reserved.

Published by HarperCollins Publishers Ltd

First edition

No part of this book may be used or reproduced in any manner
whatsoever without the prior written permission of the publisher,
except in the case of brief quotations embodied in reviews.

HarperCollins books may be purchased for educational, business,
or sales promotional use through our Special Markets Department.

HarperCollins Publishers Ltd
Bay Adelaide Centre, East Tower
22 Adelaide Street West, 41st Floor
Toronto, Ontario, Canada
M5H 4E3

www.harpercollins.ca

Library and Archives Canada Cataloguing in Publication
information is available upon request.

ISBN 978-1-4434-5726-2

Printed and bound in the United States of America
LSC/H   1 2 3 4 5 6 7 8 9 10

For the Bower family—Nancy, Cindy, Barb and John Jr.—
with respect and admiration.

And for Jayme Poisson, who amazes and inspires me every day.

CONTENTS

BOWER

PROLOGUE
LEDGERS IN THE CLOSET

LONG BEFORE HIS LIFE BECAME LEGEND, THE BOY'S NAME WAS forgotten. Reverend Napoleon J. Gilbert scrawled it in the baptismal records of Sacred Heart Cathedral in Prince Albert—a small city set on the North Saskatchewan River, where the province's prairies meet its pines. It was the 10th baptism recorded that year. The priest's pencilled cursive was hastily scribbled. In the margin of the 71st page, in the 10th volume, Napoleon wrote—and misspelled—the child's name: "Kizkain, John."

That day, the 27th of February in 1925, James Kiszkan and Elizabeth Jacobson had carried their sixth surviving child, their only son, through the arching red-brick façade of Sacred Heart Cathedral. They presented the three-month-old infant to the Church, dedicating him to the Catholic faith. Having immigrated from Eastern Europe and focused their best efforts on learning

English, neither parent spoke French. Regardless, the reverend recorded the baptism in his preferred language. The child, he wrote, had been born "le huit Novembre, 1924."

The entry was just one of thousands of church records, inside dozens of volumes of leather-bound ledgers, that sat in the back of a clerical closet at Sacred Heart for nearly a century. It was the earliest and most definitive record of the truth behind a mystery that would later baffle sportswriters and league officials for decades. But the record and the truth stayed hidden in Prince Albert, along with so much of the boy's past, untouched among the stacks in Sacred Heart.

As the boy grew up, he'd repeatedly change the story of his origin, twisting and turning the truth until even he wasn't quite certain of the line between fact and fiction. In fact, the fiction became inseparable from his identity. Fibs born of simple practicality or a desire for privacy—or sometimes just for mischief—became part of his mystique, while the forgotten boy became one of the most beloved figures in hockey history. But he became much more than that too. To many he was an unmatched athlete—a toothless, scar-faced conqueror of time and nature. Famous for those daring poke checks and dazzling saves; for the Vezinas and the four Stanley Cup parades; for the wonder of his ageless ability, as the game's oldest goalie and still a star. In later years, he became a steadfast, happy reminder of past glory for a downtrodden franchise and their many long-suffering fans. And to those who were closest, he became a faithful friend, a lovestruck husband, a tender father and a doting grandpa. As he became a legend, the boy also became a special kind of man.

That boy's long journey began just beyond the doors of Sacred Heart Cathedral, around the corner at 526 Sixteenth Street West, where his family's small bungalow, its unpainted shingles faded grey, once stood. The house is long gone, replaced by a store that sells drug paraphernalia. But if you stand in the parking lot and look around, you can still see much of the world he explored beyond those doors. The barren field across the street leads to the same tracks that once carried lager from the old Molson Brewery, which still stands there today. You can picture a game of shinny on frigid winter days on the ice pad the brewery built each year, or a game of sandlot baseball by the tracks on warm summer afternoons. At the west end of the road, the old nurses quarters still stand next to where the hospital the boy was born in used to be. You can follow the streets, with a couple of turns, to find the way to Sacred Heart, where his family wore their best outfits once a week. And across the road, where a modern high school now stands, you can imagine the two-storey brick school with a small bell tower, where he used to daydream at St. Paul's middle school. The army barracks where the boy would lie about his age, hoping to go to war, still sit on the east edge of town. But the Minto hockey arena downtown—where his unusual talent gave him his first real opportunity to become something more than he thought he could be—burned to the ground long ago. It's now a parking lot.

Much of Prince Albert today traces the city as it was then, although parts have crumbled and changed with time. But pieces of the boy's life are everywhere. Parts that made it into his legend, and fragments he left behind. His story is similar to many just like him, the child of immigrants in a new land, searching for a better life. The beginning is almost identical to that of the other boys and girls who called Prince Albert home. They grew up through the Great Depression, watching parents and siblings struggle to survive in an uncertain world. There was little time for dreaming through those harsh years, running towards the second global war in a quarter-century. The Stanley Cup was an unimportant fairy tale, told over scratchy airwaves on cold Saturday nights. But in some imaginations, those faraway heroes came to life as young players traced their paths along iced-over rivers and ponds. They were Charlie Conachers, Eddie Shores, Busher Jacksons and Tiny Thompsons. They used sticks and pucks made of whatever twigs and frozen droppings they could find. And they played through the blowing snow, in temperatures that often dropped to 50 below. It was cold and harsh—and unlikely to lead them far from life's hard realities. But it was what their dreams were made of. Although few would ever discover where those dreams could lead, they'd find some brief respite in the carefree rush of their winter game. And that was how the story of Johnny Kiszkan began—a boy on ice, slipping in his boots as he chased frozen horse dung against the prairie wind, having the time of his life.

PART

ONE

01

BRANCHES

DOWN IN THE BASEMENT OF AN OLD FIREHOUSE AT THE END of Central Avenue, on the edge of the North Saskatchewan River, are stacks of books and maps that tell the untold story of how it all began. Ken Guedo, a retired volunteer with the Prince Albert Historical Society, looks through a folder of poster-sized maps that divide the land surrounding the small city in central Saskatchewan into a grid. Guedo, in his 70s, is one of many volunteers who proudly preserve and share the history of their hometown. They are an oracle of Prince Albert knowledge. He can show you how things are now and paint a picture of how they once were: the empty parking lot that was once the magnificent Minto hockey arena, where thousands flocked each week . . . the Burger King where the massive Pat Burns Meat Company building once stood . . . the old army barracks, where Prince Albert boys signed up for war.

Guedo scans through the grids page by page, each marked by a hand-printed name. The Cummins Rural Directory Map shows the names of the people who owned homesteads in the rural reaches of Saskatchewan around the time of the First World War. He runs his finger across the page until he comes across the name he's looking for—at homestead land location NW 12-50-25 W2. "There he is!" Guedo says. "Dmytro Kiszkan." He flips through a binder with photocopy prints of other maps, showing the area cut off from the larger one he'd been scanning. He finds a map that appears to be an extension of the original. The grids match up. And with the pages side by side, two squares away—two real-life miles—is the other name he's hunting for: Jacobchuk.

"Who knows if they met out there," Guedo says. "I don't know. But there must be some sort of connection."

The old homestead documents offer a glimpse into how Johnny Kiszkan's world came to be. Dmytro Kiszkan was just 18 years old when he left behind life as a peasant farmer, working land he didn't own, to chase the promise of new opportunities overseas. He was from a rural community known as Sniatyn, on the northeastern edge of what was the Austrian Empire, in the region of Galicia— now the western edge of Ukraine. Although he was unable to speak, read or write in English, Dmytro believed his life prospects were better across the ocean than in his fractured homeland, which would soon be engulfed in humanity's greatest war.

Dmytro journeyed to the port city of Rotterdam in the Netherlands with his 14-year-old sister, Marya. On July 9, 1909, they boarded the SS *Noordam* and travelled across the Atlantic in steerage. They were the only passengers on the ship's manifest who hadn't listed themselves as Russian. Dmytro was listed as single. His profession was recorded as farm labourer, and it was noted that he was unable to read or write. When they arrived at Ellis Island in New York, Dmytro and his sister set out for Boston, where at least one of his three brothers had already settled.

It's not entirely clear why Dmytro decided to move to Canada—but two years later, on December 14, 1911, he applied for a homestead in rural Saskatchewan. It was an area where many Ukrainian immigrants, skilled at farming, settled at the time. In fact, the promise of the prairies was luring people at a rapid pace. The population of Saskatchewan would jump from a little more than 90,000 people in 1901 to more than half a million in 1911. The Dominion Lands Act of 1872 was intended to settle the vast, fertile land of the Canadian prairies. The Canadian government would grant a 160-acre plot of land to any settler able to pay a $10 entry fee, build a house and barn, and break and crop 30 acres of land over a three-year period.

Dmytro was young and single, with farming experience, trying to carve out a life in the wilderness of a foreign world. He was an ideal homesteader. After submitting a sworn statement explaining how the homestead duties had been completed, he'd be granted a title to the land and would become a naturalized British subject. He described himself in the application as a labourer, with no kin—and signed his name with an X.

Surrounded by stunning forests, Prince Albert had long been a region that relied heavily on logging, providing lumber to the treeless prairies beneath it. But through the early 1900s there was a surge in demand for homesteads in the area. To keep up with the demand, the government opened up much of the land that had already been extensively logged above the North Saskatchewan River to homesteading. The Prince Albert Board of Trade marketed the region as a place of incredible opportunity for people interested in mixed farming in a forested landscape with fertile land. It was described as a place where the overhead costs of building and maintaining a farm were much cheaper than in the open plains of the south, because so many natural resources were already available. It was also, in many ways, a more appealing place to live—not only because of the beautiful terrain but also because it was arguably safer. The prairies were prone to deadly blizzards, including a historically vicious one that took an enormous toll on human and animal life in the winter of 1906–07. A series of storms caused massive delays of food and fuel deliveries, leaving many people in the open plains hungry and without coal to heat their homes.

Between 1906 and the start of the First World War, more than 15,000 homestead claims were filed at the Prince Albert Land Office. The most sought fertile land was farther north. But Kiszkan's homestead was about 15 miles northeast of Prince Albert, not far from the Honeymoon, Saskatchewan, post office. It was an area replete with Jack pine on the edge of the sandy Nisbet Forest Reserve, then known as Sand Hills. It's unlikely that the land was ideal for farming.

Dmytro arrived at his quarter-mile plot sometime in 1912, a young man in a new land. He set to the busy, painstaking work of clearing what he could and laying out a place to build a home. And, quickly, he sought another essential part of building his new life: starting a family. There is little recorded history of how Dmytro Kiszkan and Elizabeth Jacobson came to be wed. But, as Ken Guedo discovered, homestead maps from the time show that a Jacobson family owned a plot just two miles east. Elizabeth had just arrived that year from the region of the Austro-Hungarian Empire that is known today as Slovakia. It appears that she moved in with her brother, who was also a homestead settler. She went by the name Lizzie and turned 18 on November 12, 1912.

The next day, the couple-to-be travelled 15 miles to Prince Albert where they were married by the parish priest, J.M. Caffrey. The newlyweds were listed as "Mitir Kiskan" and "Lizzie Jakubso." It was the 32nd marriage in the church that year, scrawled in the same series of ledgers that would record their son's baptism a dozen years later.

And so, the two young strangers—he just 21, and she 18—in a world that offered them little else, set out to survive in a harsh, alien landscape. Theirs was a common immigrant experience in Canada at the turn of the century. The kind of story that built a familiar narrative of the Canadian heartland: that of restless drive, resolve and humility in a make-it-work-or-die reality. With effectively no capital besides the property they owned, the Kiszkans were incredibly poor. They had few alternatives to life on the homestead. But they also had little money to invest in what they needed in order to actually farm the land profitably. Together, Mitir and Lizzie built a 14-by-24-foot log cabin that winter. They moved in on April 1,

1913. They also built a stable out of logs with the same dimensions, where they'd keep two cattle. The cabin and the stable were worth $50 each at the time. Then they set out to clear the land. At the time, clearing was done mostly by axe and by burning. It was slow, gruelling work. A general rule was that if 10 acres were cleared in a season it was considered a big job.

In their first year, they managed to break and crop two acres, while Elizabeth was pregnant with their first child. Mary was born on September 22, 1913. They cleared another acre the following season—and eight more by the time the three-year term of the homestead was complete. By then they were a family of four; their second daughter, Therisia, was born June 15, 1915. By that time, Dmytro had started to go by a more anglicized name, James. A third daughter, Anne, was born on November 3, 1918.

By 1920, after the First World War, James and Elizabeth had practically nothing to their names besides the log cabin and barn they'd built near Honeymoon. They ate the food they were able to produce, but they had no money for anything else. The young couple worked to bring the land to life, but they realized there was no future for them near Honeymoon. Over those years, James had spent several months working as a labourer in Prince Albert. The girls were getting older. The city was the only place to find regular employment. In the early 1920s, James sold the homestead and found a job at the Pat Burns meat-packing factory in Prince Albert. It was gruelling work with long hours. It didn't pay much, but it was steady.

The family rented a small home on the east side of the city before buying the house at 526 Sixteenth Street West in 1926. By that time, the household had grown even bigger. Helen and Rose were born in 1921 and 1923, respectively. At some point, Elizabeth and James had a son that they named John. He died in infancy. Then— November 8, 1924—Johnny was born. Just 14 months later, on January 26, 1926, Elizabeth had another son, named Michael. In the coming years, Elizabeth would have two more daughters, Betty (in 1928) and Margaret (in 1935). According to her family and a baptismal record, Elizabeth lost at least two other babies to early deaths through that time: Joseph and Margaret. All told, by the winter of 1935, when Johnny was 10, he had seven sisters and one brother.

WHEN THE GREAT Depression struck in late 1929, its vicious blow hammered Canada. The nation would endure a brutal decade. Across the country businesses crumbled. Farms were wiped out. Nearly a third of Canadians would lose their jobs. Even the government would be pushed to the edge of bankruptcy.

But despite the hardships of life in the Great Depression, Sixteenth Street in Prince Albert was often a happy place. The Kiszkans' yard was one of the busiest places on the block. It held a small barn, a work shed and the outhouse. It also had one of the best natural wells in the area. There was a lane behind the yard, which the neighbours often crossed through on their way to downtown on Central Avenue. They would stop by the well to chat and fetch some water. If no one was home, many just grabbed a drink of water anyway. There was a huge tree in the backyard, and James built a bench beneath it. A swing hung from one of the branches. Naturally, the yard bustled with kids.

A single wage from a meat-packing plant just wasn't enough to support a large family through those rough years in the 1930s, and like many, James Kiszkan struggled to provide for his children. He tried to find odd jobs to bring in extra money with the little spare time he had. Along with chickens and sheep, James kept a cow that they named Nelly, whose milk he'd deliver to paying neighbours to make some extra money. (Nelly later became a rug that lay next to James's bed.)

James was a handy, capable man—having cleared his own land and built his own home. He was constantly fixing up the small family home in Prince Albert, adding to what could never be enough space. The home's entrance opened into a living area, with the parents' bedroom off to the right. Beyond the living room was a large kitchen, with two more bedrooms off a hallway. Each bedroom housed three double beds. When night fell, the house was lit by the glow of kerosene lamps. In time, James would build a couple of extra rooms—a bathroom and a sewing room—and the exterior would be redone. But in those early years, through the '30s, the large family made do in the small space. When the house got too crowded, James fixed up one half of the barn so Johnny and Michael could sleep in it, while the animals shared the other half.

The harsh realities of living through the Great Depression were central to the man that Johnny would become. Sometimes it was hard for James to stretch out enough money to support the family between paycheques. There were times that Johnny would ask his father for a dime so he could go to the movies, but James couldn't give him one. Undeterred, Johnny would scheme up a way to go to the movies anyway. Once, he and a friend tried to sneak down the coal chute at the Strand Theatre on Central Avenue. But the plan was poorly measured. The friend was a touch plump and got stuck partway down the chute.

But even though the family struggled financially, James and Elizabeth did their best to celebrate what they could. Every Christmas, James brought home a tree that they kept in the living room. They'd each light little candles on holders and place them on the branches. James played carols on a violin. On Christmas Day, James would open up a trap door in the kitchen floor that went down into a small dug-out basement. He'd come up with an orange for each of the children. Sometimes, they'd also get candy, like a chocolate cigar.

For the little they had, the Kiszkans were one of the fortunate families on the street who owned a radio. Johnny and a pack of friends gathered around it every Saturday night, snacking on popcorn, as Foster Hewitt's voice crackled over the airwaves across Canada, bringing live visions of the game from the brand new Maple Leaf Gardens in faraway Toronto. The National Hockey League was a distant dream that offered some relief from the hard realities of life during the hardships of the time. The league itself had been hit hard by the economic disaster, shrinking after years of growth and prosperity, losing nearly half its teams between 1931 and 1942.

With the temperature sometimes dipping near 50 below zero, there were frozen patches across Prince Albert: the river, ponds, schoolyards, and even city streets serving as makeshift rinks. Unable to afford skates, Johnny made do on the ice with boots through his earliest years. He collected empty beer bottles around town to take in for a refund to try to save enough money to buy a pair, but he never quite got there. He used sticks planed down from the branches of poplar trees, and pucks moulded from frozen droppings of passing horses. Johnny and his friends found their local heroes at the arena downtown, where the Prince Albert Mintos senior hockey team delighted local crowds who withstood the winter wind coming through the open-sided rink to watch the local heroes play against teams from across Saskatchewan.

Johnny became a rink rat, helping to clear and maintain the ice beneath the arching wooden roof. He and his buddies idolized the Mintos players and would carry their gear in and out of the rink. Don Deacon, one of the players, called Johnny over in the dressing room one day and handed him a pair of battered old tube skates. They were several sizes too big for Johnny, who was about 10 years old at the time. He had to stuff paper in the toes so he could fit in them. But Johnny didn't care. "I worshipped those skates," he later said. With skates, he was able to join the kids down on the North Saskatchewan River, which was full of cleared-off improvised rinks, lined up side by side. The middle of the ice was always clear of snow because of the swift wind that swept though. Johnny learned how to manoeuvre the oversized tubes as the wind blew him in any direction it desired, gliding along the North Saskatchewan for miles. The wind was so sharp and cold that Johnny and his friends often had to turn around and skate home backwards to shelter their faces from the extreme cold—something he'd later credit with making him so swift moving backwards in goal.

In fact, all of Johnny's improvised gear would help lay the foundation for his future success in hockey. Johnny used a heavy stick carved from a poplar branch that his father had found and given to him for Christmas. It took an enormous effort just to shoot with it. Whenever he needed a new stick, he'd find a new branch from a Jack pine or poplar and shave off the bark and carve it down himself. A stocky, big-boned kid, Johnny found that he wasn't the quickest at forward. He often volunteered to play goal and learned that he was decent at it. There was only one problem: He didn't have any equipment. So he and a neighbourhood pal, Eddie Helko, had the ingenuity to carve up an old baby-crib mattress that was being tossed out. They cut the foam lengthwise to make pads for his legs and stitched up the sides, then cut up inner tubes to strap the pads on. They sewed a piece of cardboard onto a wool mitt to make a blocker, and stuffed an old work glove with two thick socks in the palm to use as a catcher. The pads gave off enormous rebounds, but the improvised gear did the trick. The boys flooded a patch of ice in the Helkos' backyard. They took turns shooting pucks made of cord wood, wrapped in tape, at each other. They switched position every five goals that smacked against the wooden board they used as a net.

After receiving that first pair of oversized skates, Johnny started playing organized hockey at his school. He gradually picked up pieces of equipment, here and there, while playing school hockey. He also played in a local municipal league, quickly developing a reputation as a naturally gifted goaltender. He started in what was called "peanuts" and would go on to play at the peewee, midget and juvenile level. His teams played in local loops, while sometimes competing against teams from across Saskatchewan, like nearby Humboldt, Battleford and Saskatoon—or as far away as Flin Flon, five hours northeast, or Moose Jaw, four hours south.

Although Johnny went to school, he wasn't very interested in the lessons taught by the stern nuns at St. Paul's Catholic School. He'd later make several differing claims about the level of education he completed, sometimes saying he'd completed up to the 11th grade, other times that he'd stopped after grade eight—having repeated three grades along the way. However, in other official records he'd state that he'd completed only grade three and parts of grade four. These small inconsistencies in simple facts would become commonplace over the decades, creating an aura of mystery surrounding Johnny's life—whether it was intentional or not.

But one thing that was always clear was that when it came to school, Johnny much preferred to be out on a patch of ice, kicking aside horse dung and wooden pucks with his friends on cold winter afternoons. On hot summer days, he'd find a neighbourhood game of baseball to play and loved to go swimming in the river. But there was only so much time for fun. When he was about 10, Johnny worked as a pin-setter at the Bowl-a-Drome in Prince Albert. He would run out and set the pins after every turn, because there weren't automatic machines at the time. The young pin-setters worked each evening until the Bowl-a-Drome closed at midnight. The kids hired were usually from large families where the father's hard-earned paycheques weren't enough to make ends meet. Although Johnny admired his dad, he was determined that his life would be different. But how, exactly? A hockey career wasn't a reasonable goal. It was something Johnny was good at, but it was just a brief escape from reality. He harboured few illusions of finding his future in a child's game.

Through his adolescence, Johnny had built a wide-ranging resume. As a teenager, he worked for a year at the Coca-Cola bottling plant in Prince Albert as a washer. He also worked as a delivery boy. And as a butcher. He spent two years making some extra money by fishing. And, at some point, according to documents he'd later fill out, he worked for six months as a welder. For his industrious pursuits, Johnny said, he'd managed to earn about $15 a week. It's hard to see where he found the time to become a local hockey star.

But the game did, perhaps, help Johnny find some escape from some tumultuous years for his family. Despite their many children, the hastily arranged marriage of 18-year-old Lizzie and 21-year-old Mitir wasn't meant to last. It had fallen apart several years before Elizabeth finally left James. By 1938, Elizabeth Jacobson was living separately, a couple of blocks away at 519 Eighteenth Street West, just south of the Molson Brewery. Five years later, in 1943, Betty would move to 731 Sixth Street East, on the east side of town. By that time, she was living with Mike Dupay, a labourer at Northern Wood Preserves—whom she'd marry and live with until she died. James later left the Catholic Church and joined Prince Albert's Greek Orthodox congregation, which worshipped on the opposite side of town.

The breakup was difficult on the entire family, especially because marital separations were uncommon at the time and scandal spreads quickly in small cities. Johnny took it hard. His relationship with his mother would become particularly distant. Later in his life, he would rarely discuss the split, aside from saying that "a separation in the family" was the reason he decided to change his name. It was one of several stories he would spin on that topic. But at that time, Johnny Bower was still Johnny Kiszkan—although his origins were about to get blurry.

02

BEST AS A BUTCHER

THE FIRST TIME THE TORONTO MAPLE LEAFS' MOST FAMOUS goalie appeared in newsprint, he was playing for the Canadiens. Johnny "Kizkan," as the name was misspelled, made his debut in the *Prince Albert Daily Herald* in December 1940, while playing in the town's Church National Hockey League, when he was 16 years old. The local minor hockey league played its games at the Minto Arena and was made up of four teams: the Canadiens, the Maple Leafs, the Red Wings and the Rangers. They played back-to-back games every week. Johnny played goal in his regular midget level as well as with the older juvenile team. He modelled his style on the way he imagined his favourite goaltender, Frank Brimsek, played. Mr. Zero, as Brimsek was known, started his NHL career with the Boston Bruins during 1938–39 season and became an instant star, twice posting three consecutive shutouts. As Johnny read about

Brimsek in the *Daily Herald* and heard Foster Hewitt's excited descriptions of the Bruins goalie, the teenager started to dream of the same happening to him one day.

For the time being, though, the Church League would have to do. The weekly games were something of an occasion for family and friends who came out to Minto Arena. The rink was nearly full on the evening of Friday, December 27, 1940, as the Prince Albert City Band played while all the teams skated onto the ice to kick off the season. Mayor George Brock dropped the ceremonial puck. Johnny's Canadiens played in the second game of the evening's doubleheader, losing 1–0—of course—to the Leafs.

The young netminder was an instant star. He posted his first shutout on January 20, 1941, in a game with the midget team and then picked up his second shutout four nights later, playing for the juvenile team. And a week after that, in a loss to the Red Wings on January 31, Johnny received his first recorded puck in the face. It was one of many to come. The *Daily Herald* reported that the wound required several stiches to close. Johnny still wore those stitches when he played for the Prince Albert Nationals, an all-star team selected to represent Prince Albert in a provincial championship series against a team of the best midget players from Saskatoon. Despite losing both games, Johnny was lauded for his effort. "Johnny Kiszkan in the P.A. nets was the outstanding player of the game," the *Daily Herald* reported, noting that he'd saved his team from what had seemed like certain goals.

A fun Saturday night watching hockey at the Minto Arena might have provided the crowd some levity in Prince Albert, while elsewhere the world was burning. By 1941, World War II had already been engulfing much of the globe for two years. Great Britain had declared war on Germany after Hitler's army invaded Poland. A few days later, on September 10, 1939, Canada had joined Great Britain and entered the war too. A country of only 11 million people at the time, Canada had a navy fleet of just 15 ships, an air force with just 275 planes, and a standing army of 4,261 officers with 51,000 more in the reserves. But the small nation would give everything it could to the effort to fight the war alongside its allies.

In the coming years, the Canadian sacrifice would be enormous. The Canadian Army would increase 10-fold to more than 400,000. Canadian troops would be sacrificed at Dieppe and in Hong Kong. They'd fight in North Africa and Italy—and in the clouds over Britain and Europe. They'd raid Normandy, liberating northern France. They'd die in multitudes in the bloodiest conflict in human history.

There wasn't the same sense of jubilation when Canada entered the Second World War as there had been a quarter-century earlier, at the start of the First. The memory of the more than 61,000 Canadians sacrificed in the War to End All Wars was still too horrible and raw. But in 1939, many young men who had endured a brutal decade signed up for the opportunity war provided. Unemployment was high. The army offered three meals each day, a uniform and a trip overseas. Many were motivated by a sense of duty and the belief that Nazi Germany had to be stopped. If Hitler's plans were realized, no democracy in the world would be safe. It was much more than a faraway war, and eventually every Canadian man, woman and child would be fully immersed in the effort at home and abroad. That fall, young men signed up to serve in even greater numbers than the previous generation had in the Great War. By the end of September 1939, militias across Canada had enrolled 58,337 volunteers. The mostly unmarried young men came almost equally from large cities, small towns and farms. Many had slightly stunted builds due to malnourishment during the realities of the Great Depression. Only 2 percent held university degrees, while 16 percent had completed grade six or less.

The enthusiasm didn't escape Johnny. He was almost 15 when the war began. As he'd later tell the story, he unsuccessfully attempted to lie about his age so he could sign up for the Prince Albert Volunteers militia. He did, however, attend a weekly training program at the Prince Albert barracks on Friday evenings with some of his hockey friends. They were given uniforms and put through basic drills, with designs on joining the fight once they turned 18. While there was certainly a genuine sense of duty behind his motivation to join the army, Johnny was likely to have also viewed it as an opportunity for stable employment and adventure in military life. Decent work was hard to find in Prince Albert, and Johnny had little in the way of technical skills, beyond his remarkable ability in net, of course. His plan had been to find a working-class occupation at one of the local factories or, if he was fortunate, on the railway. The war offered something more than that.

In September 1941—two months before his 17th birthday— Johnny officially joined the Volunteers militia but was told he had to remain in Prince Albert for several months. That winter, Johnny once again starred in the Prince Albert National Hockey League and continued to gain local attention for his talent on the ice. He'd moved over from the Canadiens to the Red Wings in the juvenile division and easily earned his spot on the city's all-star team, the Nationals. The *Prince Albert Daily Herald* declared that John Kishkin (another misspelling) would be the centre of attention in the Nationals' two-game series against the Humboldt Hot Shots for the northern juvenile title. An illustration in the paper featured Johnny's smiling young face overlaid on another photo of a stock image of a goalie standing with his pads together, wearing a number 1 sweater with "John Kishkin" written across the front, while the rest of the players' faces were pasted around him in their various positions on the ice, in similar fashion on stock images of hockey players.

During the back-to-back playoff games, fans at the Minto Arena donated cigarettes to the "Smokes for P.A. Boys Overseas" campaign, which—as the name suggests—collected smokes to send to the local boys at war; 2,700 cigarettes were collected over the weekend, bringing the grand total from the season to more than 206,000, just 50,000 off the mark they hoped to hit by the end of the week.

After losing the first game of the aggregate series 4–3, Kiszkan saved the Nationals in front of a full house at the Minto Arena by rising to "great heights with sensational saves," in what the *Daily Herald* praised as the most exciting game Prince Albert had played all season. Because of the 17-year-old, 160-pound goalkeeper's incredible goaltending, the Nationals managed to pull off a close

2–1 win, which tied the aggregate score over the two games at five goals apiece.

As a tiebreaker, Prince Albert proposed an overtime period at the end of the second game to decide the championship. But because the game had finished just before midnight, the Humboldt team refused to play overtime as it would technically fall on a Sunday—something that was frowned on at the time. So the final tiebreaker was back held in Humboldt that Tuesday, where a crowd of 500 cheered the home side to a 4–1 win to claim the northern juvenile title. Despite the loss, Kiszkan was once again heralded as the Nationals' star player for his "outstanding" performance. That season, Johnny was called up to play a few games with the Prince Albert Black Hawks junior team to replace their injured goalie. He was nervous about playing at a higher level but played remarkably well. The coach, a local priest, asked him to stick with the team for the rest of the season. "If you keep playing the way you are, I'm sure you'll make it to the big time," he told Johnny.

But although his reputation as one of the best goaltenders in the region was growing rapidly, Johnny held little interest in sticking around Prince Albert. There was much more at stake in the world beyond the confines of his hometown. The war overseas had escalated at a terrifying rate. Japan had attacked Pearl Harbor in Hawaii on December 7, 1941—killing 2,403 Americans and bringing the full force of the United States into battle. Canada also suffered its first great loss in December 1941, when the Japanese invaded Hong Kong. Canadian soldiers had been asked to defend the British colony and sailed from Vancouver that fall. Over the course of the defeat, 290 Canadian soldiers were killed and 493 were wounded. Canadians who surrendered faced horror at the hands of the Japanese soldiers, who embarked on a rampage of torturing and killing the wounded. In the military hospital, patients were bayonetted in their beds. Nurses were raped and murdered. Those who were captured suffered greatly as prisoners of war, forced to work in brutal conditions and with little food. Of the 1,975 who set out across the Pacific Ocean, 550 wouldn't make it back to Canada.

Meanwhile, over in Europe, Germany's brutal advance expanded rapidly. Hitler's army had trampled through Europe—devastating Denmark, Norway, Luxembourg, the Netherlands, Belgium and France. In January 1942, Nazi officials held the Wannsee Conference in Berlin to discuss a "Final Solution," expanding its systematic campaign of genocide against the Jews. Through the next two years more than four million Jewish people would be brutally murdered in Nazi death camps. Almost six million would be slaughtered before the end of the war.

As the war machine continued to churn in the spring of 1942, Johnny again went to the barracks in Prince Albert to meet with the Prince Albert Volunteers recruiting officer and enlist in the Canadian Army. On March 16, 1942—when he was 17—he filled out his enlistment forms, stating that he'd been born on November 8, 1922, claiming to be 19. In the loopy cursive reminiscent of a signature that would one day be famous, Johnny signed his name under a declaration that he was telling the truth and under an oath that he would be "faithful and bear true allegiance to His Majesty." He might not have read to the bottom of the form, where a warning noted that "any person making a false answer to any of the above questions is liable to a penalty of six months' imprisonment."

When Johnny filled out the particulars of his family for the record that day, he also noted the ongoing division at home. He stated that his father, James Kiszkan, still lived at 526 Sixteenth Street—but that Elizabeth Kiszkan now lived on the other side of town, at 840 Fifth Street West.

As non-commissioned personnel, Johnny was enlisted as a private. In a photo of him in uniform taken at the time, he looks like a red-cheeked boy, much younger than he was. Johnny was assigned to Military District 11, which meant he'd be sent to the military training facility in Vernon, B.C., to join other members of the Prince Albert Volunteers. A few weeks later, Johnny boarded a train in Prince Albert and went west across the prairies and into the mountains. He arrived in the Vernon Army Camp in the northern Okanagan Valley on April 6, 1942.

The camp had been constructed during the First World War and brought nearly seven thousand military personnel to a town of just three thousand people. As World War II began, the Vernon camps had been upgraded with new water and sewer lines, and new buildings were constructed before units began to arrive in 1940. As the war escalated, as many as 7,000 troops were stationed at the camp at the same time. While far away from actual battle, the town was a constant reminder of war. The sounds of bugle calls, the shouts of drill orders, the constant rumble of military trucks, and the echo of gunfire and exploding mortar shells punctuated the daily soundtrack of life in Vernon. The town was a revolving door for young lives, passing through before being sent across the world's oceans to be counted as the living or the dead. The majority of the temporary population were young men in their late teens and early twenties. Vernon's manner shifted accordingly. In the evenings—every night except Sunday—the sounds of the week's military grumble were replaced with live orchestras playing in half a dozen dance halls. The town's cafés, ice cream parlours, bowling alley, and theatre were always packed. Young love flourished on the edge of war. The local Anglican church quickly went through an entire book of marriage certificates and had to order more.

Canadian historian and journalist Pierre Berton, then in his early 20s, had arrived at the training camp in Vernon just a few weeks before Kiszkan. Berton was among the only university graduates at the camp. The others, he noted, mostly had completed somewhere between middle school and two years of high school. In his letters, Berton said most of the men in the camp fell into two age groups: a smaller group in their early 20s, or a much larger, older group, closer to 25. Berton noted that the men in camp found a strong sense of unity among their platoons and of competition against others in their daily drills. Sometimes, he wrote, they even practised together in the evenings. "In just ten weeks, the army had taken seventy-five strangers from all walks of life and turned them, for a little while at least, into the closest of comrades." Johnny was part of that rigorous training as a private through his first few months in Vernon. He and his platoon were pushed through drills, learning signals and how to shoot. They took on assault courses in the woods, climbing ropes over obstacles and crawling beneath barbed-wire mazes while Bren gunfire zipped overhead; crossing through frigid streams and hip-deep mud as explosives went off nearby, covering them in muck—all under the taunting charge of a drill sergeant. Johnny managed to survive the elements. He was appointed to the rank of lance corporal, a small promotion, that July.

Overseas, the Allied war effort looked dire. By the summer of 1942, virtually all of continental Europe was under German occupation. In a grim position, the Allied army tried to find a way to gain a position in Western Europe. They settled on a large raid of Dieppe, a French port, involving 6,100 soldiers—of which nearly 5,000 were Canadian. After several years of training in England, the Canadian generals and politicians were eager to see Canadian troops play a crucial role in battle in Europe. The operation was codenamed "Jubilee." Early in the morning on August 19, 1942, Allied troops attempted to surprise the German army occupying the port. But the planned four-flank attack on Dieppe, followed by a raid up a sloped pebble beach, was a disaster.

The South Saskatchewan Regiment and the Queen's Own Cameron Highlanders were involved in the western flank of the attack. They landed successfully on the coast and managed to destroy a battery of German guns, but they were overcome on the withdraw across the beach. They took heavy fire from the east and west. On the Eastern flank, Canadian soldiers of the Royal Regiment of Canada were delayed in attacking a narrow passage between the cliffs. Instead of having the cover of darkness, they attacked at dawn and were pinned down by the heavy machine gun of the alerted Germans. The main attack on the beach leading into Dieppe was a slaughter. While some soldiers managed to cross the beach into the town, others were hammered by German firepower, as tanks ran aground at the seawall and on the pebbled incline. The Essex Scottish Regiment, les Fusiliers Mont-Royal, the Royal Hamilton Light Infantry, the Calgary Regiment and the Royal Marine "A" Commando all suffered heavy casualties. Overhead, a brutal battle in the sky cost the Royal Air Force 106 aircraft, the highest single-day total in the war. The Royal Canadian Air Force lost 13 aircraft.

Despite its failure, the Dieppe raid provided the Allies with valuable information and lessons about the enemy-held French coast, which would be credited in helping plan the successful invasion of Normandy on D-Day on June 6, 1944. But the human toll of Dieppe was devastating. The Canadians suffered enormous casualties, including 1,946 prisoners of war; 916 Canadians were killed.

Back home, newspapers downplayed the totality of the disaster while relaying stories of the young Canadians who fought valiantly for liberty on the French coast. But as the casualty lists came in, more and more mothers and fathers learned of the boys who weren't coming home. In Vernon, soldiers waiting for their own turn to join the war were told of their friends who'd been killed. Johnny knew several from Prince Albert.

In the echo of lives lost overseas, Vernon pushed on with life in a typically Canadian way. That November—shortly after Johnny *actually* turned 18—it was announced that the Army Training Camp was putting together a hockey league. The five-team grouping would play its games in the state-of-the-art Vernon Civic Arena, built in 1937. The rink—with its peaked roof and rectangular, saloon-like façade—was a central part of life in the town. With the talent accumulated in the training camp from across the country, the league promised some of the most entertaining hockey Vernon had ever hosted. The teams consisted of entries from different militia units: the Military Training Centre 110, the Winnipeg Light Infantry, the Royal Canadian Engineers, the Irish Fusiliers and the Prince Albert Volunteers. The players in the league had mostly competed at the junior hockey level, with a few having played professionally—like Training Centre's Stan Smith, who played a few games in the NHL with the New York Rangers. Prince Albert's star players were Jim Logue, a 230-pound defenceman, and his younger brother Lefty Logue, a swift winger. But as the youngest in the league, Johnny was about to shed his khaki uniform for a hockey sweater and become the camp's star player. The teams practised on Tuesday and Friday afternoons for a couple of weeks in preparation for opening night, wearing skates and equipment sent to the camp so the young men could play.

More than a thousand fans, half of them soldiers in uniform, packed the arena on November 27, 1942. Army musicians played in a remodelled bandstand at one end of the rink. With the lively music filling the arena, soldiers in the stands cheered and hollered at the frenetic, violent action on the ice. The Volunteers played the Royal Canadian Engineers team in the first game of the evening's doubleheader. The boys from Prince Albert impressed the crowd with their speed and skill, winning 7–3. "The P.A.V representatives know their game," the *Vernon News* noted. And John Kiszkan put on a "flashy bit of netminding."

Excited reports of the hockey matches were printed alongside news stories that underscored the constant concerns of a country at war. Headlines like "What Must Be Done, if Air Raids Occur in Vernon" and "Incendiary Bomb Demonstration in Polson Park" informed civilians how to protect their loved ones if the city came under attack. But despite the grim backdrop, the military hockey league captured the town's attention. Even more fans showed up a few nights later to watch the Volunteers play the Winnipeg Light Infantry—"Two Prairie teams that played a banging brand of hockey," according to the *Vernon News*. During the game, an army truck knocked down a power line outside, causing a 40-minute blackout before the start of the third period. The Light Infantry's military band played in the dark as the soldiers and civilians sang along through the duration of the delay. When power was restored, the Volunteers finished off a 3–2 victory, with Johnny making several "miraculous" saves. After the win, the local news raved about the Volunteers, noting that the team of unknown players had the most "evenly balanced club" in the league. And Johnny quickly emerged as the league's standout player. "The team's beaming star is young Johnny Kiszkan," the *Vernon News* reported. "[He] hasn't gone higher than the junior ranks, but his goaltending in the army league brings him out as one of the favourites seen in the Vernon Civic Arena."

As Christmas approached, the Army Training Centre put out a special edition of its *Rookie* newsletter informing soldiers that, for those who hadn't been granted leave over the holidays, the base was bringing in "950 pounds of superlative turkey, 50 pounds of succulent cranberries, 400 pounds of juicy mincemeat, 500 pounds of fruity Christmas cake, 500 pounds of ye olde plum pudding" for Christmas dinner. Each soldier would receive a Christmas gift box containing packages of razor blades, fruit and cigarettes, arranged by some generous civilians in Vernon. And there would be a special showing of *A Christmas Carol*, starring Lionel Barrymore, in the Drill Hall. For many soldiers, the *Rookie* noted, it would be their first Christmas away from home. Johnny, who wasn't granted leave until New Year's Eve, was one of them.

But any homesickness he felt might have been allayed by the fact that he'd become something of a celebrity among the thousands of soldiers in the training camp. In a lengthy section on the new hockey league, the holiday edition of the *Rookie* singled out Johnny's performance on the ice. "A youngster at the game but has the makings of a born goaltender," read one entry on Johnny, highlighting the league's top players. "Looks like a cat on ice and is responsible for more saves than any other goalie in the league. A comer." Next to that entry—beneath the headline "Kiszkan, Vol's Goalie Proving Series Star"—the *Rookie's* reporter elaborated on the young netminder's unexpected success:

"Winning a healthy respect for himself, admiration from friend and foe, scene-stealer of the series is young, blonde Johnnie Kiszkan in the Volunteers net, who is fast making himself the most valuable man on the ice," he wrote. "With nothing more than two years of junior play with the Prince Albert Black Hawks, the youngster has natural goal-keeping qualities making him the one man to beat on the Volunteers team."

In the early weeks of 1943, the Volunteers met the Light Infantry in the league semifinals. More than 1,500 "uproarious" soldiers and civilians packed the arena throughout a see-saw affair that was tied at five after regulation. Johnny played the entire game with a large bandage on his face, after being struck by a puck shot by his own teammate during the warm-up. Despite the injury, the *Vernon News* reported, he was "his usual starry self" even though the Light Infantry picked up the victory in overtime. The Light Infantry would win the second game of the two-game playoff as well, earning the right to go to the final.

While Johnny had impressed his fellow soldiers with his puck-stopping ability, his superiors were less impressed with his prospects for war. Early in the new year, he was interviewed for his personnel selection record. The interviewer, Lieutenant M.S. Prince, recorded Johnny's long list of previous jobs, from Coca-Cola bottle washer to welder. The young corporal, Prince wrote, was "best as a butcher" and was also interested in being a warehouse storeman. In his spare time, Johnny said he enjoyed playing hockey and baseball. When it came to matters of faith, he was an "irregular" Roman Catholic, who smoked and drank moderately. The lieutenant wrote that the "sturdy Ukrainian lad" suffered from a lack of schooling and was limited in his ability to learn. "Appears alert, but is of rather stolid type," Lieutenant Prince reported, reiterating that Johnny was "an unimaginative lad, who might be useful as a butcher." It was, perhaps the most scathing review the goalie would ever receive.

A month later, Johnny drew the ire of his superiors when he failed to report to his assignment as a mess orderly. He later said he disliked the duties he was required to do as a lance corporal, especially ordering others to clean dishes and the mess hall. He was charged with conduct to the "prejudice of good order and military discipline." The next day, Johnny asked that he be reverted to the status of private and was granted the demotion.

But that did little to affect Johnny's status in camp as a hockey player. With the Western Canadian intermediate hockey playoffs taking place in Vernon, B.C., that February, the town was represented by a team of the best players in the training camp league. It was no surprise that, despite his youth, Johnny was selected as the goaltender for the Vernon Military All-Stars—the only lowly private on a team made up of corporals and sergeants. Prince Albert's Logue brothers—Jim, a sergeant, and Lefty, a corporal—were on the roster. They'd finished first and second in league scoring. While the hastily thrown together All-Stars had talent, they didn't have much time to play together. That year there was no competition for the Coy Cup, the intermediate title for B.C., so the Military All-Stars had won it by default. But there was still lots of enthusiasm for Vernon's military squad. When the playoffs opened, more than 2,000 fans packed the Civic Arena to cheer for the best the army boys had to offer. They played the Notre Dame Hounds of Wilcox, the Saskatchewan champions, in the semifinals for a chance to play the Alberta champions in the final. Johnny gave up only eight goals in three games as the All-Stars beat the Hounds two games to one.

The All-Stars then faced the Calgary Buffaloes for the Western Canadian title. The Buffaloes were a dominant team that played together regularly—and it showed. After losing the first game in front of their fans, the Army All-Stars managed to pull off a win and a tie against the Buffaloes—forcing a final game for the Western Canadian championship. Through the first three games, Johnny gave up just 10 goals. But in the fourth and final match, Calgary silenced the home crowd and outclassed the military grunts, taking the championship with a 9–2 win. The Buffaloes accepted the Edmonton Journal Trophy as Western Canadian champs on the ice, while the Vernon squad was given the Coy Cup they'd been granted by default.

Despite the disappointing finish, Johnny's selection to the Vernon Military Camp All-Star Team was an honour he'd always cherish. A photo of the team sitting in front of the Coy Cup, wearing serious, unsmiling looks, appeared in the *Vernon News* on March 25, 1963. Johnny sits right in the middle, his head hunched slightly forward, looking like a young teenager among a team of men in their early 20s. He picked up a copy of the photo and carefully wrote out the names of teammates on ruled lines he drew on the back. Along with the brown leather goal pads he'd been given by the team, he'd keep that photo for the rest of his life. While training for war, Johnny had emerged as something of a hockey star for the first time beyond the confines of tiny Prince Albert. Perhaps there was hope for a future in the game, after all. But Johnny had only a short time to enjoy his semi-celebrity status in Vernon. In just a matter of weeks, he was on his way to war.

03

WARHAWK

THE FIRST TIME JOHNNY TRAVELLED ACROSS CANADA WAS WHEN he was on his way overseas to defend it. In early April 1943—shortly after receiving a pay increase of 20 cents per day—he'd been told he was part of the next group of soldiers being sent from the relative safety of Vernon to the edge of the war. On May 9, he boarded a train with his fellow soldiers that carried him back through the mountains, across the prairies, past his hometown, through Manitoba, down through Ontario and Quebec, all the way to the Atlantic Ocean. From Halifax, Kiszkan embarked on his 10-day journey across the sea. He arrived in the United Kingdom on May 22, 1943, and reported for duty the next day.

In England, Johnny was assigned to the Queen's Own Cameron Highlanders, in with the 2nd Canadian Infantry Reinforcement Unit, which had been the main force behind the Operation Jubilee mission in Dieppe. Despite making the deepest penetration in the raid, the Cameron Highlanders had suffered enormous casualties. The Highlanders were a Scottish-Canadian infantry regiment formed in Winnipeg ahead of the First World War. The Highlanders—who wore traditional Scottish kilts with their uniforms—fought valiantly and with great sacrifice at the second Battle of Ypres, in the Somme, at Vimy Ridge and at Passchendaele. A quarter-century later—now wearing army-issued trousers instead of kilts—the Cameron Highlanders once again made a great sacrifice. Of the 503 Camerons involved in Operation Jubilee, 60 were killed in action and eight died of wounds after being evacuated; another 167 were captured and made prisoners of war. Only 268 returned to England, of which 103 were wounded.

Kiszkan was one of the many soldiers brought in as part of an attempt to rebuild and prepare a battle-ready unit for an invasion that would hopefully liberate Europe, planned largely on the lesson learned in Dieppe. The 2nd Canadian Infantry Reinforcement Unit was based in the city of Guilford, in South East England. While Vernon took precautions out of fear of potential attack, England was a war zone. From September 1940 through the spring of 1941, German bombs fell night after night in the Blitz—and had levelled much of London and industrial cities across the country. More than 40,000 civilians would be killed by bombs dropped by German planes. Back in Canada, newspapers ran stories of human toll without mentioning the total casualties. The CBC broadcast live reports from the scenes, with recordings of bomb blasts and machine gun fire, connecting the distant listeners to the destruction and horror. Thousands of families across England lost their homes, their possessions and in many cases their loved ones. At night, every light was blacked out for the entire evening. The country was battered and broken but remained steadfast beneath the weight of total war. All industrial spaces, from large factories to small workshops, were turning out products for battle. Grazing land was plowed for wheat, and flower beds were used to grow vegetables. Food was heavily rationed and never wasted. Even soap was scarce. The trains were worn down and dirty; homes went without paint; beer was watered down; whisky was scarce, with wartime taxes shooting the price of a bottle to about $5 Canadian.

Most of the Canadian soldiers had never been to England before—or anywhere beyond Canada, really. With war echoing around them, there was a sense of excitement in a new place. The Canadian soldiers drew considerable attention from the English women who lived nearby, likely because of their exotic allure and the fact that they were better dressed and paid more money than their British counterparts. To help them get accustomed to the country, the Canadians were given a booklet, which Johnny likely received, called *A Guide for Guys Like You*. It was distributed in 1943 to Canadian soldiers telling them how to understand English culture and conduct themselves in their new home. It covered typical issues like differences in the kind of money they used, driving on the left side of the road and drinking warm beer. It also tried to explain sports like cricket, rugger and British football.

"Once again, look, listen and learn before you start telling the British how much better we do things," the guide advised. "British automobiles are little and low-powered. That's because all the gasoline has to be imported over thousands of miles of ocean. British taxicabs have comic looking front wheel structures. Watch them turn around in a 12-foot street and you'll understand why. The British don't know how to make a good cup of coffee. You don't know how to make a good cup of tea. It's an even swap."

When Johnny arrived at the Canadian camp in Guilford on May 29, 1943, his qualifications were assessed in an interview by Captain S. Norman Keston. The captain recorded Johnny's age, *correctly*, as eighteen and a half years old. The private was five foot eight and 173 pounds. The record indicates that Johnny had only completed up to third grade in elementary school, which was inconsistent with other records that stated he'd completed up to the eighth grade, and his own claim to have completed school through the 11th. The card filled out by Captain Keston also indicated that Johnny had one brother and seven sisters—but that he was the seventh child in the family, when in fact, he was the sixth. But Johnny also shared some of the softer details of his childhood back in Prince Albert. He enjoyed skating and swimming, he said. He played shortstop in baseball and goal in hockey. He told Keston he had signed up for the army because his friends had joined. And after the war, Johnny said, he hoped to return home for he had lined up a job as a bottle sorter.

Keston determined that Kiszkan had a pleasant disposition. He was well groomed, with a husky build. And, Keston said, he had average understanding of military knowledge and map reading, while his mechanical knowledge was "deficient."

"A young sturdy lad of poor learning ability due to lack of education," he wrote on Johnny's solider qualification card. "Has been very erratic in his employment. Says he could handle and would like to be a Bren gunner."

That June, it poured nearly every day in Guilford. Through the constant patter of rain, the soldiers could also hear the occasional buzz of German planes flying nearby. The soldiers were put through drill after drill on those damp, wet days. Sometimes they'd do group marches through a stream of water, with their rifles held up high in the air. They trained for any and every scenario they might face when sent into the heart of battle. Johnny felt his body starting to cramp and ache in the dank climate. His muscles grew tired and sore. His back started to throb with pain he'd never felt before. His knuckles swelled. His fingers swelled too, tingling. As it grew worse, sometimes his entire hands went numb. He felt sick and lost interest in doing anything at all.

The Canadian Army played a crucial role in the invasion of Sicily that July, with the battle raging on for more than a month. There were 2,330 Canadian casualties, with 562 soldiers killed and another 84 captured as prisoners of war. With Germany beaten back, the Allies began a slow, deadly advance across Italy's mainland, through mountainous terrain lined with swift rivers. Through more than a year and a half of fighting in Italy, the Canadian Army would suffer 25,264 casualities, with more than 5,900 killed. As the fighting continued in Sicily and elsewhere, the 2nd Division remained in England, rebuilding its ranks after the devastation in Dieppe. Johnny maintained his training through the pain. But eventually, the agony in his hands and back were too great. In the middle of September 1943, Johnny spent a couple of days in the hospital. He was in and out of the ward several times over the next couple of months, including several weeks through November. There seemed to be no cure for Johnny's damaged body. He was given all kinds of treatments. They put his hands under heat lamps, and the nurses would massage them. Johnny was even sent to several different hospitals, including one in Birmingham, two hours away. But nothing worked.

Finally, in December 1943, Johnny was deemed unfit for service, as he could use his hands only with great difficulty. He was diagnosed with acrocyanosis, because his hands would turn blue in the cold. Later, it'd be determined that he suffered from rheumatoid arthritis in both of his hands—a fact that would make his future longevity as a goaltender all the more remarkable. On December 27, 1943—seven months after his arrival in England—Johnny was "struck off strength" from the Canadian Army and began his journey home.

The next day, in Italy, the Germans retreated from the cobblestoned streets of the medieval city of Ortona. It was a crucial victory for the Allies in the battle for Italy. The 2nd Division would play a role in the Canadian Army's crucial involvement in Normandy on D-Day in June 1944. Johnny very well might have seen action and wound up among the many dead. Instead, after another journey across the Atlantic and a cross-country trek by train, Johnny arrived in Regina, Saskatchewan, on January 9, 1944—one of the fortunate souls who'd made it home.

Upon returning to Canadian soil, Johnny had been told he could remain in the army working at the military district in Regina for another six months, but he had little interest in the job and declined. He was granted disembarkation leave with pay for a couple of weeks and given a subsistence allowance to purchase some new clothes and personal goods. Kiszkan quickly returned to Prince Albert where he wasted no time getting back to hockey. On January 22, he was in goal playing for a local all-star team in an exhibition game against the Saskatchewan RCAF Tech Aeronauts. The *Daily Herald* celebrated Johnny's return in an article ahead of the match: "An added attraction will be Pte. Johnnie Kiszkan, late of the Prince Albert Black Hawks and Victoria Army, who will be netminder for the All-Stars. Johnnie recently returned home from action overseas." With Johnny in net, the All-Stars won 6–3.

He returned to Regina to complete his service interview on February 7 at the #12 military district, where he was evaluated by Lieutenant D.A. Cummings. His record indicated that Johnny was being discharged for acrocyanosis because he couldn't meet the physical requirements of the army. The soldier, Cummings wrote, had a good attitude and was cooperative and willing—although his ability was below average and he hadn't sought out any courses in education or trade training to change that. Johnny told him he hoped to be hired as night watchman at the Pat Burns meat-packing plant in Prince Albert, where his father worked. Cummings agreed that the 19-year-old would be suitable for the job. For his service, Johnny was issued a defence medal for non-operational service to the British Commonwealth during the war and a Canadian Volunteer Service medal. He was officially discharged from the Canadian Army on February 14, 1944.

As a result of the war, Prince Albert had only a four-team intermediate-level league through the 1943–44 season. M&C Aviation, a company in Prince Albert that chartered flights into northern Saskatchewan, also ran a large aircraft maintenance facility in the city during the war. They were a huge employer of the community during World War II. The M&C Repair Depot sponsored one of the hockey teams in the local league, called the Warhawks. The team finished first in the Prince Albert loop, and because there was no other intermediate team competing in northern Saskatchewan, they played the champions from southern Saskatchewan, the Notre Dame Hounds, in a playoff for the provincial title. With Johnny's recent homecoming, the Warhawks looked like they had a shot at the Western Canadian championship and quickly became the talk of the town.

More than a thousand fans packed the Minto Arena to watch the playoff series in late February, 1944. Adults paid 35 cents for admission, students and members of the armed forces paid a quarter, and kids got in for a nickel and a dime. The fans hollered at Hounds coach Dean Griffing throughout the game, while he chomped on his cigar. A five-foot-four Warhawks forward tried to take out a six-foot-two Hounds defenceman, only to bounce off him—much to the crowd's comedic delight. In goal, Johnny was back in his element, "staving off volley after volley of flying rubber," the *Daily Herald* reported as the Warhawks won 5–2.

Apparently no longer feeling the debilitating effects of the arthritis in his hands, or playing through it, Johnny was just as remarkable in the second game. He made two saves on what looked like sure goals in the first five minutes. He continued to shut down the Hounds' attack with a series of tremendous kick saves as the Warhawks won 4–0—winning the series on aggregate. Frustrated by the same goalie who had shut them down the previous winter when he was playing for the Vernon All-Stars, the Notre Dame Hounds argued hat Johnny wasn't a legally registered player and that the Warhawks should be disqualified. But the Saskatchewan hockey officials found that the scene-stealing goaltender was previously registered in Prince Albert and ruled he was legally allowed to play. The Warhawks were declared provincial champions.

For the second time in two seasons, with two different teams, Johnny would play for the Western Canadian intermediate championship and the Edmonton Journal Trophy. This time the best-of-three championship was hosted at home in Prince Albert, where the Warhawks would face the Canmore Briquettes, the Alberta champs who travelled by train for the showdown. A couple of weeks later, in the middle of March, fans in Prince Albert rushed to Northern Hardware, Duncan's drugstore, and Amos' Cigar Store to pick up their 35-cent tickets. (Three-game series passes were sold for $1.) It was an exciting distraction as the war effort raged on. It was announced that all the profits from the series would be donated to the Red Cross, in much need of the extra funds.

The largest crowd of the season showed up to Minto Arena to watch the Warhawks and Briquettes play the first game of the final. Both the Prince Albert City Band and the local army band played throughout the game. The fans jumped from their seats in wild applause several times, as Johnny's fast footwork put on another show. Trailing by a goal in the third, the Warhawks scored two in front of the frenzied home crowd to win 3–2.

The Prince Albert crowd returned in triumphant force the next night, as Johnny again kicked away shot after shot from the desperate Briquettes. He "bore the brunt of the attack" early in the second period, the *Daily Herald* reported—and then held off a "veritable barrage of rubber" when the Warhawks were down a man in the third. Minto Arena erupted in triumph as the horn sounded on the Warhawks' 4–1 victory to claim the Edmonton Journal Trophy as the Western Canadian intermediate champs. In just a few months, Johnny had gone from a broken-down solider being shipped home from war with a debilitating condition to a local hero on the ice.

But beyond the game, Johnny had returned to Prince Albert with few prospects. In the spring of 1944—as the world teetered on the edge of an uncertain tomorrow—19-year-old Johnny found himself right back where he'd started. He was still the poorly educated son of impoverished immigrants, whose most practical outcome was to find work as a bottle sorter, or perhaps storeman or night watchman. Maybe he'd be best as a butcher, after all. Johnny didn't have the luxury of grandiose dreams. Just like his father, he seemed destined to work hard and endlessly for little in the way of compensation. But the story of his life was about to change forever.

BARON

IN AN ERA OF LITTLE OPPORTUNITY IN PROFESSIONAL HOCKEY, an untold amount of talent remained in small communities across Canada, playing in the junior and senior ranks, becoming local legends but nothing more. Lefty Logue, Johnny's teammate with the Prince Albert Volunteers in Vernon, remains a well-known figure in Prince Albert to this day. Lefty was adored for his crafty pitching and consistent hitting on baseball diamonds through the summers. And on the hockey rink, he was one of the best goal scorers the area ever produced. He represented Prince Albert at the senior level in both sports. He was even offered a tryout by the New York Rangers but decided he didn't want to leave his hometown. Stories of Lefty's ability are still told in Prince Albert. He's a member of the community's Sports Hall of Fame. But that's where his legend ends. And there are many stories like Lefty's across the country.

Those who might have been good enough but just didn't get discovered—or didn't take their chance when it came. But Johnny
Kiszkan wasn't going to become one of those guys.

The buzz around his talent had reached all the way to Cleveland,
Ohio. His old teammate from the area, Bob Solinger, had played
with the Cleveland Barons of the American Hockey League and
had told the team's management about the young goalie who
was starring with the Prince Albert Black Hawks. Intrigued, a
Cleveland scout named Hub Wilson came out to watch Johnny
play. He liked what he saw. He asked Johnny to officially sign a
contract that would make him property of the Barons. The idea of
playing pro hockey excited Johnny. But he had recently managed
to land a job with the Canadian National Railway, signalling trains.
It was the best he could hope for in Prince Albert. The pay was
decent and the hours were steady. It wasn't the kind of job he could
just easily walk away from. Many men wouldn't have.

But Wilson had added an unexpected perk, offered Johnny a
$50 signing bonus. Johnny had never seen that kind of money
thrown around before. It was a lot to turn down, even if it risked a
steady job with CN. Johnny decided to take a chance on himself—
and the 50 bucks. He happily took the money home and offered
$40 of it to his father, a gesture for all he felt his father had done
for him. But James Kiszkan couldn't quite believe it either. He
turned down his son's generosity, Johnny later claimed, because he
believed the money was stolen.

A couple of weeks after World War II officially ended in September 1945, Johnny crossed the U.S. border at Detroit, heading to

Ann Arbor, Michigan. At the time, he thought he was taking a chance as a rookie in the Barons' training camp. He wanted to see what might come of it, while fully expecting to be back on the railway in a matter of weeks. The Barons were coming off a Calder Cup championship, so he figured the team wouldn't have much use for him. He was no pro. He was just a shy 20-year-old who was still wearing the tube skates he'd been given when he was 10. Johnny had never been able to afford a newer pair. When he went to put the skates on during camp, a trainer pulled him aside and said he couldn't go on the ice in his ratty old skates. It was a professional league, after all. The Barons gave Kiszkan his first pair of new goalie skates. He hated them—but there wasn't much he could do after they'd given him a new pair and he'd thrown out his old ones.

The Barons had a veteran goalie, Harvey Teno, who looked likely to return as the team's starter. But Johnny managed to impress the Barons enough through training camp that he earned a spot as Teno's backup. Cleveland offered Johnny a salary of $1,700 for the season, the equivalent of about $24,000 today. It was hard for him to believe he'd actually be getting paid to play hockey. But it would only get more unbelievable from there. By mid-October, Johnny was in goal at the massive Cleveland Arena in downtown—with room for 10,000 spectators. It was by the far the biggest rink he'd ever played in. It was also by far the best team he'd ever played against. The Barons were playing their annual exhibition game against the Detroit Red Wings. But Johnny more than held his own. In fact, he shut the Red Wings out in the first and only period he played. Teno and rookie goalie Albert Tomori played the second and third periods, with the Red Wings scoring seven goals on them. The 5,000 Cleveland fans in the stands might have suspected they had found something special in the young kid from Saskatchewan. They likely didn't know they'd just witnessed the player who'd become the greatest goalie in the league's history.

One person who did realize the Barons had found someone special was Bob Ochs, a 17-year-old rink rat who helped out in the team's dressing room. Johnny was a shy, nervous 20-year-old who had just moved to one of the largest cities in the United States to play professional hockey. It was a lot to take in. Ochs volunteered to help him get settled in the big city. Johnny was still a wide-eyed, fuzzy-cheeked kid. He wasn't very social. Away from the ice, he mostly kept to himself. At the time, he didn't smoke or drink. He rarely inhabited the customary hangouts of the hockey crowd. On road trips, he would often sit in the corner by himself. Johnny boarded in a house on Euclid Avenue, which they called the haunted house because it was so large and dark. It was conveniently located right next to the Arena, which was helpful because Johnny certainly couldn't afford a car. Ochs would often come and get him. In this awkward rookie phase, Johnny and Ochs would become lifelong friends. Sometimes after practice, when Johnny stayed late to work on his own drills, Ochs would put on skates and come out and shoot on him. Ochs, who had been born with one hand, had figured out a way to flick the puck with a stick.

Initially Johnny had a difficult time adapting to life in pro hockey. Early in the season, when the team was leaving for a road trip to Pittsburgh, Johnny arrived at the bus in his old team jacket from his days in Prince Albert. The team's coach, Bun Cook, pulled him aside and told him he was supposed to wear a suit and coat to away games. Kiszkan had no idea. He wasn't used to wearing dress clothes unless it was Sunday. Cook quickly had a team staff member drive Johnny to get a jacket to wear on the road. Shortly afterwards, he asked Ochs to take him out shopping for some dress clothes so he'd look a little more like he belonged.

On the ice, though, Kiszkan was fitting in just fine. He lost the season opener to Hershey, filling in for Teno who was out with an infected toe, but his play further impressed the Barons brass. After appearing in a couple of winless games as Cleveland struggled through the early part of the 1945 season, Johnny was actually in goal during the Barons' first victory of the season—while playing for the other team. During a game in late October against the visiting Providence Reds, Johnny was lent to the Reds as a courtesy goaltender after the team's only goalie, Paul LeClerc, was knocked unconscious by a shot. So Johnny played in goal for Providence in front of nearly 11,000 Barons fans at the arena. The Barons' Fred Thurier scored on Johnny late in the third period to give Cleveland the 4–3 win. He picked up his first actual professional victory on December 1, with a 4–3 win over Providence. Shortly after that, he earned his first shutout in a 2–0 win over the Buffalo Bisons. Then he stopped 66 shots in a 7–3 loss to the Pittsburgh Hornets. With Teno often injured, Johnny played 41 games in his rookie season with the Barons. But through the playoffs, the Barons went with their veteran, and Kiszkan found himself stuck on the bench. Cleveland would make it to the league final but lost to the Buffalo Bisons in seven games.

Regardless, the fans in Cleveland already loved the team's rookie goaltender—and it was clear that he'd be sticking around for a long time. The boy with so few prospects had grown into a pro. John Kiszkan had made it.

Anne Batting's world is pinned up all around her. There are photographs of each her 10 children. Of her dozens of grandkids and great grandkids.

There's a photo of her father, James, in middle age, wearing round-rim glasses, an overcoat and a bowl cap, staring stoically into the camera in front of his house on a wintery day. He has a familiar chin. There's one of Elizabeth sitting in a chair in a floral dress. She has a familiar nose. On the wall across from Anne's bed at Castle Wood Village nursing home, there is a black and white photo of the Kiszkan kids standing in front of their house. Anne stands in the back of the photograph with her two older sisters, the rest in the middle, and the two boys on either side—in baggy white dress shirts and ties, with matching buzz cuts.

Anne is 99 years old and the only sibling left in the family—although she's not certain of what happened to her brother Michael. The family lost track of him years ago, she says.

There are photos of Anne in her early 20s, young and fashionable on Queen Street in Toronto when she went to live there with a friend. Anne looks at the photo of her wedding day, sitting next to her husband, Tom—her brother Johnny standing behind them, wearing a shy smile. He was Tom's best man at the ceremony. Nearby is another photo of Anne standing beside Johnny, in his khaki soldier's uniform. He's handsome but youthful—like a boy dressing up for a party. "He wasn't supposed to be in the war," Anne says. "He was too young."

Anne remembers when he came home from the war. And when his life started to become something more than anyone who grew up on that house on Sixteenth Street could have dreamed. She'd watched him play when she could. The family was proud when Johnny starred with the Prince Albert Black Hawks the season after he'd strolled back into town and casually won the Western Canadian championship with the Warhawks. While she can't recall if James or Elizabeth ever made it to the Minto Arena to watch their son play, she knows that some of his siblings who were still in the area did. She knows the family was proud throughout that 1944–45 season when reviews like "Kiszkan was up to his usual good form" . . . "Kiszkan sensational in goal" . . . "Johnny Kiszkan, outstanding goalie in the northern league, was the most spectacular figure on the ice last night" were commonplace.

And Anne remembers when her brother went away to Cleveland and his life took a new course.

In the process, he changed his name to Bower. "They changed it for him," Anne corrects, sharing her theory that the Barons told Johnny he had to do it. It didn't matter much, though. No matter what he called himself—Kiszkan or Bower—he'd always be her little brother Johnny.

Anne and Tom had moved their life to Castlegar, B.C., and had 10 children—starting a life and legacy all their own. Anne and Johnny stayed in touch, as did most of the siblings scattered across

Canada. The Kiszkan kids diverged on separate paths, in that way that large families often do—apart but always connected by those shared beginnings. Johnny and his success on the ice would be one of those points that bound not only them but also distant cousins generations on. History might remember Johnny by a different name, but to the relatives that share the blood of a legend, he'll always be a Kiszkan.

Over the years, in a distant valley in the Selkirk Mountains, Anne would gather her family around the television every Saturday night to watch the boy who used to play goal in his boots carve out an unparalleled legacy in the game. Anne would watch him on the ice, distant but connected, filled with pride and joy. The feeling would never fade.

"That's my brother," she'd say.

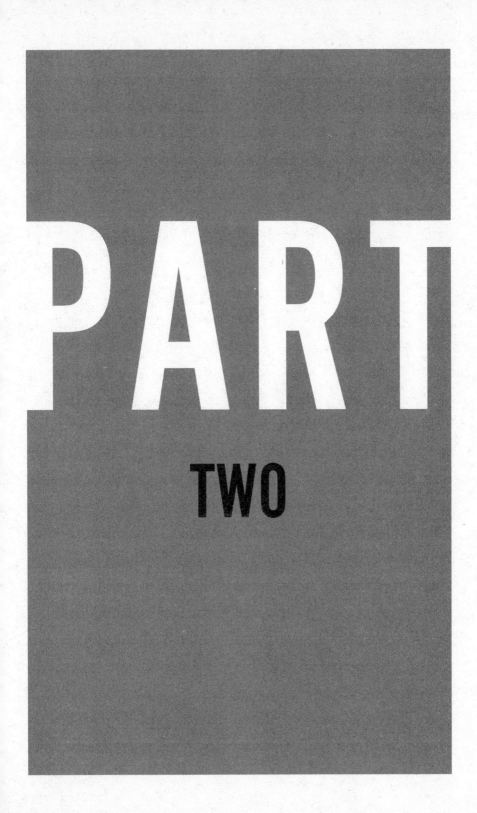

PART

TWO

05

WHAT'S IN A NAME?

MIKE KVASNAK HAS NO INTEREST IN THE BULLSHIT. AND IT'S all bullshit, as far as he's concerned. He slips an empty cigarette cylinder onto the edge of a self-rolling machine, packs in some tobacco and snaps down the lever. The last butt still burns in his ashtray, and its grey vapour wafts slowly across the smoking room in his house on the east side of Prince Albert. He's kindly stepped away from the old western he was watching on television to answer a few questions about his famous uncle.

"You've got to be careful," he warns. "Is this going to be fiction? You can talk to 10 different guys and they'll give you 10 different stories."

The 85-year-old has heard many tall tales told in his hometown. A common product of small places and big imaginations. He's a gruff but kind man—nice to chat with, if you can get through the front door. Kvasnak grew up on Sixteenth Street a couple of houses down from the Kiszkan family. His mother, Mary, was the eldest of James and Elizabeth's children. When Mary got married, she and her husband started their family on the same street where she'd grown up. Mike was born in 1933, and he and his older sister were just like another couple of kids in the family. It was a time of struggle, but also one of adventure and fun. He shares all the happy memories and hard lessons of those good old days. And he remembers his uncle Johnny, who went away to the war and brought chocolates for the young kids on the street when he came home. Kvasnak was a rink rat—and eventually a damn decent player in his own right—and he remembers his uncle starting with the M&C Warhawks and the Prince Albert Black Hawks on those packed winter evenings at the Minto Arena. He remembers when Kiszkan left for Cleveland for his first season of professional hockey and when he came home and changed his name. It wasn't a big deal then, he insists, and it isn't a big deal now.

"What's in a name?" Kvasnak asks, quoting Shakespeare. "Well, there's a lot in a name. There really is."

But as far as he's concerned, it doesn't matter how one of the most famous names in hockey came to be. What matters is what his uncle accomplished and what he left behind.

When John Kiszkan returned to Prince Albert from Cleveland after his rookie season in the American Hockey League, he asked his older sister Rose to help change his last name. She was a clerk in a law office and knew her way around the process. That September, when he attended the Barons' training camp in Winnipeg, a small newswire brief about an exhibition game against the Minneapolis Millers stated: "John (Kiszkan) Bower will be in the nets at the opening whistle." The "Kiszkan" qualification remained with Bower's name through most of his second season with the Barons.

The change wasn't actually official until a couple of months later, on November 30, 1946. That day he became John William Bower—and the name John Kiszkan would be reduced to a trivia question, while the name Bower would be raised to the rafters.

Questions about Johnny's age had already started to emerge when he returned from the war and immediately started in net for the M&C Warhawks, like some goalie superhero sent from another planet. Whether by way of typo or intent, the birthdates listed in his military records give three different years of birth, ranging from 1924 to 1921. His early claim on his attestation paper of being born in 1922 appears to be the lie he told to get into the army early. But the claim that he was born in 1921 in his discharge interview is way off and may very well be a simple typo in the report.

Questions about Johnny's age and origin would become central to the media's fixation on his remarkable story. By virtue of what he'd accomplish on the ice, Johnny's fame would grow far beyond what that little boy strapping a cut-up mattress to his legs had ever dreamed. The mystique that he carried would only fuel the interest. Johnny would become one of those unforgettable names, synonymous with the era—a part of the game itself. The phrase "Johnny Bower poke check" would become as commonplace as "Gordie Howe hat trick." Johnny would transcend the game's mere history; he'd become part of its lore.

All the while, even those closest to him would remain in the dark. His family would swear he never told them more than that he changed his name because it was too hard to spell—and that he simply opened up a book, saw the name Bower and chose it. It seemed reasonable enough. Why not? The Bowers were their own invention—a new life, built beyond a great escape. But while he'd always be a private, humble man, Johnny did little to quell the tales that would inevitably rise with his growing celebrity. It's not clear that it was intentional, but the mystery did fall squarely on him.

What's in a name? Well, about a half-dozen different stories for starters.

The name change was never a secret for Johnny. After his one professional season as Kiszkan, it never could be. But it was never something he liked to discuss. When he did, his answers frequently changed. They ranged from straightforward to complex.

The most common answer: He changed his name because reporters had a hard time spelling Kiszkan. Or Kishkan. Because the two were pretty much interchangeable when the young goalie first started making headlines. As far as difficult names go, Kiszkan was a novice problem. But some reporters clearly struggled and just dropped the confusing middle consonant, simplifying the spelling to Kiskan. Like many immigrants, especially at the time, Dmytro Kiszkan had been a constant victim of name-butchering since he'd sailed across the Atlantic. With Johnny's rising fame, it's feasible that the change was just a basic self-marketing decision. This was the simplest of the versions Johnny would tell. But that kind of savvy self-promotion would be a touch out of character for a humble young man intent on working as a railway night watchman had hockey fizzled out.

The other version of that story, told by some of Johnny's family members—like his 99-year-old sister, Anne—is that the Barons made him change his name. The rosy lens on this is that Cleveland's management had the promotional foresight and sharp sense of alliteration to know that a name like Johnny Kiszkan could never carry the soft, poetic symmetry of a name like Johnny Bower. While it would seem a bit aggressive for a minor-pro hockey team to go about suggesting complete rehauls of a 21-year-old rookie's identity, it's certainly a possibility. The darker take is that the change had more to do with the name's origins than its sound. Prejudice against Eastern Europeans was prominent through the early 20th century and certainly continued to the epoch's middle. Kiszkan's Ukrainian roots might have been a detriment to his popularity, and the Barons might have seen more value in a player with a less distinct heritage. But Johnny himself is not on record with this version of history.

He would often suggest that a split in the family had prompted his name change—which seemed to suggest the divorce of his parents, James and Elizabeth. However, in some tellings of that version, he said the name Bower was his mother's maiden name. This, by every other known record, was false. The world's most creative anagrammer couldn't find a way to turn Elizabeth Jacobson's last name into Bower. And throughout his adult life, Johnny's relationship with his mother was strained. The common story was that she had left James, although there is no fair way of knowing how their union fell apart. Regardless, it was a scandal in its time. Even Kvasnak admits that. It was a shocking, painful split for everyone involved, he says.

But Johnny told another story that lent credence to the idea that he had chosen to take his mother's last name. An in-depth feature in *Blueline* magazine, several years into his career, casually mentions that Johnny actually hadn't been born to the Kiszkans at all. The feature explained that Kiszkan had been adopted at an early age and that he'd changed his name back to the name of his biological parents when he turned 21. The story of his adoption would be repeated several times in different features throughout his career—so much so that he'd finally deny it in his autobiography. That there was a large orphanage at the end of Sixteenth Street offers some suspense to the claim, but a simple glance at James Kiszkan's chin and Elizabeth Jacobson's nose, or the shared features of any of his siblings, suggests the adoption talk was likely fiction.

Perhaps there was a different family in Johnny's life—not necessarily at birth, but rather in adolescence. As the family went through hard times and a painful separation, it's been suggested that Johnny moved in with another family in town, the Bowers. He lived with them and thought of them as his own family, and when he had the chance, he decided to officially join the family by changing his name. But why would he never speak of the family that took him? Why take their name but keep them hidden? It seems like another tale born of rumours and not one that Johnny ever harboured himself.

Stories like these flourish in small towns. And in Prince Albert today, there are still whispers of a split within the Kiszkan family that has little to do with the separation of James and Elizabeth. Johnny's brother, Michael, was known as a quiet guy who liked to keep to himself. But he grew up in difficult circumstances—poor kid, poor town, poor time—with few prospects for a better future. He didn't have the athletic ability of his older brother, just 14 months his senior. The two brothers, born so close together, had taken their lives in completely different directions. While Johnny was at war, Michael fell in with a tough crowd in Prince Albert. He'd had run-ins with the law a few too many times. When he was caught for petty theft as a teenager, Anne says, instead of showing leniency, the judge came down hard. He sentenced Michael to two years in jail, which he'd served at the Saskatchewan Federal Penitentiary in Prince Albert, on the outskirts of town, just west of where he'd grown up on Sixteenth Street. After doing time in prison, as his sister Anne says, Mike would sometimes show up at the Minto Arena and watch his brother play. But when Johnny tried to find him afterwards, he'd be gone.

Although he'd always be affable and kind in person to his family, Michael could also be distant and aloof—especially when he got out of prison. Faced with a dire reality, Michael stuck with the wrong crowd. He left home at a young age. The Pen, Anne believes, likely further entrenched his criminal behaviour.

In Prince Albert, the legend of Michael grew alongside Johnny's. The younger brother had not just fallen into a life of petty theft to get by in brutal times—he'd become a master safecracker and gotten involved with the mob. Or so the stories go. In this Cain and Abel prairie myth, Johnny allegedly returned to Prince Albert to find his brother signing cheques in his name. Compromised and angry, Johnny decided he had to change his name to separate himself from the fraudulent criminal path of his younger brother.

That's a story that gets Kvasnak heated. He stayed in sporadic touch with Michael through the years, after he left town and lost contact with most. He was just an ordinary guy, he says, who wanted to be left alone. They wrote letters back and forth, until Kvasnak somehow made his uncle angry and he never heard from him again. But back home in Prince Albert, he says, even though the man is long gone, the legend of his sins continues to grow.

"People don't know. It's just bullshit," Kvasnak says. "Well, like the safecracking—he gave demonstrations in the city hall parking lot."

He pauses to let the point settle in. "No," he says, bluntly. "But you see, the legend grows."

It's true. Legends only rise when freed from the bonds of truth. But it doesn't help that Michael stayed in sporadic contact with his family until he finally disappeared. His only living sister, Anne, still isn't certain if he's dead or alive. Everyone just assumed he was gone. And in a way, he was.

06

STANDING CLOSE

Waskesiu Lake sits in the heart of Prince Albert National Park, a coniferous expanse filled with wildlife on the northern edge of the prairies, about an hour north of Prince Albert. Each summer, the resort town surrounding the lake swelled with vacationers in search of respite from life in Prince Albert, Saskatoon or further south in Regina. The well-off kept permanent cabins, while others camped or set up temporary lodgings. In Saskatchewan, it was the place to be.

After the Barons' season ended in Cleveland, Johnny found work as the assistant golf pro at Waskesiu Golf Course, alongside head pro Johnny Chad—who played junior hockey in Prince Albert, spending a couple of seasons in the NHL with the Chicago Black Hawks before settling into a successful minor-pro career with the Providence Reds.

One afternoon in late June 1948, a group of six young women from Saskatoon walked into the pro shop and booked a tee-off time. None of them appeared to have much experience with golf, so Chad—as Johnny would always tell it—told his assistant golf pro to keep an eye on them. Johnny accepted the assignment without complaint. It helped that one of the young women, in particular, had caught his attention.

And so there, on the first tee at Waskesiu Golf Course, Johnny Bower met Nancy Brain. She was 22 and had recently finished her college studies in shorthand and typing and was working for the department of income tax in Saskatoon, assessing returns. It was meticulous work that could be a headache, so she was grateful for the week-long vacation she'd taken with her friends to Waskesiu.

Johnny didn't know anything about her when he approached the young women as they warmed up, swinging their clubs wildly. Bower politely interjected.

"Girls, you're standing a little close to each other, with the way you're swinging those clubs," he said, advising the apparent rookies that they should be careful of their surroundings and give each other plenty of room.

"Oh, are we standing too close?" one of them mocked as the group laughed.

Johnny, shy and affable, added that it'd be advisable that they not stand in front of the person who was teeing off.

The show of assistant golf pro authority didn't go over well. Nancy Brain gave Johnny a sharp, dirty look. She had grown up in a strict English home. Her father, Frank, served as a soldier in the

First World War for Britain and as a major in the Second World War for Canada. He was a man of rigid rules and firm principles. Frank always called Nancy "Joe" because he'd wanted her to be a boy. (The nickname would stick with Nancy throughout her life.) And much like her father, Nancy "Joe" Brain did not suffer fools.

"What right does he have to tell us?" she said as Johnny walked away.

But Johnny wasn't exactly wrong. The course was mostly empty, but it took the group several hours to play eight holes. Perhaps there was a delay by design. After first being annoyed by Bower's apparent condescension, Nancy decided he was rather cute. And most of the sixsome's focus on the fairway after that first-hole introduction shifted from golf to discussing the handsome assistant pro, so set on abiding by the rules.

Johnny, too, was taken by the beautiful girl with short brown hair and those stunning eyes that had cut straight through him. But he was shy and quiet. Not necessarily nervous, but certainly not overly forward. And so, small as Waskesiu was—and given that spark of attraction on the tees—it's perhaps not surprising that Johnny *just happened* to run into the group of girlfriends as they were out for dinner later that evening.

He asked them what they were up to, and Nancy told him they were heading to a show. Coincidentally, Johnny said, he was also going to check out the new film at the local movie theatre. And, conveniently, he noted, he happened to be going alone.

"Do you want to come to the movies with me?" Johnny asked Nancy, specifically, ignoring the other five.

Nancy glanced around the table for a quick sisterhood consultation. The committee's decision—signalled by quick, quiet nods—was unanimous. Nancy delivered the verdict.

"Sure," she agreed. "We'll go."

But the *we*, of course, was *who* exactly?

Nancy was cautious. She wasn't about to walk solo into a date with a stranger. So, after Johnny and Nancy took their seats for a movie (which neither would remember, because who was watching, anyway?), three of her friends quietly snuck into the row directly behind them, standing guard. Partway through the film, assured that Johnny was as sweet and innocent as he seemed, Nancy gave her pals the signal that it was okay to go. They left Johnny and Nancy sitting there, side by side, just as they would spend the next 70 years of their lives.

JOHNNY AND NANCY kept in touch when she returned home to Saskatoon from Waskesiu. When he had time off from the golf course, he'd take the train down, two hours away, to visit her. It was apparent, immediately, that their courtship was much more than just a summer fling. Nancy was drawn to Johnny's quiet, tender manner. "He has character," she thought. Johnny was the kind of man she wanted to settle down and start a family with.

It helped, too, that he played hockey. When Johnny told Nancy he was a goalie for the Cleveland Barons, she was impressed. Being from Saskatoon, she knew of several local boys who'd gone on to play in the National Hockey League. (One named Gordie Howe, from nearby Floral, had just finished his second season with the

Detroit Red Wings.) And although Nancy's family was distinctly British, Canada's beloved sport had quickly grown on Frank Brain and his family.

He and his wife, Esther, came from the tiny village of Avening, in Gloucestershire, South West England. After the Great War, Frank had worked several odd jobs, while Esther worked in a bakery owned by her grandmother. In the early 1920s the couple took a chance on a new life, deciding on either Canada or Australia as their final destination, but not certain which. With their 18-month-old daughter, Heddie, the young family sailed across the ocean and landed in Halifax. There, the couple settled on giving Canada a shot. They travelled by train to the prairies and started their new life in Saskatoon, where Frank found work with the Canadian National Railway.

Soon the Brain family added three more daughters. Nancy, born in 1925, was the second eldest. Frank never had the son he was looking for, and so Joe would have to do. She used to sit in the family's living room with her father listening to Foster Hewitt broadcasting Toronto Maple Leafs games over the radio, every Saturday night, after he'd worked a long, hard week on the rail lines. The frozen sport—and Hewitt's rapid, colourful descriptions—intrigued Frank, and he quickly became a hockey fan. A strict rule of silence was implemented in the Brain household as Mr. Hewitt shared his weekly poetry. The littlest daughters were to take a bath during Leafs games. There was to be no noise, zero distractions, in the living room. It was Saturday night—hockey night—and that was that.

And after all those cozy winters next to her dad, listening to Hewitt, imagining the plays unfolding far away in mythical Maple Leaf Gardens, Nancy had grown to love the game too.

Near the end of summer, Johnny called Nancy and told her he'd be leaving soon to head back to Cleveland. But he had no intention of leaving her behind. In just a couple of months, he'd fallen madly in love with the girl he'd met by chance that day at hole number one in Waskesiu.

"I'd like you to marry me," Johnny said.

Nancy stuck to protocol.

"You'll have to come and talk to my parents first," she said.

And so Johnny took the train to Saskatoon to ask permission to marry Nancy. He stood nervously before Frank and Esther and shared his intention to make their daughter his wife.

"Well, what do you do?" Frank asked with a sharp English accent.

"I play hockey," Johnny said.

Despite his fondness for the sport the young man played, Colonel Brain wasn't about to let Private Bower off easily.

"You're a hockey player," Frank said. "Well, how much money do you make?"

"I don't know," Johnny said, timidly.

"And you want to marry my daughter?" Frank replied, incredulous.

"Yes, sir," Johnny said. "I think, in time, hockey could really pay off."

In time?

"I'm not worried about 'in time,'" Frank said. "I want to know what's going to happen to her right now."

"We'll be fine," Johnny mustered the courage to say. "I want to marry your daughter."

Frank stared sternly at Johnny, remaining quiet for what must have felt like minutes. Then, finally, he said: "Well, what do you think, Mother?"

Esther had sat quietly through the entire conversation. She adored the polite young gentleman who'd captured her daughter's heart. But she was going to play it out just a little longer. Without saying a word, she got up and walked to the French doors that led into the adjacent room, pushed through them and left. The young couple sat there, unsure of what to do. For a moment, Johnny worried that she might have gone to grab a gun.

Then, after a few moments, she returned with a small piece of paper in her hand. It was Nancy's birth certificate. She handed it to her daughter with a smile.

"You'll need this."

With the Barons' season starting in the fall, Johnny and Nancy agreed they'd get married in Cleveland. Johnny left that September for training camp in Winnipeg. He told his coach, Bun Cook, about his plans to get married. Cook looked at the team's schedule and saw an opening of several days without games in early November.

"I think I can give you a few days off, if you want," he said.

It was considered a kind gesture for the era, and Johnny was grateful. (The Leafs, he'd later note in his autobiography, were known to send a player to the minors for having the audacity to get married and cause such a disruption during the season.)

In late October, the Barons faced the NHL's Detroit Red Wings in an exhibition series. The Red Wings had been runners-up for the Stanley Cup that spring, falling to the Toronto Maple Leafs, winners of the second of what would be three straight championships to finish off the 1940s.

In a prescient write-up in the *Akron Beacon Journal*, Johnny was described as having given every indication that he'd soon be on the AHL's list of greatest goalies, even though he was still splitting duties with fellow netminder Roger Bessette. The paper called Bower youthful and catlike, a precursor to his first nickname—the Panther Man—which would appear in the press later that season. The Red Wings had no trouble revealing the NHL's superiority, beating the Barons 6–3. Gordie Howe, starting his third pro season at just 20 years old, scored a hat trick. It was one of many battles Howe and Bower would have on the ice, even though they'd become great friends off of it. Even though Howe managed the hat trick, Johnny still got the better of him as none of the three were scored on him. Johnny blanked the Red Wings in the third period after Bessette allowed all six goals in the previous two.

Around the same time that Bower was facing Howe, Nancy was packing up her life in Saskatoon—a couple of trunks full— to take the CN train overnight en route to Cleveland. It was the farthest trip she'd ever made alone.

Compared with Saskatoon, Cleveland was enormous. Sitting on the edge of Lake Erie, the city was an essential manufacturing centre and a key transportation hub, a conduit between the Great Lakes and the rail lines that connected the country. At the time, Cleveland's population was close to 900,000 people, ranking among the largest cities in the United States. (Today, after difficult decades of decline through shifting trends in manufacturing, Cleveland's population sits at less than 400,000.) Nancy quickly fell in love with the city. While the region was expanding into suburbs and new shopping malls, Cleveland's downtown centre was still lined with restaurants, parlours and famous department stores, like Halle's and Higbee's. For a time, Euclid Avenue, Cleveland's main downtown thoroughfare, was considered one of the biggest retail districts in the United States. Streetcars rumbled up and down busy streets. But although Cleveland bustled with life, it still had some of the small-town charm that Nancy had grown up with back in Saskatoon. It was a welcoming, comfortable place.

It was also a proud sports town. The Barons' Calder Cup win the previous spring was just part of the city's athletic success. A few weeks before Nancy arrived, the Cleveland Indians beat the Boston Braves to the win the 1948 World Series. The championship, the team's first in 28 years, capped a historical season in which 42-year-old pitcher Satchel Paige, a long-time star of America's black baseball leagues, was finally given a chance to play in the major leagues with Cleveland. He was the oldest player to ever make a major-league debut and became the first black player to pitch in a World Series. At the same time, that fall, the Cleveland Browns football team was on its way to a third straight All-American Football

Conference championship (in the team's first three years of existence). Cleveland was dubbed "the City of Champions."

Nancy spent her first week in Cleveland making the arrangements for the wedding. Frank and Esther Brain took the train trip from Saskatoon shortly after she arrived. The night before the wedding, Bower asked his father-in-law-to-be out for a drink at a bar across the street from the Cleveland Arena. Frank was partial to libations of the strong, warm English type. He ordered a Black Forest Ale and then had a few more, as the two men bonded over pints. The next morning, Frank was a little worse for wear but still happy to see his daughter get married. Had he opened the Cleveland *Plain Dealer* that morning, he would have discovered that his little Joe's life was suddenly newsworthy. In the paper's sports section, under the headline "A New Baroness," word of her nuptials was shared with all of Cleveland: "Goalie Johnny Bower of the Cleveland Barons will take that jump to the benedicts league this morning . . . The girlie who goaled the goalie is Nancy Muriel Brain, of Saskatoon, Sask."

And so, just six months after that first movie together—now in the city of perpetual winning—Nancy Brain was to become Nancy Bower. The ceremony was held at noon at Cleveland's Trinity Church on Euclid Avenue. Bun Cook kindly scheduled practice for 10 a.m. that morning so that all of the Barons and the team management would be able to attend. Roy Kelly, Johnny's teammate, stood up as his best man. No one from Johnny's family was there.

After the ceremony, Johnny and Nancy walked up the aisle under a canopy of hockey sticks held up by the Barons players. The team's captain, Freddie "the Fox" Thurier, paraded the newlyweds from the church to a reception at the Belmont Hotel, where the party continued into the night.

But any honeymoon for the happy new couple would have to wait. Ever the company man, Johnny was back to work, between the pipes, just a couple of days later. To his credit, Bun Cook had generously suggested the couple travel to New York City for a few days to celebrate, but Nancy declined. She liked it just fine in Cleveland, she said. Manhattan had zero appeal to her; it never would.

THAT YEAR WOULD turn out to be a momentous one for the groom. On the ice, Johnny picked up more playing time when Bessette went down with a leg injury, and he took full advantage of the opportunity, winning his first four starts. It turned out that having the wedding early in the Barons' season was a wise choice. Early that December, Spike Jones and His City Slickers had the 1948 holiday hit "All I Want for Christmas Is My Two Front Teeth," which would reach number one on the pop charts in 1949. A couple of weeks later, as the catchy tune hummed from radios across America, an errant stick whacked Johnny in the mouth during a game against Providence. The blow sliced open his tongue, knocked out one of his front teeth and left the other dangling, until it was pulled by the team dentist, Dr. Marty Seymour. With Bessette out, Johnny couldn't miss a game. The toothless tender was back in net for the Barons the next evening in Buffalo, fuelled by three bowls of soup because he wasn't able to chew.

By Christmas Day, less than a week later, Johnny had indeed been blessed with the gift of a full grill, the recipient of some rushed bridgework by Seymour. "I sure wanted 'em for Christmas," he told the Cleveland *Plain Dealer*, with a big full grin. Johnny sported his brand new pearly whites in a 4–0 win over the Indianapolis Capitals on the 25th. After the shutout, the Capitals' 18-year-old rookie goalie skated down the ice from his crease to shake Bower's hand. His name was Terry Sawchuk.

The Panther Man, as Johnny was now being called in the press, followed up that whiteout performance with back-to-back shut-outs early in the new year. By the end of the regular season—his fourth in Cleveland—Johnny had earned his position as the Barons' number one goaltender and was being discussed as one of the best in the 11-team American Hockey League. But while the AHL was filled with top talent, it wasn't the league that young players grew up dreaming of playing in. It was a fine living, sure—and it certainly beat working in the railyard back in Prince Albert. But as an independent franchise, the Barons didn't have (or want) affiliation with an NHL club, like several of their opponents did. The Barons had been owned by local businessman and sports pro-moter Al Sutphin, who had been key in the development of the AHL (and had a hand in creating the Ice Capades). Sutphin ran his organization like a major professional team. When he sold the franchise in the spring of '49, he handed the management reins over to Jim Hendy, who had been president of the United States Hockey League, a minor-pro circuit in which the Barons had a farm team. Hendy had every intention of maintaining the Barons' reputation as a top pro team, with designs on one day joining the NHL. So, while a young star like Terry Sawchuk was only in Indianapolis to prepare for his inevitable rise to the Detroit Red Wings, the NHL team that owned him, the Barons wanted to keep 24-year-old Bower around just as he seemed to be reaching his prime. Johnny was fine with that, of course. Intensely loyal, he was grateful for the opportunity the Barons had given him to play the game professionally. And as he and Nancy started their life together, Cleveland felt like home.

Still, the hope lingered that Johnny might one day find his way into one of the only six goaltending spots available with a National Hockey League team. At the time, in 1949, those spots were occupied by legendary goalies: his boyhood hero Frank Brimsek in Boston, Turk Broda in Toronto, Bill Durnan in Montreal, Chuck Rayner in New York, Jim Henry in Chicago and Harry Lumley in Detroit. If it was difficult for many talented forwards and defencemen to make it to the six-team NHL, it was even harder for a goalie. So, Johnny would have to bide his time in Cleveland—and it was quite possible that he'd have to end his time there too.

Riding Johnny's incredible goaltending, with his league-leading five shutouts and 38 wins, the Barons made it all the way to the Calder Cup final in 1950. They faced the Indianapolis Capitals for the championship, but Bower was outmatched by Sawchuk, who was playing his final season in the AHL before joining the Red Wings in what would be a Hall of Fame career. Sawchuk would give up just 12 goals in eight games in the 1950 AHL playoffs. The Capitals swept the Barons in four games to win the Calder Cup.

In the off-season, the Barons asked Johnny to work on his rebound control, which had emerged as his most vulnerable weakness. The arthritis that kept him out of action during the war also made it difficult for him to hang on to pucks fired at his glove side. To compensate, Johnny had developed the habit of simply knocking the puck down in front of him. He also tended to leave pucks in scoring position instead of driving them into the corner out of danger. Johnny worked on his weaknesses relentlessly, almost obsessively, seeking to perfect his game in practices—a trait he would become famous for throughout his career.

In training camp that fall, Johnny faced new competition for his starting job from a younger goalie named Lou Crowdis, brought in by Jim Hendy, perhaps to keep his star goalie on edge. The added pressure forced Johnny to keep quiet about an injured leg, which he endured throughout training camp in order to prove that he deserved to keep the number one spot. He did, of course, and Johnny was the Barons' most important player through the 1950–51 season. Often left to his own devices as the Barons focused their attention on the offensive attack, Johnny bailed out his teammates in heroic fashion game after game. His play garnered comparisons from head coach Bun Cook to that of Frank Brimsek of the Bruins. The compliment thrilled Johnny, who was humbled to be mentioned in the same sentence as his hero. Once again Bower led the AHL in wins, with 44, and he earned AHL All-Star Team honours. The Barons made it to the Calder Cup final for the second straight season. This time they faced the Pittsburgh Hornets. Johnny was peppered with shots in the series, stopping more than 50 twice, as the Barons and Hornets battled to a seventh and final game. There, Johnny kicked aside 38 in a 3–1 victory to win the Calder Cup.

The following season, Johnny's reputation for resilience continued to grow. He took a skate to the chin and mouth in a game against Indianapolis just after Christmas. With blood pouring from his face, Johnny was rushed off the ice into the locker room. He lost another tooth and needed seven stiches to tie up the gaping wound. But 10 minutes later, after what the Cleveland *Plain Dealer* called "an injury that would have benched a less courageous player," Johnny returned to the ice to finish off the 5–1 win.

That year, Johnny battled for the league's best goals-against average and won the Harry "Hap" Holmes Memorial Award as the AHL's top goaltender. He was named a First-Team All-Star and was the unanimous choice by Barons fans for the team's most valuable player. Cleveland was knocked out of the first round of the playoffs by the Providence Reds, but Johnny's status in the game was solidified. There were more and more whispers that the Barons' 27-year-old veteran goaltender could easily play in the NHL, if given a chance.

"He's the world's best goalie, in my book," Barons coach Bun Cook told the Cleveland *Plain Dealer*.

Perhaps. But although Johnny was well on his way to becoming the greatest goaltender in AHL history, he still hadn't had his chance to prove he was the best in the game.

CHINA WALL

Nancy Bower woke up in the middle of the night to the sound of rustling downstairs in the kitchen. She looked over to her husband's side of the bed. He was gone, but his pillow was drenched through with blood.

Panicked, she rushed down the stairs to the kitchen, where she found Johnny struggling to tend to the terrible wound that had split above his lip. Nancy had seen her husband carry many cuts and bruises home from the games he played. He'd had his nose broken a few times and been knocked out now and then. It was commonplace for Johnny to come home with a new lump or cut on his face. (Team trainers often kept leeches to place on lumps and bring down the swelling.) Up to that point in his career, Johnny had already lost eight teeth. It was always scariest when an injury was close to an eye or the mouth. This was by the far the worst she'd seen.

Earlier that evening in late January 1953, Nancy had been at their house in Cleveland listening to the live broadcast as the Barons played the Hornets two and a half hours away in Pittsburgh. She'd heard the reports that Johnny was down on the ice after taking a shot in the face. The puck fired by the Hornets' John McLellan smacked him directly in the mouth. He was nearly knocked unconscious by the blow.

The impact drove his teeth through his flesh. It knocked out a four-tooth bridge he already had in his mouth. A pivot tooth broke. Another front bridge was shattered, one anchor tooth was knocked out, and another was cracked. One of the broken teeth exposed a nerve.

The game slammed to a worried halt. Pittsburgh's goalie, Gil Mayer, rushed across the ice to see if Johnny was okay and helped with first aid when Bower was taken to the locker room. Dr. Philip Faix, the Pittsburgh team physician, said it was the worst injury to a goaltender he'd ever treated. To Faix's shock, Johnny asked the doctor to let him continue the game. Dr. Faix refused. Plastic surgery was needed to repair the damage to his lip.

A Barons front-office worker, Floyd Perras, had to come in from the stands, get dressed and finish the game. It was one of the game's quirks that a team employee would take over in net if a goalie was hurt. The cost of keeping a second goalie was deemed too expensive, so the Barons' promotional manager would have to do. To Perras's credit, he did sometimes practice with the team. But the single-goalie system remains one of the most illogical rules of the game's history.

Back in Cleveland, Nancy was still waiting for news on the radio. She hoped the team would have the sense to take Johnny to a hospital in Pittsburgh. When Nancy got a call saying her husband was travelling home on the team bus that night, she was incredulous. She waited and waited for him to arrive. Hours later, when he finally walked in the door, Johnny held a filthy-looking towel to his face, covered in blood.

"Didn't they do anything for you?" she asked.

The doctor had cleaned up the wound, bandaged it and given Johnny an anesthetic to freeze out the pain.

Nancy tried to get Johnny to go to the hospital, but it was already late and he planned to get checked out in the morning. She had packed up some ice for him to put on the wound. But now, in the middle of the night, his pillow was drenched in blood and her husband was puttering around the kitchen, trying to mend his own face.

"That's it! We're going to the hospital."

At 3 a.m., she took her husband to get his face fixed.

The next morning, Nancy got a call from team management, asking why she'd taken Bower to the hospital.

"He never should have come home on the bus," she said. "He was bleeding so bad."

Nancy was told she should have taken Johnny to the hospital affiliated with the Barons, instead of the closest one to their house.

"Well," she said, "that's just too damn bad."

After being transferred to the Barons' infirmary of choice, Johnny spent the next several days lying in a hospital bed. It took

12 stitches to close the bloody gash above his lip. He'd need to have a full plate put in during the off-season, but Johnny wasn't concerned about going toothless for a while. The Barons were battling for the top spot in the regular season, and he just wanted to get back on the ice.

After missing just three games, Johnny returned—wearing a brace on his jaw and a big white bandage across his upper lip. He'd spent the week on a liquid diet, unable to chew solid food. Still, Johnny made 20 saves. It was a 3–0 loss, but he was heralded for his courage in returning to the team so quickly. But Johnny didn't think much of the feat. His face would just go numb when he got hit with a puck, and later, when the pain set in, it wasn't unbearable. Johnny simply viewed it as a test. If he didn't get right back in the net—or if he did but flinched when a puck was shot at him—it would show that he was scared to play. He had to show that he wasn't. At the time, wearing a mask in a game didn't cross his mind. Sometimes he wore one in practice. It was a clear piece of Plexiglas that looked like something a welder would wear. Johnny hated it. Every time he wore it, it would fog up and he wouldn't be able to see anything. So, despite his missing teeth, Johnny wasn't about to start wearing a mask in games.

And anyway, he seemed to thrive in painful settings. Two nights after his return, the Barons tied the Syracuse Warriors 4–4 in an overtime draw. Johnny made 52 saves. A few nights later, he made 35 saves in a 4–2 win over the St. Louis Flyers. The following week, the Barons travelled to Buffalo to face the Bisons and a young netminder named Jacques Plante, who was his rival for top-goalie honours that year. The future Montreal Canadiens star would become the first NHL goaltender to wear a mask in games on a regular basis. A still-bandaged Johnny made 47 saves on 50 shots—while the Barons put seven past Plante on 40 shots, including one from the Barons' end that skipped over his stick.

That season, Geoffrey Fisher, a reporter from the *Cleveland News*, started to refer to Johnny as "the China Wall" in his reports. Fisher first used the reference to describe how impenetrable the Barons goalie was after he'd posted a couple of shutouts. Johnny picked up the paper one morning and saw Fisher's China Wall reference. He loved it. The Panther Man, as Johnny had been previously, just didn't have the right ring to it. The idea of a vast, ancient wall was the perfect way to describe Johnny's play—and it would become increasingly relevant as time went by. After Fisher first used the term, it stuck. And ever since, in the world of hockey the China Wall would be synonymous with Johnny Bower.

As the season wound down, in late March, Johnny had a bone chip removed from his upper jaw—and in the process, the doctor discovered that his jaw had been broken the entire time. "The dentist lanced the jaw, but Bower will play tonight," reported the Cleveland *Plain Dealer*. "Complications are still arising from a terrific face wound received by the star goalie." Despite those lingering complications, Johnny finished the regular season with a 2.54 goals-against average and six shutouts.

In the league final that spring, the Barons battled the rival Pittsburgh Hornets for the Calder Cup. The Hornets were then a minor-league affiliate of the Toronto Maple Leafs and were coached by King Clancy, a former player with the franchise. Clancy would move up to coach the Leafs the following season and eventually settled into a role as the team's assistant general manager, alongside Punch Imlach. Clancy was about to get a taste of what his future goalie was capable of.

Throughout the playoffs rumours swirled that the New York Rangers were planning to make a deal with the Barons that would finally bring Bower to the NHL. While he did his best to downplay the chatter, the battered Bower played like a man with something to prove. After putting up two shutouts in the first series over Syracuse, Johnny blanked the Hornets 2–0 in the opening game of the final series, as 8,500 fans packed into the Arena in Cleveland. Later, in Game 6, Johnny made 78 saves in a game that took four overtime periods to lose. The 3–2 victory by the Hornets in Pittsburgh forced a seventh game. During the game, Johnny was struck in the face by a puck that was thrown from the stands. Police officers were unable to track down the perpetrator. The match lasted for 121 minutes and 46 seconds of playing time, less than a minute shy of the AHL record. It ended just before 2 a.m.

"Yes, I'm tired," Johnny admitted at practice the next day. "And I didn't get much sleep. I was playing the game over, I guess. But I'll be rested by tomorrow."

Johnny was rested enough to post another shutout—his fourth of the playoffs—in Game 7 as the Barons and Hornets battled once again to overtime, this time tied at zero. In one of the more bizarre ways to win a championship, the Barons' Bob Chrystal lobbed a high shot on goal from 70 feet out that bounced awkwardly, changing direction in front of Hornets goalie Gil Mayer and finding its way into the net. The Arena erupted as the Barons celebrated on the ice, crowding around the Calder Cup. It was the "longest and hardest-fought playoff series" in league history, the *Plain Dealer* would declare. The Barons pumped their fists in the air and let out a cheer as a camera captured the moment. Johnny, kneeling on the far left, had the biggest toothless smile of them all.

IN EIGHT SEASONS with the Barons, the shy kid from Prince Albert had become an AHL star. But could his success in the minors translate to the National Hockey League? Johnny himself didn't doubt it. There was certainly a difference between the skill level of the NHL and AHL, but with only six teams in the top tier, Johnny had faced plenty of talent in the minors. Cleveland had been kind to Nancy and him. It was as much of a home as any other place he'd lived in his life. But the New York Rangers were knocking on the door, and answering would mean an opportunity to finally prove what many had long suspected—that Bower was one of the best in the game, period. The rumours excited him. A move to New York would also mean a higher salary, and in an era where even the best players had to pick up side jobs in the summers, turning down a raise just wasn't an option.

As Johnny unstrapped his heavy, sweat-soaked leather pads after the Barons celebrated their Calder Cup win on the ice, he was asked about his future. Any deal made by the Barons required his approval.

"If they will match the National League salary here, I'll stay,"

Johnny said, making it a matter of simple economics. But Jim Hendy had already said he'd match any NHL salary his goalie was offered—while adding that he wouldn't stand in the way if Bower wanted to leave. Still, he knew that after eight seasons in Cleveland, Bower was too good for the AHL. "We can't hold him back any longer," Hendy said.

But quietly, at the time, Johnny wasn't entirely sure he wanted to stay in the game at all.

In the summers, he and Nancy would return to their favourite paradise at Waskesiu Lake. Their friends, Ken and Jean Turnbull, had opened a restaurant there called the Saratoga Grill in 1949. Johnny had found that he preferred playing golf to teaching it, and he wasn't a fan of the hassles that came along with his assistant golf pro job at the course. Instead of focusing on golf, Johnny had spent much of his time chasing down young caddies who had stolen balls—to sell around the block at three for a dollar. Or he was sent out to quiet down unruly foursomes distracting the other well-heeled golfers on the course. While that job had worked out once—in meeting Nancy—he grew tired of playing the course policeman. Just as he had declined an authoritarian role in the military, Johnny had little interest in enforcing golf course rules. So, when Ken Turnbull asked if he and Nancy would be interested in helping out at the Saratoga Grill they decided to give it a try.

The Saratoga offered them a chance to make some extra money in the summer, side by side, in the lakeside town they loved. Johnny worked the grill along with Ken, while Jean and Nancy worked up front, waiting tables. Johnny was content in the repetitive, constant flow of flipping beef patties and grilling whitefish. He created his own signature burger. Something of a local celebrity because of his success in Cleveland, Johnny was already a popular draw for guests.

The Saratoga Grill sat next to the Red Deer Chalet, where lots of tourists stayed. It was near the breakwater, where kids took swimming and diving lessons—and it was right next to the boat dock. The Saratoga had quickly become a popular place for local youth, wealthy tourists and golfers from the nearby course. By 6 a.m. every morning, golfers would come in for a pre-round breakfast. Throughout the day, families came in to eat after spending hours on the beach and in the water. Music floated through the diner during the day from boats in the bay, or from the nearby roller rink in the evenings. Crowds of young people would come on weekend nights from the dance hall down the street for hamburgers and Cokes, which went for seven cents. Ice cream went for five. The restaurant served fresh whitefish caught in the lake every day. A sign on the wall in the diner read, "The fish on the menu today slept last night in the Bay."

Johnny enjoyed his time on the grill so much that he even thought about opening up a place of his own. And in the summer of 1953, as rumours that he was heading to the NHL persisted, Johnny actually considered retiring from hockey. At 28, he'd already gotten more out of the game than he could have imagined as a boy growing up in Prince Albert through the Great Depression. Although the bright lights of Manhattan were luring, they were also a long way from the serenity of his life with Nancy on the lake. He'd also just undergone complicated dental surgery to repair his mangled teeth that off-season. By Johnny's count, to that point, he'd sacrificed nine teeth for the sport.

The phone rang at the Saratoga on July 20, 1953. It was the Barons' general manager, Jim Hendy. And it was official: Johnny Bower was the property of the New York Rangers. His rights had been traded to the Rangers, along with Eldred Kobussen, in exchange for cash, Neil Strain and goalie Emile Francis, who had been the top goalie with the Vancouver Canucks of the Western Hockey League the previous season. Johnny had mixed feelings when he got the call. He wasn't sure if Manhattan was a risk worth taking. Hendy didn't try to soften the decision. The Rangers had finished last in the six-team league during the 1952–53 season, with just 17 wins.

"It's going to be rough up there for you," he told Johnny. "They're developing their team."

It also wasn't apparent that Bower had a guaranteed job with the Rangers. New York already had an excellent young goaltender in Gump Worsley, who had been called in to replace the aging and injured Chuck Rayner during the 1952–53 season and was so impressive that he earned the Calder Trophy as the NHL's best rookie. At just 24 years old, Worsley seemed like the goalie of the future for the Rangers. When the Rangers announced they had traded for Johnny, the team stated he would compete with Worsley in training camp for the top job. But despite his excellent rookie season, the Rangers seemed to have doubts about the diminutive Worsley, who was just five foot seven and 150 pounds. The Rangers had given up a lot for Johnny. It was clear they had serious plans to use him. With Johnny hesitant to sign with New York, the Rangers sent Muzz Patrick, a member of the team's front office, to Waskesiu Lake to try to convince him. Patrick walked into the Saratoga one afternoon, right in the middle of the lunch rush. Bower was busy flipping burgers at the grill, and he told Patrick he'd make him something to eat. He made the Rangers coach one of his signature burgers, and they sat down to chat when the lunch rush died down. Patrick had brought along his own sweet dessert. When he showed Bower just how much he'd make with the Rangers, Bower decided Manhattan was worth a shot and he signed the deal.

That summer, Worsley was working as a bartender at a hotel in Saskatoon, where he'd played previously with the Saskatoon Quakers in the Western Hockey League. The goalies had never met before. Johnny walked in and took a seat at the bar, while Gump eyed him from behind the counter as though he looked familiar. Gump was a bit on the chubby side, and the first thing Johnny thought was that he was going to spend the summer getting in shape and beat his rival out of his job in training camp. Johnny had a drink and then, before he left, said: "Gumper, I'll probably be your standby come training camp."

"I *thought* you were Johnny Bower," Gump replied. "Well, the only thing I can say to you is good luck, because you've got your work cut out for you."

There were few pleasantries when Johnny reported to the Rangers' training camp that September. He arrived as slim as he could, contrasting himself to the short, plump Gump—and he outduelled the

Rangers' returning goalie. New York handed the starting position to Johnny, sending Worsley across the continent to the Vancouver Canucks of the Western Hockey League. Worsley and Johnny would eventually become great friends. They still had a camaraderie, years later, when they'd play against each other in the NHL. They even went on a number of cruises as couples together with their wives. But at the time, there was no love lost between them. Before Worlsey left, he stopped Johnny and let him know he didn't intend to stay gone for long.

"I'll come back," he said. "And I'll get you."

JOHNNY, THE STUDENT, stood square in his stance and stared at the puck in front of him. Everything else in the arena escaped his mind. He had one task—one simple but critical task. To dive forward and drive that puck as far away from the net as possible, regardless of the collateral damage caused to any poor soul trying to manoeuvre it by him. It was about precision and speed. It was about surprise. Before coming to New York, Johnny had rarely used the poke check he would become famous for. But in the faster pace of the NHL, a goalie had to be aggressive. It wasn't enough to merely get in front of the puck. No, he had to attack. He had to shock the opposing forward with agility and force. He had to make the move before his opponent did.

Charlie Rayner, the New York Rangers' veteran keeper whose career had been cut short by a knee injury, had assumed the role of the Rangers' de facto goalie coach, which was something no team bothered to keep at the time. Rayner started working with

Johnny right after training camp. It was an apprenticeship that would shape his Hall of Fame career.

Rayner watched Johnny closely from the stands each game, making notes on what he thought the aged rookie was doing wrong. He felt that Johnny flopped too much—something that might have worked in the minors but would be picked apart in NHL. He also warned Johnny about his weakness managing the puck.

"You have got to know how to handle the puck," Rayner told him. "You can't always stop it. You have to know how to handle it, stop it, and shoot it ahead . . . and you have to know how to poke check."

The poke check was a split-second decision, Rayner explained. It was also a huge gamble. One wrong calculation and the net would be left wide open. Johnny learned that as soon as a player reached the lower edge of the faceoff circle, he could drive out and catch the puck with his stick.

After Rangers practices, Rayner put his pupil through a series of rigorous drills. He'd place six pucks in an arc from the bottom of the faceoff circle and make Johnny dive stick-first into each of them, one after the other, again and again, until he mastered the skill. It was exhausting repetition—like burpees in full soaked-leather goalie gear. Rayner also taught Johnny the sweep check, a full-body version of the poke check that would cut off a player coming across the net and usually ended with the player flying out of control through the crease.

The Rangers' season started on the road, in Detroit, on October 8,

1953, where things got off to a rough start for the 28-year-old rookie. Gordie Howe—another Saskatchewan kid and a close friend who happened to be the world's best player—welcomed him to the league by scoring one of the Red Wings' four goals in the Rangers' loss. A few days later, Johnny picked up his first NHL win, 5–3 over Chicago—in a game that would be much more indicative of his rookie season.

When the Rangers returned home a couple of weeks later, the Bowers stayed at a hotel next to Madison Square Garden. But, evidently, Johnny didn't realize just how close to the rink they were. Leaving for the Rangers' game, Johnny walked out of the wrong entrance at the hotel, leaving him around the corner from the rink. Oblivious, he found a cab and asked the driver to take him to the arena. "Hop in," the driver said, because a fare is a fare. He made two right turns and pulled up next door in front of the Garden.

But the Bowers' transition into life in New York City would take much longer. They rented a place out on Long Island, where many of the other players lived. To get to the games in downtown Manhattan, they had to take the subway or travel through the city's infamously thick traffic. Although world famous, New York didn't appeal much to the Bowers. They tried to settle into the city's hectic, bustling pace. But the gargantuan metropolis had none of the warmth of tiny Saskatoon, none of the serenity of the prairies, none of the beauty of Waskesiu Lake, or even the personal connections possible in a relatively large American city like Cleveland. New York was bright, loud and obnoxious. It was a monster of a city. And it certainly wasn't home. Nancy hated it.

Even the Rangers fans were unlikable. Spectators were notoriously rough in New York. They would throw stuff on the ice if a goalie let in a bad goal. During one game, Johnny was bombarded with full cans of beer after allowing three goals. Johnny crouched inside his net to avoid getting hit. And unlike Cleveland, where fans were loyal and dedicated, hockey had much less appeal in New York. While the Yankees had well-known stars like Mickey Mantle and Yogi Berra, the Rangers players were relatively anonymous. Johnny felt that the fans in New York didn't really understand the game they were watching. It was just a show to them—and they let players from both teams have it. Sometimes, playing on home ice, he wished he was back in Cleveland where the fans understood the game and appreciated him.

The team even seemed like an afterthought at Madison Square Garden. The rink was dark and the lighting system cast shadows all over the ice. It was busy too. The Garden would often host basketball or boxing in the afternoon, with boards placed over the ice. The Rangers would play later in the evening, when the ice was soft and terrible for skating. And because of all the events coming through the venue, there was little time for actual practices on the main ice surface. The Rangers had to settle for small upstairs practice rinks, which had steel boards. Otherwise the team practised on the outskirts of town.

But it wasn't all bad in New York. In fact, Johnny, under the close guidance of Rayner, was excellent. He was by far the team's most valuable player, especially early in the new year when he led the Rangers to the best record in the NHL between January 1 and

February 21. Johnny had two shutouts and six one-goal games through that stretch, with a goals-against average of 2.14. Dubbed the "veteran-rookie," the press often gave Johnny a hard time about the top row of teeth that he'd pop out of his mouth and place in a glass in his stall during each game. But he'd also quickly earned respect around the league.

"Bower is key to our team," said Muzz Patrick, who stepped in as the Rangers' coach partway through the season. "He gives us a good crack at any game. He may not have the fine moves of a Sawchuk, or a Lumley, but he gets his work done. He has something special—a lot of guts."

By March, Johnny was being discussed as the potential winner of not only the Calder Trophy as rookie of the year but also the Hart Trophy as the league's most valuable player—up against players like Red Kelly, Gordie Howe and Maurice Richard (whom Johnny considered the best goal scorer he ever faced).

While the accolades were nice, off the ice much bigger things were happening. On March 11, 1954, in New York City, Nancy went into labour. She gave birth to their first child, a son. They named him John. Johnny held the newborn boy tightly in his arms. From that first moment, regardless of what his success in the game would bring, greater than any legacy left on the ice—above it all— Johnny's family would always be the piece of his life that he carried closest to his heart.

The Rangers finished in fifth place, just behind the Boston Bruins for the final playoff spot. But it was an 18-point improvement from the previous year. And Johnny, who played all 70 games that season, posted a 2.54 goals-against average—the lowest posted by any Rangers goalie in 14 years. Despite the objects thrown in his direction, the Rangers fans showed their appreciation by voting Johnny as the team's most popular player.

He earned a wristwatch for the honour. But, just as Gump Worsley had learned a year earlier, a goalie's individual success on the ice wouldn't secure his place within a dysfunctional Rangers organization.

And just as quickly as Johnny had made his mark in the NHL, he was gone.

08

MINORS CONSOLATION

THE BLIZZARD HIT AS THEY REACHED THE MOUNTAINS. IT WAS a complete whiteout. Johnny strained to see the road ahead. Nancy sat nervously beside him, watching over their infant son. She was still trying to process how they had gotten there.

It had been mere months since Johnny had been discussed as a possible Hart Trophy winner and Calder Trophy winner. But New York was known as the graveyard of goalies for a reason. Just as Gump Worsley had been tossed aside in favour of the older rookie a season earlier, Johnny knew he could face a similar fate under the unpredictable Rangers management.

The decision came down to Muzz Patrick, who just a year earlier had journeyed out to Lake Waskesiu to convince Johnny to sign with the Rangers. Starting his first full season as the Rangers' coach, Muzz said he planned to make his decision on the team's goaltending based entirely on what he saw in training camp, and nothing else.

Johnny arrived at training camp that fall a little overweight, coming in five pounds heavier than he had the season before—perhaps due to the added responsibilities of fatherhood. He felt sluggish. But Worsley had returned from exile in impressive condition. During his time in Vancouver, Worsley had continued the excellent play he had put on display in New York before Johnny took his spot. He started 70 games for the Canucks and posted a 2.40 goals-against average, winning the WHL's MVP award. When he said he'd be back for Bower, he meant it.

The Rangers took both Bower and Worsley on an exhibition tour through the west coast, playing their farm teams in Vancouver, Kamloops, Kelowna and Seattle. Worsley outduelled Johnny through that stretch. Patrick felt that Johnny sometimes let in soft goals that others would stop. He felt that Worsley was a more complete keeper. Then the Rangers travelled to Saskatchewan for another series of games in Regina, Saskatoon and Prince Albert—but only Worsley got to play. And he played spectacularly. Having outperformed Johnny throughout camp, he won back his starting job in New York.

After Johnny was told he was being sent to Vancouver, he returned home to the apartment to share the bad news with Nancy.

"How can they do that, John?" she asked.

Everyone in the hockey world was puzzled by the decision. Johnny, trying to take the responsibility, would blame his conditioning and criticize himself for not working hard enough in the off-season—even though neither his work ethic nor his physical condition had ever been, or ever would be, brought into question throughout his career.

One theory, later printed in *Blueline* magazine, was that Johnny didn't get along well with his teammates. Despite his affable nature with fans, in the locker room, he'd earned a reputation of being a loner. Although Johnny would mellow later in his career, he had very much played the part of the oddball goalie early on. He didn't hang out at the usual spots with teammates away from the rink, and he didn't spend much time boozing or smoking. On the ice, he was a perfectionist. Johnny was often bitter about defensive lapses that led to goals—sometimes openly.

"I have always been a bad loser," he told *Blueline* magazine a few years after his debut season in the NHL, admitting he would get a bit too worked up when his teammates made a mistake.

"A goaltender shouldn't get mad at his defenceman, because it just brings on more strain," Johnny said. "Still, it's so darn hard to swallow your feelings when one of your own defencemen gets in your way and deflects a shot into your cage . . . I realize now that I didn't do some things I should have done. I never patted a defenceman on the pants after a good play. I never said any kind words when I got a bit of cover. When I look back I guess I was too hot-headed."

At four years younger than Johnny, Worsley was clearly the Rangers' choice for the future. But there was also speculation that this was a demotion that related to cash as much as anything else. New York didn't seem to want a goaltender to get too comfortable.

Shuffling around two good ones meant that neither could make hefty demands, because they'd be swapped back down to the minors. In fact, Bower, Worsley and Emile Francis would each play for the Rangers' affiliate in Vancouver over a three-year span.

Now, in early October 1954, it was Johnny's turn. He and Nancy had packed up their apartment in Long Island after training camp and set out on the long road back to the minor leagues. They drove from the east coast through the Midwest, heading north through Minnesota and crossing into North Dakota before reaching Saskatchewan. They listened to the radio and sang along. Nancy read to John Jr., trying to get him settled. After stopping back home in Saskatoon, they set out again to report to the Canucks in Vancouver. But a relentless blizzard in the Rockies threatened to stop them. Johnny hadn't put snow tires on the car yet. The weather had been great when they left, but now the wheels slipped in the mounting snow. Finally, the vacancy light of a motel blinked through the white. Johnny pulled in and booked a room for Nancy and John Jr. to get some sleep. Then he set out for a nearby town, to find snow tires to put on the car and continue the journey. Nancy didn't get any rest. She sat next to the window of the motel room, holding John Jr. and watching worriedly, waiting for the headlights to return through the blizzard.

Nancy was upset that the Rangers had sent Johnny away. After waiting so long for his opportunity to play in the NHL and after proving that he belonged, he was tossed aside—tossed across the continent—to toil once again in the minors. Nancy would never forgive the New York Rangers for the way they treated him. The whole organization was mixed up, she thought. But Vancouver wouldn't be the end. Johnny had worked too hard, for too long, to simply give up. Decades later, Nancy would look back and be grateful it hadn't worked out with the Rangers. "I'm just glad we didn't stay," she'd say.

JOHNNY FOUND IT difficult to be back in the minors in Vancouver, even though he quickly became the talk of the Western Hockey League. He was tremendous on the Canucks' first road trip, to cities like Calgary, Edmonton and Saskatoon. But it was hard to be pleased with his demotion. Johnny had no doubt that he was good enough, but the politics of professional hockey were impossible to navigate.

"Don't tell me this is going to be the end of my career in the NHL," he thought. "I just need another chance."

That opportunity came quickly, when Worsley took a slap shot off the inside of his ankle, chipping off a piece of the bone, on November 21. Worsley was unable to put any pressure on his leg and was forced to leave the game. That evening, Johnny received a call telling him to get back to New York City. He was on the first flight out of Vancouver the next morning and in goal at Madison Square Garden two nights later to help the Rangers beat the Bruins 2–1. But his triumphant return didn't last long. Johnny played a few more games, including a 4–1 win over the Montreal Canadiens. In the four games since he had returned, Johnny had allowed just seven goals. Patrick told the press that "the job is his until further notice." It seemed like an endorsement, but it also left open the possibility that if Johnny faltered the job could go back to Worsley, who was watching intently from the sidelines and begging the team's doctors to clear him for play.

A few nights later, after a 6–1 loss to the Detroit Red Wings, that notice was given. Worsley's ankle had healed, and Bower was sent back to Vancouver.

Discouraged but determined, Johnny continued to impress in the Canucks net. He helped the team make a push for a playoff spot, coming up huge in several games—including one in early February in a win over the New Westminster Royals, in which he made several point-blank saves in a flurry of attempts with his arms and legs—and then finally one with his head. Johnny would finish out the season in Vancouver by recording a WHL-best 2.71 goals-against average and seven shutouts.

That spring rumours swirled that the Montreal Canadiens, who were reportedly unhappy with the play of Jacques Plante, were thinking about trading with the Rangers for the rights to Johnny. The Canadiens had fallen to the Detroit Red Wings in the Stanley Cup Final in seven games for the second straight season. But the move that would have dramatically altered the course of NHL history never came to pass.

Johnny returned to the Rangers' training camp in Saskatoon that fall hoping to outduel Worsley for the team's starting position. But he was disappointed once again. The Rangers—who had finished fifth in the NHL standings with 17 wins in 1954–55—had hired a new coach, Phil Watson, to replace Muzz Patrick. Watson had played right wing for the Rangers for more than a decade, until he retired in 1948. This was bad news for Bower. Watson had it out for him from the start. He'd known Gump Worsley for some time, through his association with the Rangers organization. His preference was clear. During his time as a right winger, Watson had apparently become a goaltending expert.

"The only way to get along with Watson was to keep your mouth shut, and that's what I tried to do," Johnny later recalled. "Phil would get under my skin."

Watson felt that the 30-year-old had developed the bad habit of turning to look at the net after every shot he faced. Johnny argued that it was just his natural way of turning with the shot, controlling the rebound. But Watson kept criticizing him, until Johnny finally relented and agreed to try to make a change. It didn't work. The pucks started landing right at Johnny's feet and would get lost in his pads when he didn't do the slight turn. He'd lose sight of the pucks entirely, and opposing players would crash in and nudge the free puck past Bower and into the net. Frustrated, Bower quickly returned to his own style. Watson, in the end, would prove to be widely unpopular with his players.

At the end of training camp in Saskatoon, in early October 1955, Johnny was again left off the Rangers' main roster. But this time, instead of being sent to Vancouver, Johnny was assigned to the Providence Reds, in Rhode Island, marking his return to the American Hockey League.

Once again Johnny, Nancy and their 18-month-old son, John Jr., packed up their car and drove across the country, hoping to find a way back to the NHL.

But with Johnny about to turn 31, how much time would he have left?

WHENEVER NICHOLAS LAMORIELLO could, he'd take his family to the Rhode Island Auditorium to watch the Providence Reds play. He was enamoured with the game. Lamoriello ran a fish shop and would deliver fresh products to local restaurants in town. The work provided a livable middle-class income for him and his family. The Lamoriellos lived in a modest two-tenement house, split with Nicholas's brother and his family, in nearby Johnston. They were one of many proud Italian families living in the Rhode Island area who worked hard for what they had. They also lived and breathed hockey. One of the few extravagances they splurged on were season tickets to Reds games, which ran for about $1 a game at the time. Through his job delivering fish, Nicholas often made deliveries to restaurants that were frequented by the Reds. When he saw the players he admired, he couldn't help but stick around to chat—and would sometimes invite the players over to his house for some home-cooked Italian food. That was how, in the fall of 1955, Johnny and Nancy Bower got to know the Lamoriello family. Johnny and Nicholas had similar temperaments and got along incredibly well. John Jr., then a toddler, would take rides in the backyard on a small horse the Lamoriello family kept. The Reds' new goalie was also a huge fan of Mrs. Lamoriello's cooking—a feast of steak, chicken, pasta and desserts that helped make Providence one of Johnny and Nancy's favourite places to live.

Nicholas's son, Louis, inherited his father's passion for hockey. He was practically raised in the old Auditorium, with its chicken-wire-lined boards and bench doors that opened out onto the ice and occasionally hip-checked passing players. He was a young teenager when he first met Bower—a star by the standards of the American Hockey League. Louis already had dreams of pursuing a career in the game and was becoming a decent player in his own right. But his real talent would always lie within the way he saw the game from the sidelines—the way he could envision how an athletic franchise could come together as a whole and succeed. Louis looked up to Bower, whom he viewed as a kind, humble man who always put the team ahead of himself. As a dinner went late at the Lamoriello house one evening, Johnny excused himself because the Reds had a game the next night and he felt he needed to get to sleep early so he would play well. It left a lasting impression on Louis—better known as Lou—who would become known for enforcing strict expectations on professionalism and dedication to the team throughout his own Hall of Fame career in the game.

Over the years, Johnny would stay in touch with the Italian family from Johnston that had shown his own family so much kindness and hospitality. And six decades later, in 2015, when Lou Lamoriello took over the position of general manager of the Toronto Maple Leafs, one of the very first calls congratulating him on his new role with the storied franchise was from an old legend named Bower.

. . .

THROUGH NEARLY A decade in the minor leagues—and that one sparkling season in New York—Johnny had proven time and again that he deserved to play among the best players in the game. But the limitations of the six-team NHL, with all its politics and complete mismanagement (and with only six permanent positions for goaltenders) meant that Johnny was perpetually the best player not in the NHL. Despite the accolades he'd earn as the greatest goalie the minor leagues had ever seen, he had no legacy to leave the game. Without making it in the NHL, his success in the minors would mean relatively little in hindsight.

In truth, Johnny was bitter that he hadn't received a real opportunity to stay in the NHL after his remarkable rookie season. If given the chance to return, he wasn't sure he would have accepted it. He'd already proven he was good enough, but it wasn't enough to keep him there. "I knew that in the NHL I'd never be sure of the situation," Johnny later reflected. He was reaching the prime of his career, and even by the modest standards of an AHL paycheque in the 1950s, he was still doing much better than he might have had he walked away from the game and remained in Prince Albert. Could he risk the instability of the NHL, when he had respect and reasonable certainty about his future in the minors?

Those questions swirled, but in his heart, Johnny knew he was too competitive to not want to play at the game's highest level. And his drive to show he belonged was enough to keep him going. In their early 30s, most players would begin their inevitable decline. Not Johnny. He was about to enter the ageless era of his life, a period in which what he accomplished was so unbelievable and his origin story so hazy that it seemed to many as though it was all too good to be true.

It started in Providence through the 1955–56 season, in front of an always packed audience, as Johnny's play was so exceptional in the Reds goal that he was named MVP of the AHL, becoming the first goaltender to ever win the award. (The win came with a $300 bonus.) Perhaps fuelled by Mrs. Lamoriello's spaghetti, Johnny led the Reds to a first-place finish through the regular season. Providence would go on to meet the Cleveland Barons in the Calder Cup final. Johnny offered his former team no mercy. After the Reds won the first two games of the series handily, he made 39 stops in a 4–2 win in the third game of the championship.

"Unless the Cleveland Barons figure out some new way to get the puck past Johnny Bower, it looks like the American Hockey League's Calder Cup will go to the Providence Reds," one sportswriter declared.

The Barons tried everything, but they just couldn't do it. In Game 4, Johnny stopped 23 shots in the third period alone. The Reds won 6–3, claiming the team's first Calder Cup since 1948–49.

At a parade down Main Street in Providence celebrating the win, Johnny held John Jr. in his arms and kissed Nancy, as fans lined the thoroughfare to congratulate their heroes. MVP of the league, Johnny was first among them. It was his fourth time hoisting the Calder Cup. It was a thrilling accomplishment, but Johnny knew the one trophy he'd dreamt of carrying was still out there—in another league entirely.

• • •

IN THE FALL of 1956, Dwight Eisenhower was president of the United States. Richard Nixon was vice president. Charlton Heston hoisted up holy tablets in the blockbuster film *The Ten Commandments*. Elvis Presley crooned "Heartbreak Hotel." In Canada, that December, John Diefenbaker—who started his political career in Prince Albert, Saskatchewan—was elected as the leader of the Progressive Conservative Party of Canada.

And if there was a year when the legend of Johnny Bower truly started to take shape, it was then—in the fall of 1956—in his second season in Providence, that an aging minor-leaguer made himself impossible to ignore.

Naturally, though, it started with disappointment. Surely, now, there was no doubt that Johnny deserved a spot in the NHL. But once again, he battled to crack the Rangers roster—and once again New York sent him packing for Providence in early October.

This time Johnny was even more spectacular. Shortly after being sent to the minors, he made 48 saves in a 1–1 overtime draw with the Rochester Americans. Then he picked up a shutout in a special showcase between the Reds and the AHL All-Stars—making 47 saves. It was unheard of. Just after his 32nd birthday, Johnny was called back up to the Rangers for a couple of games while Worsley was injured. But he lost both and was quickly returned to Providence, where he continued to make headlines with his remarkable play. Johnny would never play for New York again. And that was fine by Nancy. She absolutely loved Providence. Later in life the couple would return almost every year to visit. The fans were wild, passionate—and supportive. Johnny never had to duck a beer in Rhode Island. If the Bowers were going to be stuck in the minors, Providence would suit them just fine.

In January, there were rumours that the Rangers might trade Johnny to the Boston Bruins to replace Terry Sawchuk, who had left the team to attend to personal issues. But the deal never happened. Meanwhile, Johnny was busy setting records. On March 10, with an 8–0 win over Rochester, he picked up his 37th career shutout—more than any goalie before him. He was well aware that he was on the verge of pulling off the record. Johnny called the final 60 seconds of the win the longest minute of his life. He would finish his AHL career with 45 shutouts, a mark that would stand for almost 59 years, until Michael Leighton of the Rockford IceHogs posted his 46th in 2016.

The incredible season ended with Johnny posting a dazzling 2.42 goals-against average—his lowest ever. (It was the fifth straight year he'd average less than three goals a game.) Johnny was named league MVP for the second straight season. He was only the second player in the league's history to win the award twice. He picked up another $300 bonus for the win—adding to two other $300 bonuses he received for having the lowest goals-against average in the league and for being a unanimous selection for the All-Star Team.

For good measure, Johnny was also named the Rhode Island athlete of the year. John Crawford, the Reds' coach, declared that Bower was "the best goalie of all, in any league, without reservation."

Although the Reds failed to defend as Calder Cup champions, Johnny returned to the grill in Lake Waskesiu that summer knowing he'd accomplished just about everything he could in the AHL. At the end of the 1956–57 season, Bower had played in 528 career AHL games—one less than the record at the time, set by Harvey Bennett. It was already a full career, by any standard. He was grateful for that. And knowing that his window for the NHL was shrinking rapidly, he prepared to finish his hockey career in the league that had given a shy, poor kid named Kiszkan a chance to live his dream.

During the off-season, the Rangers wanted to trade Cleveland's goalie Marcel Paille, whose rights they owned, to a different AHL team. But Jim Hendy had a contract with the Rangers that said Paille could only play for Cleveland in the AHL. To get out of it, the Rangers offered to give Cleveland back the rights to Johnny. Hendy leaped at the opportunity to get his old goalie back. The Barons sent Ed MacQueen and cash to the Rangers as part of the deal. Johnny was heading home.

Having followed their ambition to start a restaurant of their own, Johnny and Nancy had found a second income that, along with their savings, could support their family after Johnny's playing days were over. Their new coffee shop and grill in Waskesiu had a cook and six waitresses. It opened every morning at 8 a.m. and stayed open until 2 a.m. to catch the late-night revelers. The grill featured Johnny's specialty, "Bower's Big Boy"—a fully loaded burger with double patties that he stuffed with extra bread crumbs. The shop operated for only four months through the summer, although Johnny believed it could stay open through the fall hunting season.

But with the news that they were heading back to the Barons, the Bowers closed up the restaurant and returned to Cleveland to arrange a place to stay before Johnny left for training camp in North Bay, Ontario, in September.

Despite loving his time in Providence, Johnny was thrilled to return to Ohio. It was where his career began, and so it seemed only fitting that it would end there too. The Barons had just won the Calder Cup and looked like they would be a top team in the AHL again. Johnny signed a no-trade clause with Cleveland that would ensure he had complete control over his future with the organization. The 32-year-old didn't want any surprises or any more moves. He was either finishing his career with the Barons or he'd be done altogether.

"I won't play anywhere else but in Cleveland," he told the Cleveland *Plain Dealer* before heading to training camp. "When the time comes I am sold or traded, it's time to hang up my skates. My business can support me, especially if we keep open for a longer season."

But Johnny worked against his own declaration. His previous two seasons in Providence had assured his spot in the AHL history books. However, in his return to Cleveland, Johnny was *even better*. In early December—over the course of five games— he set an AHL record for the most consecutive minutes without being scored on. The streak ended on December 8 after 249 minutes and 51 seconds of shutout hockey. His run of zeros was broken midway through the third period of what would have been Johnny's fourth straight shutout, in front of 7,000 fans at the Arena. The Barons were down two men when the Buffalo Bisons finally scored. Johnny had bested the previous shutout streak record by 28 minutes. By that time, he already had five shutouts in 23 games—just four away from the AHL record of nine shutouts in a season. The shutouts came with an added incentive for Johnny, who was always happy to make an extra buck: He had a bonus in his contract that gave him $10 for every zero he posted.

"Johnny 'China Wall' Bower is apparently the hottest goaltender in professional hockey," *The Hockey News* wrote a few days later.

Johnny felt that his success was due to his vast experience in the minors. He was simply a smarter goalie than he had been before. He had learned every season and gotten better. At the same time, he knew he was slower, and quietly, his eyesight was already causing some concern. But all that mattered to the fans who packed the Arena every game, and to the Barons franchise that raked in money because of the star they had in goal, was that Johnny Bower was in Cleveland to stay.

"Just go down the line and compare him with any goalie in the National League," Jim Hendy boasted to *The Hockey News*. "I wouldn't exchange him for any man up there."

Of course, it didn't take long for the NHL to take notice.

Johnny was in the midst of the greatest season of his career at the time, with a goals-against average of 2.19 through early January, when Hendy told the press the Barons had rejected an offer from an NHL team for their star goalie. Or rather, that Bower himself had rejected it.

Jim Hendy called Bower into his office and told his goalie about the offer. The deal, Hendy said, would involve cash in the five figures and two or three good players coming to Cleveland. But it was up to Johnny, who had a no-trade clause in his contract. Hendy told Bower he could have some time to think it over. Hendy refused to name the franchise that was interested when he told the story to the press. But speculation swirled that the offer had come from Boston, the team that had shown interest a year earlier. At the time the Bruins' goalie, Don Simmons, was injured. Boston acquired Harry Lumley from Buffalo that week as a replacement. Johnny told Hendy he didn't need any time at all. He was staying in Cleveland.

"My wife and I like Cleveland and the fans here," he told reporters when news of the potential deal broke. "I said last August and I say it again now that if I am sold or traded I will not report to any other club."

Hendy expressed relief that Johnny had decided to stay. "I knew if [he] left us we might lose a lot of fans," he said.

The Toronto Maple Leafs' head scout, Bob Davidson, was a frequent patron at Cleveland Arena that year. He liked what he saw in goal. Unhappy with the play of their current goalie, Ed Chadwick, the Leafs inquired about trading for Bower. Once again, Hendy listened to the offer and left the decision up to his goalie. Once again, Johnny refused to be traded. But the Leafs had other ways of getting the man they wanted.

Part of the reason Johnny was uninterested in a move at the time was because he had much more than hockey on his mind. A few days after news of the potential trade to the Bruins broke, Nancy gave birth to their second child—and first daughter—Cindy Ann, on January 11, 1958. Their family of three had grown to four at the tiny home they rented on the leafy corner of Laverne Avenue and West 162nd Street, in Cleveland's eastern suburbs.

It seemed as though Johnny's return to Cleveland couldn't have gone any better. By March, he had earned eight shutouts and had an incredible goals-against average of 2.19. It was the lowest posted by any goalie in the AHL since 1938–39. But on March 9 in a game in Providence, he was slammed into his post in a goalmouth collision. His belly pad shifted out of position, exposing his torso as the Reds' Jimmy Bartlett crashed into him. The post pegs had little give. Johnny went down hard in the collision. He left the game. Jim Boag, the Barons' trainer, came in to replace him.

Later, lying in a hospital bed in Providence, Johnny was told he'd broken three ribs. The pain was excruciating. Of all the injuries Johnny had endured through his career—more than 100 stiches, lumps all over his face, and a mouthful of missing teeth—nothing hurt as bad as this.

"I'd rather have 20 stiches on the face than one sore rib," he said cheerfully, after arriving home in Cleveland by plane a few days later. "With those face cuts, you can still get in there and play."

Johnny could walk, but that was about it. A mangled face? No problem. But broken ribs made it impossible to move the way he needed to. The pain was just was too much. He was told he'd be out

Johnny's parents, James Kiszkan and Elizabeth Jacobson, were married on November 13, 1912. Elizabeth had arrived in Canada from a region in Europe now known as Slovakia and had turned 18 years old the day before the wedding. (COURTESY OF THE BATTING FAMILY)

Young Johnny poses with his siblings in front of the Kiszkan house in Prince Albert. Although the Kiszkans were a large, poor family living through the Great Depression, their home was known as a happy place always buzzing with activity. Johnny stands up front on the right side. Anne Batting, Johnny's only remaining sibling, stands on the right side of the back row. Johnny's estranged brother, Michael, stands to the left. (COURTESY OF THE BATTING FAMILY)

On his sister Anne's wedding day, Johnny served as best man to her husband-to-be, Tom Batting. Anne stands to the right of Tom, who is sitting. Johnny stands behind him. While the Kiszkan siblings spread out across the country, Johnny and his older sister Anne would always remain close—despite the distance between Castlegar, B.C., where Anne and Tom raised their family, and Toronto, where Johnny became a hockey legend.

(COURTESY OF THE BATTING FAMILY)

Johnny was 15 years old when he first attempted to join the Prince Albert Volunteers at the outbreak of World War II. Two years later, in September 1941, he again lied about his age, successfully joining the militia two months before turning 17. (COURTESY OF THE BATTING FAMILY)

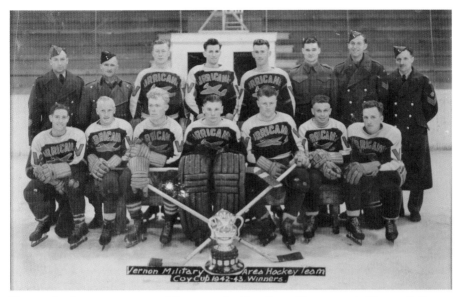

Thousands of young men prepared for war at the Canadian military camp in Vernon, B.C., flooding the town with hockey talent. Johnny Kiszkan was just 18 years old when he starred in the camp's hockey league for the Prince Albert Volunteers team. Johnny was so impressive he was named to the camp's all-star team, which played for the Western Canadian championships. (Courtesy of the Bower family)

Johnny Kiszkan, seen here leaning against a fence near his family home in Prince Albert, became a local celebrity as a goaltender playing with the M&C Warhawks and the Prince Albert Black Hawks after returning from the war. (Courtesy of the Bower family)

With Johnny in goal, the M&C Warhawks won the 1944 Western Canadian hockey championship. He played so well that word of his ability quickly spread, gaining the attention of the AHL's Cleveland Barons. (Courtesy of the Saskatchewan Sports Hall of Fame)

When Johnny Kiszkan arrived at the Cleveland Barons' training camp, he still wore the old tube skates he'd been given by an older player when he was 10. They were the only skates he owned before turning pro, when the Barons provided him with gear he'd never dreamed of owning. (COURTESY OF THE BOWER FAMILY)

Johnny became a star with the Cleveland Barons through the late 1940s and early 1950s, where his dazzling, catlike saves earned him his first nickname, the Panther Man. (COURTESY OF THE OCHS FAMILY)

As a Baron, Johnny became close friends with Bob Ochs, who was an equipment manager with the team. Ochs helped the shy young netminder get settled into life in the relatively big city of Cleveland. Born with one hand, Ochs developed a way to shoot on his friend after Barons practices. (COURTESY OF THE OCHS FAMILY)

Johnny met Nancy Brain while working as a golf pro in the resort town of Waskesiu, while she played a round with a group of her friends. Later that day, he asked her to a movie. It was the start of seven decades together, side by side.

As Johnny spent more than a decade in the minor leagues, Nancy offered the support and love—and sometimes medical attention—the ageless goalie needed to finally realize his NHL dream. (Courtesy of the Bower family)

For years, Cleveland was home to Johnny and Nancy Bower. The city was a bustling commercial and manufacturing centre of nearly a million people when Johnny starred with the Barons through the late 1940s and early 1950s. He was part of three Calder Cup championships with the Cleveland Barons, where he became the team's most beloved player and became known as the China Wall. Johnny was prepared to retire a Baron, before reluctantly joining the Leafs in 1958.

(Courtesy of the Bower family)

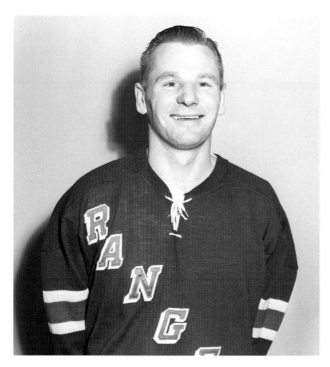

Despite a spectacular rookie year with the New York Rangers, Johnny was sent back to the minors after his breakout season in 1953–54. (Turofsky collection/Courtesy of the Hockey Hall of Fame)

After being jilted by the NHL, Johnny amazed hockey fans in the minors for more than a decade. He still holds the AHL record of 359 wins by a goalie. He won the Calder Cup four times. Here, as a member of the Providence Reds, he celebrates with Nancy and John Jr. after his fourth and final Calder Cup win. (Courtesy of the Bower family)

Johnny's father, James Kiszkan, left behind his life as a peasant farmer in a region now known as Ukraine when he was 18 and sailed across the Atlantic looking for a new start. He settled near Prince Albert, Saskatchewan, as a homesteader before finding employment at the Pat Burns meat-packing company, where he spent the rest of his working days. Here James poses for a photo in front of his house in Prince Albert in his later years. (COURTESY OF THE BOWER FAMILY)

for at least three weeks. That meant the remainder of the Barons' season. That was the bad news. The good news was that the injury put another $300 in his pocket. At the time of his injury, Johnny's 2.19 goals-against average was so far ahead of everyone else in the league that even if another goalie played shutout hockey for the rest of his season, he still wouldn't be able to post a better average. So Johnny was guaranteed to pick up his bonus as the league's top goalie for the third straight season.

Johnny wore a brace around his torso and drank milk, hoping to mend the broken bones in time for the playoffs. It didn't work. But he did pick up two more $300 bonuses when, once again, he was named to the AHL's First All-Star Team and won the league's MVP award for an unprecedented third year in a row.

The Barons, who finished second overall in the regular season, just weren't the same without their star goalie. Johnny watched from the sidelines, nursing his tender ribs, as Cleveland was upset in the first round of the playoffs. They lost to the Springfield Indians, a team they had faced many times through Johnny's record-setting season. The Indians were pieced together and led by a 40-year-old general manager and coach named George Imlach. Everyone called him Punch. He'd taken note of the aging goalie in the Barons net that year.

At 33 years old, after playing in 592 games, more than any AHL goalie ever had—and winning 359, more than any AHL goalie ever would—Johnny Bower's minor-league career was finally finished.

But his legend was just beginning.

• • •

NANCY BOWER SITS in her kitchen, looking at old photographs with her daughter, Cindy. The home today is filled with Johnny. From the bird feeder in the yard to the tools in the basement to the clutter in the garage, where he'd putter. Together, Nancy, in her early 90s, and Cindy, near 60, reminisce about all the small, happy moments that filled seven decades of love—starting with how it all began.

"Girls, you're standing a little close to each other, with the way you're swinging those clubs," Nancy says, imitating him that day in Waskesiu, when Johnny walked over to that first hole and scolded her and her friends. She recalls her feisty response after he'd walked away: "What right does he have to tell us?"

Cindy laughs at the image of her parents' early banter. The annoyance begot flirtation, which led to a date—and then three kids and an entire life together. The photographs in front of them, collected from family albums, tell the story of those thousands of in-between moments that carried them from the beginning to the end. Each story leads to another. Like the time Johnny came home with all his teeth knocked out; those summers spent by the lake and serving customers at the grill; the day John Jr. arrived and changed their lives forever; the blizzard in the mountains after the Rangers cut him loose. The joy of those years in Providence and Cleveland—and the lingering disappointment that Johnny, as he aged, might never get another shot at the NHL. And even if he did, could he trust it?

They had resigned themselves to that reality, Nancy says. They were happy in Cleveland, after all. They could see their story ending there. But this is a different city. And this house is full of logos, photographs, and blue and white artifacts that tell a different tale.

"But this is Toronto, John," Nancy says—recalling what she told him as they faced a life-changing decision in the summer of 1958.

"This is Canada. It will be different."

PART

THREE

09

BROTHERS

GEORGE ARMSTRONG WATCHES A NEW GENERATION OF MAPLE Leafs play on television, five decades removed from his days as the longest-serving captain in the franchise's history. All these years on, and he's still a fan of the game. He's impressed by their talent—they're bigger, they're faster, and every one of them shoots as hard as Bobby Hull ever could. The game has moved on, moved forward—as long-ago years of glory fade ever into the past. Watching the Leafs take on the Tampa Bay Lightning, he thinks back to those days and to an old friend, recently lost.

A hockey team, he says—a good one—is a band of brothers. That's what the Leafs of the 1960s became. And for Armstrong there was no teammate, no brother, who could mean more to him than Johnny Bower.

"I loved the man," he says. "There's no question about that."

While the two men were different in many ways, they developed a close bond that would last the rest of their lives. They were leaders of the last great era in Leafs history. The Leafs roster was known to fight each other often, with scuffles regularly breaking out in practice. That's just what brothers do. But never Johnny. "He was a teddy bear." The only way to really rankle him was to put a puck by him in practice, Armstrong says—or to tap one in when he wasn't looking. The man's work ethic was unparalleled. His determination to be the best, even as he aged, marvelled Armstrong.

"The only thing Johnny Bower didn't like was a puck in his net," he says. "Everything else in the world, Johnny Bower loved."

And Johnny loved Armstrong as much as anything. Long after their playing days, as the decades passed—after their families grew up and had families of their own—as they became old legends, their bond endured. But with time, all things expire. And now his brother was gone. It hurt like hell.

On Armstrong's television, as the Leafs battled Tampa Bay, William Nylander would pick up two goals and an assist, while Auston Matthews added three helpers of his own. Toronto pulled off a 4–3 win with a new generation that would one day watch from afar too. And high above the ice, two banners marked "Bower 1" and "Armstrong 10" hung close to each other, together among the few who will never be forgotten.

It's almost unfathomable to imagine a world in which Johnny Bower was never a Toronto Maple Leaf. But Johnny wasn't just bargaining when he bristled at the idea of leaving Cleveland.

He was almost 34 years old, for goodness' sake. He had two kids; John Jr. had just turned four, and their newborn, Cindy, was just a few months old. If the National Hockey League wanted him, it had had plenty of opportunities to get him. Like, an entire career's worth of opportunities. What use would the Toronto Maple Leafs have with an old guy like him, who had maybe a year or two left in him at best?

Those doubts cycled through Johnny's mind when he learned he had been selected by the Leafs in the intraleague draft on June 3, 1958. He'd been clear in his statements to the Cleveland papers: He intended to finish his career with the Barons.

Johnny was resentful of being dismissed from the NHL after his 1953–54 rookie campaign, even though he had a 2.54 goals-against average. He had even publicly called out his old coach for holding him back, which Watson claimed was "a bunch of baloney." But Johnny's long sentence in the minors was undoubtedly one of the biggest blunders in league history.

Regardless, Johnny had little faith in the NHL's promises. And it didn't help that the Maple Leafs were particularly bad at the time. Historically bad, in fact. Toronto had just finished last in the NHL for the first time in franchise history. The team hadn't made the playoffs in two straight seasons. And the '50s had been unkind to the Maple Leafs. They hadn't won a playoff series since they'd last won the Stanley Cup in 1951, on a goal by Bill Barilko—who would go missing after his float plane crashed in a remote region of northern Ontario just a few months after he scored the winner.

The Leafs were a young team. George Armstrong, the captain, was in his late 20s—and among the older players key to the roster. Stalwart defenceman Tim Horton was nearing 30. Forward Ron Stewart was in his mid-20s. And Toronto had a pipeline of talent developed through the St. Michael's Majors and the Toronto Marlboros, both junior teams—and fierce rivals—that the Leafs sponsored. Majors like Dick Duff and Frank Mahovlich and Marlboros like Billy Harris, Bobby Baun, Bob Pulford and Carl Brewer were all barely out of their teens. Eighteen-year-old Dave Keon was still with St. Mike's. The cohort was among the last of the key prospects that the Leafs monopolized in Ontario.

A month after Leafs coach Billy Reay drafted Bower, the team hired 40-year-old Punch Imlach away from Springfield to come in as one of the team's assistant general managers, beside the legendary King Clancy, who had been inducted into the Hall of Fame that year. Toronto didn't have a general manager at the time. Instead they were headed by a committee, led by Stafford Smythe—the son of the Leafs' founder, Conn Smythe.

After being rebuffed in their initial attempt to trade for Johnny while he was playing with the Barons, the Leafs planned to select him in the interleague draft. They hoped Johnny could help—or replace—their current starter, Ed Chadwick.

True to his word, Johnny initially told Jim Hendy he didn't intend to sign with Toronto. He and Nancy had no interest in uprooting their lives, only to be shipped elsewhere if the team changed its mind, as had happened in New York. Hendy tried to convince him that the move to Toronto was the right deal for him and his family. Johnny relied heavily on the income he earned every summer through the restaurant at Waskesiu Lake, so Hendy tried to explain the benefits in terms of burgers—which, he said, were sure to become even more popular to visiting tourists once they learned the Toronto Maple Leafs' goalie was grilling them. The notion of more burgers enticed Johnny.

Despite losing the AHL's three-time MVP, it was likely an important deal for the Barons as well. Through the draft, Cleveland made $45,000 for giving up three players. It was a considerable sum, given that the Barons had barely broken even that season, with a net surplus of about $5,000 after the sale of the players was factored into the club's financial report a few weeks later. Still—after boasting that Bower was the best goalie in hockey—Hendy appeared to want to stir up some doubt about his value in the NHL, perhaps trying to keep the fan-favourite league MVP in a Barons sweater.

"I want to make it clear that Bower is a good goalie and is in good shape, but I believe he is two years older than the record book indicates and he'll come awfully high for two years' service," Hendy told the press after Bower was drafted, sparking debate about just how old Johnny actually was—and how much time he might have left.

Questions were already arising about Johnny's age. Maybe it was the novelty of such an old goalie returning to a full-time position in the NHL—but as soon as he pulled on the blue and white sweater, he became an ageless myth. The updated National Hockey League guide that year would list Bower as being born in 1925. But the NHL guide from 1953–54 listed his birth year as 1924, meaning he was turning 34. Confusion swirled, and Johnny's claims that he had lost his birth certificate didn't help quell the discussion.

In actuality, Johnny would be the second-oldest player in the NHL that season. (Doug Harvey and Gus Mortson were a couple of months younger.) Maurice Richard was the oldest at 37.

By late June, the Barons still hadn't been paid by the Leafs for Bower's playing rights. Hendy's attorney sent a letter to the NHL head office in Montreal stating that the rights should be returned to the Barons. Meanwhile, Johnny weighed his options while running the coffee shop back in Lake Waskesiu. Knowing Bower was on the fence, the Leafs sent Bob Davidson to the national park to try to nudge him along. It was a positive conversation, Nancy Bower would recall. And for her part, she was pushing her husband to take a chance with the Leafs. It helped, of course, that two of Nancy's sisters had settled into lives just west of the city, in Oakville and London. But, more important, Nancy told him, it was his last chance to live his dream. The Leafs were the only way Johnny would ever have his name etched on the Stanley Cup.

And besides, he had little choice in the matter. While his contract with Cleveland said he couldn't be traded or sold without his permission, there was no escape clause that dealt with the draft. So he risked being suspended from playing hockey at all if he refused to sign with Toronto. But that didn't mean he didn't have any bargaining power. He was a star goalie, after all. If the

Leafs wanted Johnny to report, it was going to be on his terms.

Jim Hendy gave Leafs coach Billy Reay a photostat copy with the terms Johnny had requested. He wanted a two-year deal and a substantial amount of money, "but no more than Harry Lumley received," *The Hockey News* was told at the time, ensuring that Johnny didn't come off looking greedy. That lofty number was $10,000—or about $86,000 today, factoring in inflation. He wanted a two-year guaranteed contract, in which he'd get paid the same each year, even if he suffered a serious injury, including anything that might happen in training camp. On top of that, Johnny asked that his moving expenses be covered, and that the Leafs agree that if they no longer wanted him, the only team he could be moved to was the Cleveland Barons. By AHL standards, it was a bold ask. But in the NHL, for a player like Johnny, it was a steal.

In early August, Imlach met with Bower in Saskatoon, hoping to finalize the deal that would bring the Leafs their coveted veteran goalie. The two men were vastly different in many ways—in particular, the way others saw them. Imlach was driven by success but was also quick to cut down others who didn't appear to have the same mindset. Johnny was similarly driven by the desire to win, and his work ethic would never be called into question. Both men were rigidly old-school. They believed in order and loyalty. Although in temperament the pair were opposites, they would always have respect for each other—for the most part. Imlach's stubbornness would end a few promising careers in Toronto. Very few Maple Leafs remained on his good side, and even Johnny wouldn't be immune to Punch's antics. But there, on that August afternoon in Saskatoon, the two men shook hands on a new era for the Leafs franchise.

As would become tradition, the losing season didn't cost the Toronto Maple Leafs many fans. The hype of the Leafs' off-season had been enough to maintain support. Advance ticket sales were among the highest they had ever been, the team claimed. The Leafs brass had made bold proclamations for the upcoming season, perhaps overcompensating for the team's dreadful finish. That propaganda leaned heavily on Bower. Stafford Smythe, the chairman, declared they had picked up the best goalie the team had had in two decades and that Bower would add at least 10 points in the standings. The team's defence had been terrible, Smythe said—and all but Allan Stanley, who had just been acquired, were expendable. Then he quickly added young Bobby Baun to that list of untouchables. (No mention of Tim Horton, who was still recovering from a broken jaw and leg injury.) When the Leafs opened training camp in Peterborough on September 15, Baun looked at the team's new ancient addition in goal and thought it was unlikely he'd be able to survive in the NHL at his age. But Baun would quickly admit he was wrong. "His desire was amazing," says Baun, who developed a close connection with the goalie.

"And the dollar was amazing," he adds, noting that much of Johnny's drive was fuelled by his desire to support his family.

It had already been announced that the team would carry both Bower and the 25-year-old Chadwick. Coach Bill Reay believed no goalie could withstand an entire 70-game season and be at his best. He downplayed the notion that Bower was replacing

Chadwick. "No one is picking on Ed, or underestimating him," Reay assured reporters—while adding: "But I will say that I wasn't pleased with the excess poundage he picked up the last time I talked to him. He'll have to prove that he's better than Bower to start in goal . . . I feel that if we had been able to spell Chadwick last season we might have won a dozen games we lost."

But despite competing for the same position, Bower and Chadwick quickly became friends. Chadwick had played every game of the previous two seasons and didn't seem to mind the added help in goal. He would often seek advice from the elder Bower—who had less NHL experience but whose reputation as one of the best in the game while stuck in the minors had earned him a great deal of respect from other goalies. By the end of the pre-season, Johnny was the clear favourite. He gave up just 10 goals in four full games and four half-game splits. Billy Reay was impressed with the way he cleared out pucks and intercepted passes. It was a weakness Johnny had learned to overcome in his early days with Cleveland. And Reay liked that Bower had a reputation for never cracking under pressure (although he was still known for pointing out the mistakes of his teammates that led to goals).

But Johnny's usual calmness splintered before the Leafs' home opener. Sitting in his stall in the locker room as 15,000 fans packed into Maple Leaf Gardens on Carlton Street, he could feel his body shaking. The Leafs hadn't won on opening night since 1953. But once again, Maple Leaf Gardens was full of that wishful optimism that accompanies every new season. And the fall of 1958 seemed particularly special. It already felt like the start of a new era. The Maple Leafs unveiled sweaters with lace ties at the collar. Glass lined the boards at the Gardens for the first time. Johnny was one of eight new players in the Toronto lineup. But the visiting Chicago Black Hawks, with a 20-year-old sophomore named Bobby Hull, were a dangerous club. Usually, it was Black Hawks goalie Glenn Hall who suffered from jittery nerves. He was famous for vomiting before games. But on October 11, 1958, it was Johnny who felt his stomach rumble. The nerves continued through the pregame warm-up, as Johnny marvelled at the size of the Gardens, full of fans. And as a band belted out the national anthem, he stared at the enormous portrait of Queen Elizabeth that hung at the far end of the rink, trying to calm the jitters. He worried about the first shot. If it went in, everything would fall apart. How could he recover?

This was more than Johnny's debut in a blue and white sweater; it was the first night of his last chance.

Up in the stands, Nancy Bower was worried too. Ever since becoming the spouse of a goalie, she'd dealt with all the nerve-racking moments from the stands. Every last-minute surge by an opposing team, every blowout when the net seemed 10 feet wide, every shot that clipped Bower in the face—Nancy watched them, unable to change the outcome but carrying the stress every bit as much as her husband did. Now she sat in a storied stadium, in a hockey-mad city, knowing the outcome on the ice would decide whether Toronto would be a lasting home.

After training camp, Nancy and the children had travelled from Saskatoon to Toronto to join Johnny. They unpacked their belongings and settled into a small apartment on the main floor of a house in Toronto's west-end Junction neighbourhood, next to the train tracks. Another couple lived upstairs. The house was owned by Ron Ingram, a Toronto-born player who was with the Buffalo Bisons in the AHL. It was a cramped space for the young family of four, but it would do while they settled into their new life in Toronto. The Bowers still owned a house back in Saskatoon, which they used when they weren't up at Waskesiu Lake running the grill. That's what they considered their real home. Hockey was transient by nature. The Bowers had learned that lesson clearly enough through 11 years in the minors. They didn't plan to fully settle into life in Toronto. Johnny's two-year contract was secure in terms of pay and provided a guarantee that they'd be shipped back to Cleveland if things didn't work out. But two years was not a long-term plan. As Johnny figured, at best, he might see the contract through to the end as a Leaf. About to turn 34, there was little expectation that Johnny would remain with the Leafs for more than a couple of seasons.

The constant change of setting had been exciting for the Bowers. Nancy hadn't complained about having to pack up and move—aside from disliking the impersonal bustle of Manhattan and that drive through the mountains in a blizzard. For the most part, though, the coast-to-coast journey through the minors had been an adventure.

"Travelling a bother?" Nancy mused to journalist Margaret Scott in a feature for a Toronto Maple Leafs official program that year. "It's no such thing. I love every moment of it. I can't think of anything more educational or exciting, and it certainly broadens the outlook. Now that we have a family I find it a little harder to pack, but I think moving has been so good for our son and I hope our daughter also gets a chance to see the world."

At four years old, John Jr. was a miniature of his dad, with close-cropped blond hair, wide blue eyes and a big smile. But often when it was just his father setting off to see the world—or, the world that exists between the eastern seaboard and the Midwest, anyway—little John Jr. would break into tears. He'd pass the time waiting for his dad to return home by attending to the matters of nursery school and watching his westerns on TV. Cindy was an infant, too young to concern herself with such things.

The Bowers didn't know many of their teammates, as they had in Cleveland. Johnny's long-time Barons teammate Steve Kraftcheck made the move to Toronto too, but he'd end up playing only eight games with the Leafs. Allan Stanley was the only other member of the Leafs the couple really knew, because he and Johnny had played together in New York. Nancy had yet to meet the other wives. Soon, though, she'd be the matriarch of the group, welcoming new players' wives and taking them under her wing.

When the puck finally dropped in Johnny's first game as a Leaf, his nerves quickly dissipated and he showed the fans that the hype surrounding him was warranted. He held off the Black Hawks' feisty forwards for two periods, helping the Leafs to a 1–0 lead heading into the third. But Chicago made sure that Johnny's NHL return didn't go smoothly. Danny Lewicki, who had crossed paths with Johnny when they both played for New York, knocked his old teammate down—one of several Black Hawks who gave him a rough ride that night. Chicago finally solved Johnny in the final period, putting three past him. But fans in the Gardens knew the opening-night loss couldn't be pinned to Johnny. The next evening, the Leafs faced the Black Hawks again in Chicago. Once again, the Leafs were outmatched. The Hawks continued to crash into Johnny. And this time he faced 47 shots in a 5–2 loss. He let in a long shot from Bobby Hull from the blue line as he was heading off the ice near the end of the game. Stafford Smythe had walked into the locker room between the second and third periods and torn into his players. Imlach was apoplectic, saying his team "lacked fire" and calling their effort a disgrace. Things only got worse from there. The Leafs floundered through the first month of the season. By late November, they had won just five of their first 16 games. It looked like another lost year. The problem fell to Imlach to fix. He was promoted to general manager in early November. Eight days later, Imlach fired Reay and inserted himself as head coach. Despite their weak start, Imlach was adamant that his team would be successful. He exuded swagger and confidence, proclaiming that the bottom-dwelling Leafs were going to make the playoffs. But by March, the Leafs were still in last place.

Johnny's role as the Leafs' starter diminished as the losses piled up. Imlach decided to run with whichever goalie was hot, while the other watched from the stands. For a time, Johnny's future with the Leafs seemed tenuous. Imlach openly mused about sending Bower back to the minors. There were rumours that he might be traded or placed on waivers. Johnny spent some time recovering from an injury. But eventually (after letting those demotion and trade rumours linger), Imlach told Johnny he had faith in him. In his own way, of course.

"Play the way I tell you to play and not the way you know how to play," Imlach said. "Do like I've told all the other players, and we'll be successful."

Imlach was particular about how he wanted things done, convinced that he knew best. He believed firmly in tradition. When he joined the Leafs, he continued a team policy created by Conn Smythe that would lead to one of Johnny's most important relationships in the game. It had been Conn Smythe's policy since the 1930s that the team's two most important players room together—which meant the captain and the goalie were always paired. Thus began a span of 11 seasons where George and Johnny fell asleep in the same room during every road trip. As assignments go, it was an easy one for Armstrong. Bower was as affable and genuine as it gets. "If you didn't like him, there was something wrong with you," Armstrong says. Known as the Chief to his teammates because of his First Nations heritage, Armstrong was the kind of player who led mostly by example. He was never the most talented player on the team, but he was one of the most reliable. He was a humble team player. Armstrong joked he was given the captainship in 1957 because the Leafs were a lousy team with lousy players at the time. He simply hung onto the C when better players came along.

Armstrong also happened to be the team's best prankster. And he made his roommate the target of his finest work—some of the best pranks ever pulled in a hockey locker room. Johnny was always good for a laugh, and he always knew how to take a joke. "He'd drive Johnny crazy," says Bob Baun. "Being roommates, I don't know how they did it." The pranks ranged widely in complexity. During breakaway drills, Armstrong would stand in the corner and tap pucks Johnny's way, to mess with him. He was known to have cut the bottom off Johnny's ties and to have administered muscle relief balm to a jockstrap—all the classic juvenile antics of any locker room. Sometimes, when Johnny fell asleep in the sauna in the Leafs locker room, Armstrong would pee on the hot stones to wake him up. Johnny took it all in stride. But Armstrong's most elaborate trick took some planning. Although Johnny wore full dentures, he'd remove them for practices and games—setting them aside for safekeeping inside a plastic case he kept in his stall. Johnny's propensity to stay after practice for extra work left him particularly vulnerable to prank attack. After one post-skate session, he came off the ice and popped his teeth back in. But something was off. They didn't fit right. He fiddled around to get them in place, while everyone else in the room tried to suppress their laughter. Confused, Johnny took a closer look. Then he realized they weren't his. He'd been trying to fit a stranger's grill in his mouth. The dressing room burst into the laughs now. Johnny looked around for the culprit, still unsure where his actual teeth were. At first, he was sure it was Eddie Shack, a well-known jester in the locker room. But his inquest fell flat, until a giggling Armstrong finally copped to the crime and delivered the punchline. The teeth were borrowed from a friend who worked at a funeral home and had swiped them from a recent guest.

Johnny was also regularly teased for his thrift by his teammates, most of whom weren't old enough to remember the hard times of the Great Depression. While players like Bob Baun enjoyed the finer things in life, like designer clothes and fancy restaurants, Johnny never shook the austere habits of his youth. He owned only a few suits, and never ones that were particularly expensive. When the team went on the road, he would pocket his $3 per diem. "He's the only guy I know who bought a TV with what he saved on his road trip money," says Baun. Instead of buying beverages, Johnny brought along powdered Tang to mix as juice and a jar of instant coffee to put in hot water. He also packed oranges to eat for breakfast. On the road, Armstrong would take the oranges and put them on the windowsill while Johnny was sleeping so they'd be frozen solid in the morning.

But the gags never really bothered Johnny. They were, after all, a sign of acceptance—only played on the guys who could handle them. In fact, the gags only bolstered the bond that Johnny and George shared. They became close friends over long train rides and weeks on end away from their families. Discussions never got overtly personal. They seldom told stories about their youth or asked much of the other, aside from funny tales about growing up. Armstrong never inquired about the name Kiszkan and why Johnny had changed it. They joked about the differences being white and First Nations and took sides when they watched old westerns on the television in their hotel room. Armstrong was five years younger than Johnny, so he grilled the elder about his age. Like most of his teammates, Johnny called Armstrong "Chief," which Armstrong didn't mind. If he wasn't calling Johnny an old man, Armstrong was calling him various slang phrases for the female anatomy, like Coozie (a nickname that didn't stick). They'd smoke together in the bathroom of the team's dressing room before games and between periods, like a couple of high school pals hiding from the teacher. And in the boyish, hypermasculine way of the locker room, Johnny and George built an emotional connection. For the rest of their lives, each frequently described the other as being just like a brother.

Family, in fact, was a word several teammates would use to describe those long-ago days. The Leafs were an eccentric bunch, made of big personalities. There were plenty of insults hurled back and forth. And fights on the ice and in the dressing room were common. They might have bickered with each other, but they'd defend each other to the end. And within that family, both Bower and Armstrong were respected leaders. At first, Johnny had a difficult time mixing with his new teammates. But Armstrong urged him to spend more time with them away from the rink. Under Armstrong's wing, Johnny settled in as one of the guys. During team outings, Johnny would sip a beer, maybe two. Armstrong, who didn't drink, would have a Coke. While some guys would go out and drink all night, the pair would slip away as the others kept going. When young guys on the team felt pressured to keep up with the veterans, Armstrong and Bower would pull them away, because no one could give them hell if they left with Coozie and the Chief.

That was how it was through 11 seasons together. But during that first one, the family was stuck in last place. And for the first time as a Leaf, Bower showed his true worth. Riding on the goaltending that had made Johnny a minor-league star, Toronto went on a remarkable late-season surge. By March 14, with five games remaining, the Leafs were seven points out of a playoff position. But by the last game of the season, they had managed to catch the New York Rangers for the final spot.

The Leafs' season came down to one final Sunday night game against Detroit. The Rangers were playing Montreal that night, and if they tied or won they would clinch the last playoff spot—and the Leafs would be left on the outside for another year. Toronto trailed Detroit 2–0 at the end of the first period. But during intermission, news came through from New York that the Rangers had lost 4–2 to the Canadiens. If the Leafs won, they were in. The news appeared to bolster their effort in the second, where they quickly tied the game. But the Red Wings pulled ahead again, with two goals, despite Johnny's best efforts to jump headfirst into loose scrambles and dive to block pucks with his chest. He was so close to his first-ever NHL playoff appearance, and he wasn't going to let his friend Gordie take it away. With Johnny battling to keep the game close, the Leafs found a way to fight back and catch the Red Wings by the end of the second. Tied 4–4, late in the third, Larry Regan stickhandled through the Red Wings and fed a perfect pass to Dick Duff, who scored the winner. Toronto held off Detroit to the buzzer. The Leafs had made the playoffs, in one of the most dramatic late-season surges from last place the NHL had witnessed.

"We're the hungriest team in the world and we're just getting started," Imlach declared hoarsely in the Leafs locker room after the win, as his team celebrated their playoff berth. "I told them they could do it if they wanted it bad enough. It's work, work, work if you want success in this game."

The miracle finish, by a team of young, inexperienced players—and Johnny—helped foster the spirit of confidence that Imlach had insisted on that season. Bower finished his first season with the Leafs with 15 wins in 39 games played and a 2.72 goals-against average.

The Leafs met the second-place Bruins in the first round of the playoffs. Boston had been Stanley Cup finalists the previous two seasons, losing to the Montreal Canadiens both times, and they were gunning for another chance.

Playing in an NHL playoff series for the first time, Johnny again felt his nerves rising. It showed. With Bower in net, the Leafs dropped the first two games of the series in Boston, by scores of 5–1 and 4–2. Knowing he hadn't played his best, Johnny offered to step aside to let Chadwick play the remainder of the series. But Imlach decided to stick with Bower. Back at Maple Leaf Gardens, Johnny finally picked up his first NHL playoff victory as the Leafs beat the Bruins in overtime, 3–2. The next game at home went to overtime as well. Johnny saved the game by diving across the net to stop a shot from the Bruins' Vic Stasiuk that went off his glove and then his forehead before bouncing away from the goal. A few minutes later, Frank Mahovlich scored to tie the series at two games each.

The Leafs continued their run, winning the next game 4–1 in Boston. After the game, Imlach paraded around with a wig on his bald head, which a fan had thrown at him from the stands. But the victory march was a bit premature. The Bruins won the next game to force a final matchup between the heated rivals. In front of a hostile Boston crowd, the Leafs trailed by a goal heading into the third period. But the miracle season wasn't quite over. Bob Pulford tied it up for the Leafs—and Gerry Ehman, another old "rookie" who'd spent years in the minors, scored with just two and a half minutes remaining to win the series for Toronto.

The team that had barely made the playoffs was heading to the Stanley Cup Final for the first time since Barilko's overtime winner in 1951. The underdog Leafs, who had reignited their fan base across the country, had found a way to believe in themselves too. They celebrated as though they'd won the Cup in the locker room after the final game in Boston.

"We'll take Montreal in seven," Imlach shouted to reporters as he celebrated, referring to the powerhouse Habs team that had won three straight championships and were waiting for their new challenger.

Montreal was led by 37-year-old captain Maurice Richard and 34-year-old defenceman Doug Harvey. The Habs roster was stacked with players like Dickie Moore, Jean Beliveau and Bernie "Boom Boom" Geoffrion—with 22-year-old Henri Richard, the Pocket Rocket, right behind them. Jacques Plante guarded the Montreal goal.

The Leafs may have had momentum after beating the Bruins, but they didn't have much of a chance against the Habs dynasty. The Canadiens took the first two games of the series in Montreal, with Bower facing 44 shots in the Habs' 3–1 win in the second game. "We lost. That hurts," Johnny said contemplatively as he got undressed after the game. "If only I could have gotten a couple of them."

Back in Toronto, Johnny turned aside 29 shots and Dick Duff scored the overtime winner in front of 13,000 fans at Maple Leaf Gardens. But it was just a glimmer of hope, and it wasn't enough. Montreal won the next two to take the series in five games, claiming the team's fourth straight Stanley Cup.

Although Imlach's bold prediction about winning the Stanley Cup was wrong, the Leafs were on the verge of something special. And Johnny was an important part of the resurgence. He was receiving so much fan mail that he bought a thousand photographs of himself so he could autograph them and mail them back in return. By the end of the season, Johnny had to order another thousand.

Toronto had finally found its man in goal. And in Toronto, Johnny had finally found his place in the NHL.

10

GRAND OLD MAN

DESPITE HIS RISING FAME, ON OPENING NIGHT IN OCTOBER 1959, Johnny Bower was only the second most famous son of Prince Albert in attendance at Maple Leaf Gardens. That night, John Diefenbaker, the Canadian prime minister, was at the Gardens to help celebrate the start of a new NHL season.

Diefenbaker had grown up in various small communities in Saskatchewan and was educated in Saskatoon before serving in the First World War. He started his law career in the tiny town of Wakaw before settling in Prince Albert in 1924, where he pursued his political ambitions while practising criminal law. He was elected as a federal Member of Parliament in 1940, representing the province's Lake Centre region—and then became the Progressive Conservative candidate in the Prince Albert riding in 1953. Five years later, he was elected prime minister. Diefenbaker was actually the third prime minister to represent the Prince Albert riding, as anyone visiting the city today is quick to learn; Liberal prime ministers Wilfrid Laurier and William Lyon Mackenzie King both ran in the riding but didn't live in Prince Albert. Diefenbaker would always be the most locally revered among them.

That summer, Diefenbaker had waved at Johnny during a parade for Queen Elizabeth and Prince Philip as they travelled through Prince Albert. The local politician had Johnny's vote. But the Leafs goalie was uncertain if "Dief the Chief" even knew who he was.

"I don't know if he would remember me," Johnny said before opening night at the Gardens.

But soon it would be impossible for even the prime minister to not know about the legend of Johnny Bower.

That season, in the fall of 1959, the starting position was Johnny's to lose. His play through his first season as a Leaf had left little doubt about it. Imlach put his faith in his aging goaltender, whom the NHL record books indicated was about to turn 34. In fact, Bower was a year older than that. He tried to set the record straight in the press early in the season. "I've lied about it so long," Bower told reporters. "I have to stop and think. But here's the truth. I'll be 35 on November 8."

But even if he wasn't able to keep the number straight in his mind, Johnny already felt the weight of age. He noticed he'd been sluggish through training camp that fall. His reflexes lagged, and he was slowing down. Johnny was already suggesting a contingency plan for the Leafs goal.

"I'd like to see Ed Chadwick come back as the regular goaltender next season. I'd stick around in case of an emergency," he said. "I feel pretty good right now. But at my age, you don't know how long you can keep up with this pace."

On the ice, however, Johnny showed little sign of slowing down.

He was relentless in practice, working so hard and for so long that his teammates complained to him about making them look lazy. In games, he continued to prove that he belonged in the National Hockey League—and probably had all along. In Johnny's first season, the goaltending duties had been relatively even, but Chadwick played only four games with the Leafs through the 1959–60 regular season. Only Jacques Plante and Glenn Hall played more games than Johnny that year.

In February, the Leafs picked up defenceman Red Kelly, one of the game's most talented players. Kelly had been shipped to the New York Rangers from the Detroit Red Wings, where he'd been a perennial all-star and the team's captain, but his relationship with team management had soured. Kelly refused to report to New York, declaring that he was retiring. But Imlach stepped in to intervene—convincing the Red Wings to trade him to Toronto instead and persuading Kelly to join the Leafs as a centre.

Toronto ended the season in second place, with 79 points, its best finish in nearly a decade, largely on Johnny's remarkable play.

After picking up a shutout in a 1–0 win over the Chicago Black Hawks in the penultimate game of the season, Johnny circled the ice as fans at Maple Leaf Gardens gave him raucous applause as the game's number one star. Before leaving the ice, Johnny stopped and waved into the *Hockey Night in Canada* cameras. It was intended for his mother-in-law, Esther Brain, who was watching back home in Saskatoon, as she did each game. Johnny was fulfilling a promise he'd given a woman he'd come to love dearly. Whenever he had the chance, Esther had asked that he say hello, just to her.

"I have to wave," Johnny said afterwards in the locker room, when questioned about the unusual gesture. "Whenever I don't, I hear about it."

It was an endearing public act that helped further build the legend of Johnny Bower as a kind and humble aw-shucks boy next door who had somehow made it big. Johnny was waving to Esther, but he was also waving to all the moms watching at home, letting the fans know the game was more than just a faraway spectacle— that they were part of it too.

The next evening in Detroit, Johnny turned aside 45 shots in a 3–2 win over the Red Wings to finish off the regular season. It was just a warm-up for the playoffs, where Toronto and Detroit were set to meet in the Stanley Cup semifinals. Johnny's reputation as one of the NHL's best was growing quickly.

"The Leafs can go a long way with that kind of goaltending," said a frustrated Jack Adams, the Detroit Red Wings' general manager, after the game.

But Toronto dropped the first match of the semifinals, and Punch Imlach decided to up the ante for his team. Before Game 2, in Toronto, the Leafs' coach stacked a dozen large bundles of cash on the floor in the middle of the Leafs locker room and a wrote a message to his players on a chalkboard: "Take a good look at the centre of the floor. This is the difference between winning and losing—$1,250."

If the Leafs managed to win the series and make it to the team's second straight Stanley Cup Final, each man on the roster would receive a bonus of that amount, Imlach explained. It was more than a 10 percent bonus for Johnny, who was making $11,000, part of which went to the league's pension fund. The added cash incentive appeared to work. The Leafs took the second game 4–2 in front of nearly 14,000 fans at the Gardens. Then Johnny did his part to help earn some extra coin. He faced 66 shots as the Leafs and Red Wings battled to triple overtime in Game 3, literally holding his team in it, save after save. Before the final overtime period, the exhausted netminder pulled Frank Mahovlich aside for a pep talk.

"You're the guy. You'll get it," Johnny told him. "All you gotta do is get in front of their net."

Sure enough, Mahovlich rushed up the ice past two Detroit defenders and fed Red Kelly, who was stopped twice by Terry Sawchuk before Mahovlich tapped in the rebound for the 3–2 winner. Mahovlich was the overtime hero, but the victory came on the back of Johnny's incredible performance.

"I don't believe some of the stops he made, even though I saw them," said Red Wings general manager Jack Adams. "But how long can he keep it up?"

A few more games, at least.

Johnny held Gordie Howe to just one goal in the series as Toronto won in six games. And for the second straight year, Toronto met the Montreal Canadiens in the Stanley Cup Final.

But once again, the Leafs were no match for the mighty Habs dynasty. Montreal beat Toronto in four games to win its unprecedented—and still unmatched—fifth straight Stanley Cup. It was the eighth and final championship of 38-year-old Maurice Richard's career. The Rocket would announce his retirement that September.

Such a definitive defeat might have seemed demoralizing for the Leafs faithful, but after losing the fourth game 4–0, the fans at the Gardens gave the Leafs players a loud standing ovation as they left the ice. Having made the Cup Final in back-to-back seasons, Toronto's fans felt they had something to believe in.

But after just two seasons with the Leafs—and two chances to win the Cup—Johnny, once again, seriously considered retiring from the game. With his two-year guaranteed contract expired, he wasn't sure if Toronto still had him in their plans, or if playing hockey was still in his.

Shortly after being eliminated from the playoffs, Johnny and Nancy returned to Saskatoon. John Jr. was now an inquisitive six-year-old and Cindy was toddling around at two. The Bowers were about to welcome another child. On May 23, 1960, Barbara was born. The strain of travel was wearing down the young family. They needed stability, especially through the next few years as their children started going to school.

The Bowers still ran the grill in Waskesiu Lake in the summers and were thinking hard about Johnny's future after the game was through. If he found a decent job during the off-season, Johnny suggested he'd likely hang up his skates. About to turn 36, he would be the oldest player in the NHL if he returned for the 1960–61 season. (Doug Harvey was younger by a month.) Johnny said he didn't believe he was able to play 70 games anymore. Echoing his sentiments from earlier that season, Bower told reporters that if he returned to Toronto, he'd prefer to be the team's second goalie.

However, the Leafs ignored Johnny's apparent lack of faith in himself. That spring "the Grand Old Man of the Leafs," as one news article described him, was awarded the J.P. Bickell Memorial Award as the player held in highest esteem by the team. It was given at the discretion of the directors of Maple Leaf Gardens and wasn't necessarily awarded every year. There had been no winner in either 1957 or 1958, when Toronto had failed to make the playoffs. Conn Smythe said the directors felt Bower had best represented the team on and off the ice through the 1959–60 season. "Against Detroit in the playoffs, he was simply superb," said the godfather of the Leafs organization.

Even if Johnny was contemplating retirement, he wasn't letting his body know. He trained relentlessly that summer as he always did: strapping a bag of cement mix across his shoulders with cellophane and then running 10 miles.

Shortly after the Bickell was awarded, Imlach sat down with Bower to discuss a new contract and urge him to return. Johnny agreed to another season in Toronto. His new contract included a bonus if he allowed fewer than 200 goals in a season.

Bower missed the first few days of training camp in Peterborough that fall so he could keep the restaurant in Waskesiu Lake open as long as possible. He did, after all, have three kids to provide for now. His contract of $11,000 a season—which would be just over $90,000 today—was certainly decent, but Johnny knew he needed to earn every penny he could to take care of his family when the game was gone. He was in the midst of selling the bourgeoning restaurant, using the proceeds to become the co-owner of the new Waskesiu Lake hotel with a local businessman named Bob Webb. Bower hoped the venture might expand on the success he'd had with the grill and would be an investment that would pay off in his retirement.

When Johnny arrived, tardy, to training camp that September he was greeted in his first practice with a puck to the face, courtesy of Dick Duff. It left a rising bruise on Bower's cheek. "I don't think I'll ever be late again," Bower joked after, feeling the lump. "It might pay me to close my restaurant a couple of days early and miss this physical torture." But Johnny wouldn't shy away from a little pain. In fact, he spent five hours a day catching up on his conditioning throughout training camp, on and off the ice, making sure his creaky, old body was ready for the regular season.

Dr. J.P. McKenna, a Peterborough doctor conducting physicals for the Leafs during training camp, marvelled at Bower's physical ability. Johnny was naturally fit. He had strong hands and arms, despite the arthritis that took him out of the war. He had a rock-solid core. He was strong in that well-worn farm hand kind of way. All calloused hands and muscles that served an actual working purpose.

"If you didn't know something of this controversy about his age, you could guess it was 25—assessing him physically," McKenna told *The Hockey News*. "I never have seen a man of his reported years in such wonderful condition. I don't know what he does to stay in shape. Definitely, he is doing something."

McKenna also referred to Bower's heart as a "ticker of a Tiger" and claimed of his eyesight, "Some people have naturally good vision up to the age of 60. Bower is probably in that small percentage." On that final mark only, Dr. McKenna would be wrong—eventually Johnny's vision would betray him.

But the mythology of Johnny Bower was starting to evolve. His origins were still hazy. Reporters continually questioned him for the truth, but Johnny seemed to enjoy the aura of mystery. During an airborne road trip early in the season, he was singled out by an immigration officer who questioned whether he was actually a part of the team.

"He's no hockey player," the official said. "He's too old."

The Hockey News had fun with Johnny's alleged age ahead of the 1960–61 season, noting that "the NHL press book gives his birth date as November 8 in 1924, but nobody takes that too seriously. There have been boys who played junior hockey until streaks of silver started to show in their chin whiskers."

Johnny explained to *Toronto Star* columnist Jim Proudfoot that questions about his age had persisted since he played junior hockey, when an opposing junior team had complained to the league that he was too old to play because he had recently returned from the war.

"Hey, Johnny," one of his teammates yelled from across the locker room, overhearing the story. "Which war was that? The First?"

"Naw," Johnny replied, well accustomed to the taunts. "The Boer."

But Proudfoot, calling Johnny "the Archie Moore of hockey," noted that the goalie's age was generally regarded as "blatant fiction." Johnny stoked the rumours, telling Proudfoot that he was "35—going on 40." It was a regular act. Johnny would hem and haw to reporters about whether he was 36 now—or maybe it was 36 last year, so possibly 37. "Aw-shucks, I don't know," he told Proudfoot. "I've been lying about it so long I've confused myself."

And at times, Johnny became a philosopher.

"Your age varies with the way you feel," he said. "Sometimes when I'm tired and aching in a few million places, I think this has gotta be my last season. I just can't take this kind of treatment any longer. Then I get feeling good, as I do these days, and I decide, hell, I can go on forever."

Or an inspirational speaker: "I'm not too old to learn," he said another time. "I'll tell you that."

The press was on to Johnny now. They knew that by spring he'd groan about the grind of another long season and his aching, breaking body. He'd certainly retire soon, he'd announce. But come fall he was as good as new, fresh and limber and ready for another season.

Despite his age—whatever it was—Johnny was playing the best hockey of his career. He was doing superhuman things. During one game at Maple Leaf Gardens, Johnny chased a loose puck out of his net but got tied up with Boston's Vic Stasiuk, who grabbed hold of his stick in the melee. The puck rolled to Bronco Horvath, who fired it at the empty net. Johnny let go of his stick and dove headfirst for the net, blocking the shot with his chest as he soared through the air. Horvath tossed his stick on the ice in frustration. Milt Schmidt, the Bruins' coach, called it the greatest save he'd ever witnessed. Conn Smythe called Johnny the Leafs' "Horatius at the Bridge," referring to the myth about a Roman soldier who saved Rome from an invading army on his own.

Johnny allowed just 41 goals through the first 17 games of the season, amounting to a 2.41 goals-against average, well ahead of his counterparts on other teams. After so many years of being discussed as one of the best, Johnny found himself in position to win the hardware to prove it. Throughout the season he was in the running for the Vezina Trophy (then awarded to the goalie on the team that allowed the fewest goals), alongside Glenn Hall in Chicago and Jacques Plante and Charlie Hodge in Montreal. He was also comfortably ahead in voting for the All-Star Game—and was openly discussed as a candidate for the Hart Trophy as the league's most valuable player, along with his pal Gordie Howe; Montreal's Boom Boom Geoffrion, who had a 50-goal season; and his teammate Frank Mahovlich, who was on his way to scoring a franchise-best 48 for the Leafs.

"At 36 or 37 or 40 or even more, Cleveland's old China Wall has been enjoying the finest, most rewarding season of an up-and-down, sometimes distinguished career as a professional goaltender," wrote *The Star*'s Proudfoot.

Johnny brushed off the accolades. "I'm just more noticeable because the team is winning and I'm in the running for the Vezina Trophy," he said humbly. And he wasn't entirely wrong. The Leafs battled with the Montreal Canadiens for the first-place position throughout the 1960–61 regular season, led by Mahovlich's offensive prowess and Johnny's goaltending. But Toronto was shaping into a well-balanced contender, built on a mix of experience and talented youth.

That fall, young forwards Bob Nevin and Dave Keon cracked the Leafs lineup, becoming two key pieces of a Maple Leafs roster that looked much more promising than it had before Punch Imlach took over. Nevin, from South Porcupine, Ontario, would play on the Leafs' best line, alongside Mahovlich—another northern Ontario product, from Timmins—and veteran Red Kelly, who was now at centre. He'd score 21 goals and 58 points in his rookie season, third on the Leafs behind Mahovlich and Kelly. Nevin's rookie campaign was so good that he finished second in voting for the Calder Trophy. Instead, the trophy went to the Leafs' other sensational rookie, Keon. He set the pace for his legendary career as a Leaf by scoring 20 goals as a rookie, the first of six straight seasons where he'd hit the mark. But Keon was much more than a goal scorer. He could skate, stickhandle and check. His incredible value came from playing in both ends; he was capable of scoring goals but also wearing down opponents on a penalty kill.

The Leafs surged into 1961, winning five games in a row. Johnny's 2.54 goals-against average was the league's best when his remarkable season was hammered with sad news. Jim Hendy, Johnny's general manager in Cleveland, died suddenly on January 14, at just 55 years of age. Johnny was devastated. He viewed

Hendy as a father figure. Hendy had believed in him and pushed him to join the Leafs, knowing he'd regret finishing his career in Cleveland without taking one last run at the NHL.

Johnny was granted a brief leave from the Leafs. He hired a small plane and flew to Cleveland to attend Hendy's funeral. On the return flight, the small charter entered a dark storm and shook violently in the turbulence. As the plane dipped and tilted wildly, a white-knuckled Johnny worried that he'd end up joining his departed friend much sooner than he'd hoped. He arrived safely in Toronto but was badly shaken.

Hockey calmed his nerves. Aside from his first game at the Gardens, Johnny barely betrayed his jitters. While most goalies are known for eccentric behaviour, especially on game days, Johnny found that his pregame anxiety diminished the closer he got to puck drop. And when the game began, that puck was all that mattered. Despite the emotional stress of losing his friend suddenly, Johnny's play didn't suffer a bit. By February, he'd allowed only 132 goals in 50 games played—well on his way to collecting that bonus Imlach had agreed to when he signed.

And while Johnny worked for that extra cash and to have his name etched on the Vezina, he also took a chance at entering the record books in a way no goalie had ever done before. The visiting New York Rangers tried to score a couple of late goals to erase a 5–3 deficit against the Leafs on February 8, 1961. With their goalie, Gump Worsley, pulled for an extra attacker, the Rangers' Dean Prentice dumped the puck into the Leafs zone from centre ice with just eight seconds left. The puck took a bounce from the corner to the front of Johnny's net. Allan Stanley rushed in to clear it, but Bower had other ideas. He flipped his blocker hand to the top of his stick and gripped the shaft with his catcher.

"Look out!" he yelled at his defenceman—and wristed the puck over attacking Rangers, towards the empty net. The shot from Johnny took everyone in the Gardens by surprise. No goalie had been credited with an NHL goal at the time. And few had tried. The crowd rose and cheered in anticipation as the puck bounced just past centre ice and slid quickly towards the net. It missed by just a few feet, right before the final horn. Appreciating Johnny's entertaining attempt, the crowd stayed on its feet, laughing and clapping for their league-leading goalie as the Leafs left the ice. In the locker room afterwards, Johnny pulled his trousers up, two legs at once, with a comb stuck in his hair, as he recounted the effort for Scott Young of the *Globe and Mail*.

"I only had about four seconds," Johnny said, carrying a big grin as Young followed him to a dressing room mirror.

"It came out perfectly, and I went a way out after it," he said, as he parted his short blond crop cut. "I thought it might hit a bump or something and go in. They're always hitting bumps when they come at me. Well, you never get them if you don't try. I tried."

Across the hall, in the Rangers dressing room, Johnny's old friend Worsley—covered in bruises, with a fading shiner and several old stitch marks—offered some praise for the attempt on his empty goal.

"I'd sort of liked to have seen it go in," he said. "But he's a blind old so-and-so."

A few nights later, the Red Wings' Howie Young collided with Bower in the crease during a game in Detroit. Johnny's legs twisted underneath him in a tangle of bodies. He felt the pop right away and knew he was badly hurt. He had trouble moving his left leg, but he tried his best to pretend he was all right. He stayed in the game and stopped Alex Delvecchio on a breakaway a few minutes later. After the game, which the Leafs won 4–2, the pain was unbearable, and Johnny agreed to go to a hospital in Detroit to have his leg examined. The results were positive: Johnny's left hamstring was torn. He was told his season was over, but Johnny worked hard to be rehabilitated in time for the playoffs. The Leafs had looked like Stanley Cup contenders, but losing Johnny would be an enormous blow. He practised with the Toronto Marlboros, and the Leafs brought in former St. Mike's goalies Gerry McNamara and Cesare Maniago to play in his absence.

Johnny had still been leading the league in goals-against average when he was injured. Because the Vezina was given to the goalie on the team with the fewest goals against, Johnny's shot at having his name engraved on the trophy now depended on the two goalies brought in to replace him. To their credit, McNamara and Maniago managed to keep enough pucks out of the net to secure Johnny the Vezina as he sat on the sidelines.

The Leafs finished second in the regular season, just two points behind the first-place Montreal Canadiens. Maniago played the first two playoff games, winning the opener for the Leafs. Johnny managed to return for the final three. But the Leafs, who had lost several other players to injury, couldn't pull off any postseason magic. Toronto fell to Detroit in the first round, despite having finished 24 points ahead of the Red Wings.

But Johnny had finally carved his name next to the all-time greats, after so many seasons without even having the chance. He fought back tears as NHL president Clarence Campbell handed him the storied Vezina Trophy that spring. And while he received all the accolades, Johnny didn't forget the two goalies who stepped in to secure the prize. He unexpectedly gave McNamara and Maniago each $100 from the $1,000 prize that came along with the Vezina.

On top of his award as the league's best goalie, Bower was voted to the First All-Star team and also finished second in voting for the Hart Trophy as the NHL MVP, losing to Boom Boom Geoffrion, who was only the second player after Rocket Richard to score 50 goals in a season.

The fascination with the China Wall was just getting started.

"Johnny Bower of the Maple Leafs (age undisclosed, but 36 by the record book) is the oldest goalie to have won the Vezina Trophy," *The Hockey News* declared in the spring of 1961. "The ageless goalie (called Satchel Paige by the baseball crowd, Methuselah by the biblical crowd, Jack Benny by the entertainment crowd) is the enigma of the NHL."

11

CHAMPIONS

The tiny red-brick house at 16 Patika Avenue looked almost identical to other postwar houses on the quiet street in the community of Weston, northwest of Toronto. Each house shared a driveway with a neighbour, which led to a one-car garage in the yard behind the house. The quiet boulevard was lined with trees planted every 30 feet or so alongside a sidewalk, in front of a small patch of grass that led to a porch. The façade was just wide enough for a door and a single window, capped by a shingled roof that held a window to the single room upstairs.

It was a modest, middle-class enclave of young families. Every house, it seemed, was filled with kids and teenagers. On warm summer evenings, neighbours would chat about the news and sports as they stood on their verandas, while the busy chatter of childhood adventures filled the street all the way from Weston Collegiate at one end to the playground around the corner on Merrill Avenue at the other. In the winters, that park would come to life with the sounds of hockey on a makeshift rink next to the playground.

In 1960 when the Bower family had moved in, everyone on Patika knew exactly who their famous neighbour was. But aside from the young boys who'd occasionally work up the nerve to knock on the door and ask for an autograph—which Johnny always warmly agreed to—the neighbourhood treated the Bowers like any other family on the street. And the Bowers acted as though that were true.

Weston was a welcoming, comfortable place, akin to life in Cleveland or back home in Saskatoon. Nothing like the chaotic anonymity of Gotham. An early suburb of metro Toronto, Weston was filled with young families like the Bowers. The west end of the street ran into the entrance of Weston Collegiate Institute—one of the region's oldest high schools, which Bower's teammates Ed Chadwick and Bob Pulford had once attended. Teenagers filed busily to and from the high school during the day. Uncertain of how long they'd be staying in Toronto, the Bowers rented the house from Jimmy Morrison, a local hockey player who was with the Detroit Red Wings. Buying was far too presumptuous.

Johnny and Nancy thrived in quaint suburban modesty. As Bower's fame grew—and, eventually, his paycheque followed—they would always avoid the lure of a sumptuous life. Even though the street would later be marked "Johnny Bower Boulevard" on the signs at its intersections, the couple at number 16 lived as though they were just Johnny and Nancy from Saskatchewan.

And John had a decent job downtown, at Church and Carlton. The gig often took him away on business, for weeks at a time. So Nancy was the captain of the house. She took care of her three young kids as well as the house and the bills and all the thousands of things big and small that keep a middle-class family ticking. As the kids grew, Nancy would be the one to take young Cindy to the rink for figure skating classes or John Jr. to hockey practice. She'd tuck the girls into bed in the small upstairs room they shared—and let John Jr. stay up just a little late to watch his father on TV.

When Johnny returned from his road trips, Nancy would pack the kids into their station wagon and drive them downtown to Union Station so they could be on the platform as the train pulled in. They would run aboard, even though they weren't allowed, and greet their dad in his bunk with tiny, excited hugs and kisses. And Johnny would bring them souvenirs he'd picked up on his travels to faraway places like Detroit, Chicago or New York City. He'd hug them hard and carry them out to Nancy. Back home on Patika, he'd tuck them in and read them stories to help them dream of sweet adventures. In the morning, before he climbed back in the station wagon and slogged through the city traffic, Johnny would pull Nancy close in the kitchen, while the kids chomped down breakfast, and he'd kiss her as though it was the first time or the last time, because she—and they—was all there was and everything that mattered to John Bower, of 16 Patika Avenue, in Weston.

BUT OF COURSE, he was much better known as Johnny "the China Wall" Bower, the Vezina Trophy–winning all-star from the Toronto Maple Leafs. By the early 1960s, his fame had grown beyond anything he could have imagined growing up in Prince Albert through the 1930s. Television had changed everything.

Hockey Night in Canada's Saturday night television broadcasts were first beamed into living rooms in Toronto and Montreal in 1952—carrying on the tradition of Foster Hewitt's radio broadcasts on CBC radio, which formally started in the mid-1930s.

Those Saturday night broadcasts weren't important just to Canadians who grew up with the game. They also provided something of a bridge to many new Canadian families that hadn't. Nancy's family had no exposure to hockey in England but found a common interest with their new world in Saskatoon through the strange sport described by Hewitt's frantic descriptions on the radio every Saturday evening. In a small way, hockey played a role in connecting a vast landscape through shared experiences: workyard recollections of great plays described by Hewitt, boisterous bar debates over favourite teams, a sense of assembly within a country taking shape as cultures from around the world collided in one space. Hewitt's stories gained shape and colour through television. While the game's legends could previously have been read about in daily newspapers and seen in photographs, the action broadcast through television screens provided a new sense of awe and wonder. By the time stations for CBC and Radio-Canada launched in 1952, more than 100,000 sets had been sold. A year later, it was more than half a million. Through those early years in the 1950s, kinescopes of the televised games were shipped across the country and viewed a week later. In 1957, microwave transmission allowed live broadcasts to be viewed throughout Canada. And by the 1960s, *Hockey Night in Canada* was beaming into storefronts, bars and living rooms from coast to coast. NHL hockey further entrenched itself as part of the exterior fabric of the Canadian experience.

The players had become much more than names that captured the attention of schoolkids. They were more than faraway figures, the hazy heroes of newspaper clips and storybooks. You no longer had to live in a big city like Toronto or Montreal to witness a game, to roar with the crowd, to watch the speed of action come to life. Hewitt had built legends with his words, but television gave them life. Players from this era would transcend the decades as memorable figures of popular culture—beyond serious hockey fans—in ways that the greats of the 1930s and '40s, like Eddie Shore, Charlie Conacher or Bill Durnan, never would. Certainly, those radio-era players would be revered for their place in the sport's history. But they wouldn't, *they couldn't*, permeate popular culture in the way that the stars of the 1950s and 1960s would. This was the golden era, from which certain stars would continue to burn brightly through the coming decades—names like Rocket Richard, Gordie Howe, Bobby Hull—and, of course, Johnny Bower.

After the 1960–61 season, Johnny was already one of the most popular players in the NHL, even though he was yet to win a Stanley Cup. It seemed as though fans and players alike were rooting for him. "He's a nice man, for one thing," Dick Duff said at the time. "And he's been knocking around in the minors so long that everyone is happy to see him doing well." Whenever he was injured in a game, *The Hockey News* observed, most opposing players would lean over to see if he was all right. Detroit's Howie Young had been roundly criticized for the collision with Johnny that had torn his hamstring and ended his Vezina season. Johnny, ever affable, went out of his way to tell Young that he knew it was just an accident. Among Leafs fans, however, there was little doubt that the team's star goalie was taken out on purpose.

As Johnny turned 37 on November 8, 1961, the Leafs issued a press release to note just how old their award-winning netminder claimed to be, and newspapers across Canada celebrated the league's oldest player—noting that he was once again looking sharp enough to win the Vezina. Through the first 10 games of the season, Johnny had allowed only 18 goals. But in early December, he took a hard shot on the right ankle during a game against Montreal. Johnny helped preserve a 1–1 tie against their league rivals, but his ankle swelled into a grapefruit after the game. He couldn't put any pressure on it. When the team returned to Toronto by train, Johnny was taken to the hospital.

The Leafs called up former Boston Bruins goalie Don Simmons to take his place. Simmons had quit hockey that season to take a job as a milk salesman. But Toronto had picked him up as an insurance policy in case Johnny's fountain of youth ran out. It would prove to be a key move for the organization, which also still had a young Gerry Cheevers in the system. Toronto was once again battling Montreal for the top spot in the league. With his swollen ankle, Johnny watched from the sidelines for five games while Simmons replaced him.

It was more time in the stands than Johnny could bear. In his first game back, he took a stick to the head that sent him for seven stiches across his hairline to his ear—but he returned after being mended to complete a 31-save win over the Rangers at Maple Leaf Gardens.

Johnny was in a good mood after the game, smiling as he returned from the shower to find John Jr. sitting in his stall. The younger Bower, barely reaching his father's waist, always found his place in the stall after home games, slipping in as soon as Imlach was done addressing the team.

"See my stiches?" Johnny asked his son, pointing to the newest gash in his collection. "Yeah, did you see that fight?" the seven-year-old replied, more interested in a late-game tussle between the Rangers' Pat Hannigan and Frank Mahovlich, adjudicated in Frank's favour by Allan Stanley.

"Didn't hurt much," Johnny said, trying again.

"What didn't hurt?" John Jr. asked his dad. "The fight?"

Johnny just sighed and smiled at his son, while Hughie Smythe, one of the team doctors, came in to examine his ankle, which was still considerably swollen. Johnny had pressed hard to be allowed back in the lineup. As he got off the table, John Jr. was still going on about the fight he'd witnessed from the stands, sitting next to Nancy.

"What was it about?" he asked again.

John Jr. was an inquisitive kid. Every time the Leafs were in town, he spent as much time as he could at Maple Leaf Gardens. It was like a second home to him. During practice days, he'd wander through the concourse on each level, stroll down the aisles of empty seats and explore the ancient halls beneath the stands. The Gardens was filled with odd rooms and mysterious passageways, and John Jr. was constantly finding his way into places he wasn't supposed to be—or being shown the inner workings of the building by the familiar arena staff. Sometimes, while his father was getting treated, the team's physiotherapist, Karl Elieff, would let John Jr. swim around in his large portable tub.

On game days in Toronto, John, Nancy and John Jr. would drive to the Gardens from Weston, east across Davenport, south on Church. They'd park in the players' lot at the back of the arena on Wood Street around six o'clock, a couple of hours before game time. While Johnny got ready for the game, Nancy and John Jr. would walk to the coffee shop inside the Gardens. The mother of the Leafs' trainer worked there, and she'd make John Jr. his favourite for dinner, a toasted ham sandwich with mustard.

During games, Nancy and John Jr. always sat in the blue seats, section 48, row J, seats 7 and 8. Afterwards, as the arena cleared out, John Jr. would dash down to ice level and run around the outer edge of the boards to the hallway that led to the dressing room on the other side of the rink. When he reached the dressing room door, the usher would have him wait until Imlach was finished his postgame soliloquy. As soon as the coach walked out, either beaming or steaming, John Jr. made his entrance. The husky kid with a wide, round face would hop into the stall that held his father's gear while Johnny hit the showers or went off to get another war wound mended. Usually the team's trainer, Bobby Haggert, or equipment manager, Tommy Naylor, would hand John Jr. a Coke or ginger ale. Tim Horton would walk by and give the kid a playful shove or tousle his hair. George Armstrong often played a prank. He'd toss a towel at John Jr., pretending he was a member of the custodial staff. Or he'd pile up laundry right where he sat.

"Just throw them on the floor, Johnny," Bower would tell his son with a smile as the kid stood there, unsure of what to do.

John Jr. took it all in—the pranks, the laughter, the vulgarities of the grown men's playground. He watched his father transform back from the China Wall into Dad, all cleaned up and bandaged, in a suit with combed hair. They'd walk out of the dressing room together, father and son. In his 60s, decades on, John Jr.'s voice would crack and escape him as he thought of how much those small moments had meant. Out in the hall, they'd find his mom waiting outside the family lounge. Johnny would greet Nancy with a kiss. And together, the three would head out the back door of the Gardens, where Johnny would sign a few autographs for a handful of patient, adoring fans. John Jr. would climb into the back seat of the Rambler and watch the lights of the city go by as they drove back to the suburbs. If the Leafs had won, they'd stop for pizza at Tony's, a takeout joint in a strip plaza near their house. And Tony would make one up, just the way the Bowers liked it, loaded with pepperoni and mushrooms.

TORONTO SLIPPED DURING the second half of the 1961–62 season and wound up with 85 points—still good enough to finish second overall but 13 points behind the first-place Canadiens. Jacques Plante claimed the Vezina Trophy and would also win the Hart.

The Maple Leafs were the heavy favourites as they faced the New York Rangers in the Stanley Cup semifinals. After Toronto won the first two games of the series at Maple Leaf Gardens, they ran into trouble in Manhattan where they played in front a wild packed house of nearly 16,000 typically impolite Rangers fans. New York took the game 5–4—including a goal off a 60-foot shot that skidded under Johnny's left leg. Afterwards, Imlach singled his goalie out in the loss, saying that Bower seemed "too relaxed" while allowing five goals and called him careless for allowing a fat rebound that led to the game-winner.

Imlach was prone to sharing his opinions about goaltending. He often offered pointers to Johnny on how to better play his angles, or when it was ideal to stand up versus going down on a scoring attempt. Johnny's relaxed demeanour before games was often noted, especially in contrast to other goalies who were known for their pregame intensity and nerves. Imlach warned that he might play Simmons if his starter didn't pick up his game.

Was Johnny's age starting to show? The Leafs dropped the next game, allowing the Rangers to tie up the series at home. But Imlach stuck with Johnny as the Leafs returned to Toronto. Back at the Gardens, Game 5 went into double overtime. Up in the blue section, young John Bower Jr. was so nervous watching his dad stop 41 shots in the thriller that he turned his head every time the puck went near Toronto's net. After the first overtime period, John Jr. threw up in the washroom. Early in the second extra frame, Red Kelly scored the winner on Gump Worsley, who made 56 saves in the loss. The loss deflated the Rangers, who were flat in Game 6. The Leafs won 7–1 and were headed to the Stanley Cup Final.

This time they'd face a young, talented Chicago Black Hawks team that had upset the first-place Canadiens. Although they'd finished third in the standings, the Black Hawks were the defending Stanley Cup champions. Bobby Hull, just 23 years old, had scored 50 goals that season, mostly on the force of his booming slap shot. And crafty 21-year-old Stan Mikita was right there with him, adding 52 assists. Once again, Toronto won the first games at home but ran into trouble on the road. The Leafs dropped the third game at Chicago Stadium on Madison Avenue. Then, in Game 4, they lost Johnny. He made a remarkable split save, reaching across the length of his net to block a low slap shot from Hull in the first period. But he sacrificed his groin to do it. Once again, Johnny knew he was badly hurt but tried to play through it. From the bench, Imlach noticed his goalie moving laboriously in his crease. He sent Armstrong out to check on Bower, who told the captain he was fine. Johnny had no intention of leaving a game in the Stanley Cup Final. Armstrong reported back to Imlach. The charade lasted for four minutes, until finally, with Johnny clearly in agony, Imlach sent Armstrong back to tell him he was coming out. Johnny refused. The back-and-forth continued, with Armstrong as the messenger. He returned with an ultimatum from the coach: If Johnny didn't get his stubborn old butt off the ice, he'd be fined $25. It was just too much to spare. Imlach had him. Johnny relented, skating slowly to the bench. Don Simmons was summoned from the stands to get dressed to play.

After the Leafs lost 4–1, Johnny went to the hospital, where he learned that he'd severely injured his groin muscle. There was talk about freezing and taping his groin ahead of the next game, but it would come at too great a risk. Johnny's season was over. But his team was still hunting for its first Stanley Cup in more than a decade. He watched from the sidelines as the Leafs won Game 5 without him and returned to Chicago Stadium with a chance to win the Cup in Game 6. He desperately wanted to play and probably would have willed himself through the pain, but Simmons was healthy and played well for Toronto.

Johnny cheered as Bob Nevin scored to tie the game at one partway through the third—and then as Dick Duff put in the winner just a few minutes later. He watched the clock tick down through the final seconds of the third period as Toronto led 2–1. The final horn sounded: The Maple Leafs were Stanley Cup champions, for the first time in more than a decade.

Back in Toronto, Leafs fans celebrated like it had been a century, at least. When the team touched down at Toronto International Airport at 3:15 a.m., more than 1,500 fans were waiting for them. The team was mobbed as they left the terminal building. The Stanley Cup was ushered into a police cruiser as the crowd went wild at the sight of it. Duff, Nevin and Armstrong were hoisted high on the shoulders of fans and carried around. A loud cheer greeted the injured Bower, who was spared the piggyback treatment. Traffic around the airport was jammed as cars parked and honked near the exit of the airport.

A few days later, police reinforcements had to be brought in to contain a crowd estimated at nearly 60,000 that shut down Toronto's core during the Leafs' Stanley Cup parade. Only 50 officers had been assigned to the parade because the city had expected about 20,000 attendees, tops. Another hundred officers were called in as the wild crowd continued to swell.

Johnny sat in a convertible, smiling and waving to the mad mob, with Nancy and the kids beside him. John Jr. revelled in the moment as fans clamored to wave at his father. He'd watched the Leafs win on television. When Johnny came in the door the next day, John Jr. wrapped his arms around him and declared, "We won the Allan Stanley Cup!"

The route up Bay Street to City Hall was packed with thousands of people, mostly teenagers, in a state of pandemonium on a warm April afternoon. Only the first four of 15 convertibles carrying the victorious Leafs managed to reach City Hall. The others had to abandon the cars as fans converged on the street. They pushed through the crowds with police escorts for nearly two blocks to reach the stage. They were covered in confetti and streamers, while some fans snatched their handkerchiefs and grabbed at their neckties. "I touched him! I touched him!" several young female fans shrieked as they managed to get a hand on the passing hockey stars.

"More than fifty crying children became separated from parents and were taken to a City Hall room," the *Globe and Mail* reported.

Over a speaker, Mayor Nathan Phillips asked the crowd to give the players space to make it to the dais.

"Beating Chicago in the Stanley Cup Final wasn't as tough as this," Armstrong shouted as he struggled through the crowd.

Magistrates in the nearby courthouse had to adjourn court because the noise outside made it impossible to hear. Some fans climbed street lights and TTC streetcars that were halted by the crowd.

When all the players made it to the stage, Mayor Phillips, who had flown home from vacation in Bermuda to be there, introduced each player but his voice was mostly drowned out by the crowd, who knew them all by heart anyway. With his turn at the mic, having made it to the stage, Armstrong addressed the crowd through enormous cheers. "For once the Indians came out on top!" he said, referring to his First Nations heritage. After the drowned-out introductions, the Leafs players were escorted to the mayor's office, where they were each presented with gold cufflinks bearing the city's coat of arms—as police tried in vain to clear out fans who had infiltrated the premises and were running through the halls.

It was, Mayor Phillips said, the "greatest reception" the city of Toronto had ever seen.

12

BIG FISH

Johnny Bower stood in an old fishing boat just off the shoreline in Waskesiu Lake, reeling in a northern trout. His fishing partner, Gordie Howe, in khakis and a polo shirt that struggled to contain his massive arms and shoulders, helped snag the silver catch in a net. Johnny, sporting a white cap and black spring jacket—and much less upper body—spun the handle on his rod and pulled in the line. It was August 1962, and Johnny and Gordie were on the water doing what they loved best. The Howe family owned a small cabin in the area and, like the Bowers, spent their summers on the lake. Having grown up just outside of Saskatoon, Gordie started going to the lake during the summers as a young pro with the Detroit Red Wings, when Johnny was just getting his start with the Cleveland Barons. In fact, the first goal Howe scored in a Red Wings sweater was on Johnny, during an exhibition game against the Barons.

With similar temperaments—both kind and gentle, with a fiercely competitive edge—the two young hockey players became fast friends. They often played golf at the local course, where Johnny had worked and Gordie later found summer employment. Howe could crush a golf ball, while Johnny was a decent putter. When they went down to the breakwater to swim, the local kids clamoured to meet them. One time, Gordie broke both diving boards in the swimming area as his hulking frame dove off them. Both Johnny and Gordie would entertain young fans who riddled them with questions. They often bought the kids burgers and pop while they chatted. And if they weren't on the golf course or swimming at the breakwater, Johnny and Gordie were out on the lake reeling in northern trout. If they'd been lucky, the pair would come back to John and Nancy's shack tent—with plank wood walls, a couple of windows and a canvas roof—and they'd cook up their catch with green peas and then eat and talk and laugh into the night, until Nancy went off to bed exhausted, leaving the boys chatting beneath the stars.

In later years, after Gordie met and married his sweetheart, Colleen, they'd bring their young family up to Waskesiu too. The Bowers had bought a proper cabin by then, while the Howes settled for a shack tent. They played golf and tennis, and they went down to the beach together. On Saturday evenings the Bowers and Howes would go to the local dance hall. The area was frequented by bears, so whenever they had the chance, Gordie and Johnny would sneak up on their wives and growl—or bang on the outside toilet facilities—to give them a scare.

Gordie often came by the restaurant and helped out on the grill. Customers were thrilled to learn that just beyond the curtains separating the dining area from the kitchen, Gordie Howe was flipping their hamburgers.

The Howes' eldest son, Marty, was the same age as John Jr.— and their second son, Mark, was just a year younger. The three boys ran around finding all sorts of trouble. One of their favourite capers was to steal the sour gumballs from a jar near the cash register when no one was looking, and then lick off the sugary coating and put them back, so the pretested gumballs could still be sold. Sometimes the boys would go out fishing with their fathers. Mark Howe's boyhood imagination would capture one moment as they all sat on the pier, with their lines in the water, as it started to pour rain in the distance. The small storm drifted towards them, making the lake dance—but the rain just stopped about 10 feet out, falling in front of them like a waterfall in the sky.

But despite their long kinship through those halcyon summers, when Johnny finally made it to the NHL the famous friends gave each other a hellish time. Each was regularly bested by the other. Howe would score 49 of his 1,071 career goals on Johnny. And two of those were nearly Bower's undoing at the start of the 1962–63 season.

Gordie scored a pair on Johnny when the Leafs met the Red Wings in early November—including one in which he, rather rudely, pushed Tim Horton onto the Leafs goaltender and then tapped the puck into the net. Detroit won the match 7–3. Toronto had lost six of its first 11 games, in which Johnny allowed 36 goals. It was an uncharacteristic slump for Johnny, and Imlach worried that his age had finally caught up to him. After the game, Imlach announced that Johnny was benched. The Leafs were calling up Don Simmons from the Rochester Americans. The starting job would be his until he lost it.

Imlach was frustrated by the play of his entire team and openly discussed trading Dick Duff to Boston. He also said that Eddie Shack, Billy Harris and Ron Stewart were on the block as well. But at the time, Johnny was the prime target for change. A split-second slowdown can be the difference in the life of a goalie. A few days later, on Bower's 38th birthday, the Associated Press mused about whether "the oldest player in the National Hockey League [had] finally reached the end of the line with the Toronto Maple Leafs."

Simmons, the career pinch-hitter who'd completed the Leafs' Stanley Cup win, played admirably, winning three straight games, while Johnny watched from the sidelines, hoping for a chance to disprove the reports of his demise. Considering everything he'd faced in his career—the oversights, demotions, disappointment, injury after injury—it was hard to bet against Johnny's resilience. His spirit was never in question. But, surely, the man was mortal, and age always claims the final win. Johnny could have viewed his rough start and demotion to the stands as a sign that it was finally time to go. But he was having none of it.

Despite his relegation to the backup role, Johnny went through his game-day routines as though he were playing. He ate a steak at 2:30 p.m. and then went down for a long afternoon nap while the kids played outside. Everyone in the Bower household knew to be quiet inside on game-day afternoons. Johnny's long naps were essential. Nancy would wake him at the exact same time, and they'd make their way downtown to the Gardens together. But ahead of the game against the Montreal Canadiens, it was Leafs trainer Bobby Haggert who woke him with a phone call. Simmons was down and out with the flu. The misfortune of one goalie's bowels was another's gain. The Leafs needed Johnny to play in relief. He knew this might be his last chance to prove he could still play. Another poor showing might sink him for good.

Johnny held off the Habs in a 4–2 win and then followed the victory up a few nights later with a 3–2 win over the Detroit Red Wings. He was his old, marvellous self in both. He'd been saved by a flu bug. Imlach decided that Johnny still had more to offer. He planned to use both Bower and Simmons for the rest of the season, giving his 38-year-old goalie more rest—but giving him the primary spot in goal.

By early 1963, headlines once again sang about Johnny's "Perennial Youth." He'd finish the season with a 2.60 goals-against average in 42 games, while Simmons took over for the other 28. Johnny's rebound put him in contention for another Vezina Trophy. In late March, Imlach announced that Johnny would start the remainder of the season and through the playoffs, with Simmons on standby.

Toronto had turned its rough start around and looked like contenders for another Stanley Cup. Frank Mahovlich led the team again, with 36 goals and 73 points. Veteran Red Kelly—also a federal MP at the time—was right behind his linemate the Big M, with 60 points. And 22-year-old Dave Keon had 28 goals and 58 points. Imlach boasted that he was already the best player in the league, and on that claim he had a point. Keon's ability at both ends of the ice was just getting better. He was already one of the best penalty killers in the game. Keon won the Lady Byng Trophy for his sportsmanship and gentlemanly conduct, his second major award after claiming the Calder. Meanwhile, 24-year-old Carl Brewer was a standout on defence and would finish second in voting for the Norris Trophy.

The Leafs finished first overall in the standings, with 82 points. It was the first time Toronto had been the best team through the regular season since 1948. Then they beat the rival Montreal Canadiens in the Stanley Cup semifinals in five games; Johnny picked up two shutouts in the series and allowed just six goals as he outduelled Jacques Plante. On the other side, Gordie Howe and the Detroit Red Wings had upset the Chicago Black Hawks to reach the Stanley Cup Final. Howe—at 35 and in his 17th NHL season—had won the scoring title with 86 points to win the Art Ross Trophy and would also win the Hart Trophy as league MVP. It was the sixth and last time he'd win both trophies. Johnny's old fishing pal once again threatened to be his biggest nightmare.

Toronto picked up two important wins at home to take an early lead in the Stanley Cup Final, but the team suffered a huge blow when Frank Mahovlich strained ligaments in his left knee on a hit in the second game.

With the series in Toronto, Howe barrelled towards the Leafs goal and lost control of his hulking frame.

"Look out, John! Look out!" Gordie shouted at Johnny, who was in the path of the oncoming train. It was too late. They went down together in a twisted pile of skates, sticks and pads. Both men got up slowly. As Johnny tried to find his feet, Gordie reached over and grabbed his arm to help steady him.

"Are you all right, John?" he asked anxiously. "Everything okay?"

Johnny shrugged off the collision with his friend. The crowd, noting the act, applauded the pair of all-stars.

It was a moment of kindness in an otherwise heated series, which tensed up after Detroit won Game 3 at the Olympia. Red Wings fans were notoriously rough, and 14,000 of them didn't intend to let up on the visiting Leafs. During Game 4, they let Toronto have it before the puck even dropped.

Howe delighted the mob by scoring a couple of minutes into the game on a long slap shot from just inside the blue line that knocked aside Bower's catcher and ricocheted into the net. Imlach felt his goalie should have had it. He asked one of the team trainers to find out where Simmons was sitting and make sure he was ready to play. "We can't be patsies out there," Imlach said. But Johnny wasn't shaken. Howe hammered shots at him all night and set up several scoring opportunities for his teammates. He even crashed into Bower on a few occasions, using his enormous strength to knock the goalie off his game. But Bower made 38

Johnny was about to turn 34 years old when he agreed to join the Toronto Maple Leafs, but despite being the oldest player on the team, he was also one of the most athletic. Here he warms up with the youngsters at training camp in 1958. (MICHAEL BURNS SR./COURTESY OF THE HOCKEY HALL OF FAME)

The Bower family spent their summers by the lake, often returning to Waskesiu, Saskatchewan, where they kept a cabin for years. (COURTESY OF THE BOWER FAMILY)

Tim Horton may be the best-known hockey player in the coffee shop business, but his team-mate Johnny Bower beat him to it. Johnny started his coffee shop and grill in Waskesiu in the early 1950s. The restaurant was known for its signature "Bower's Big Boy" burger.
(Courtesy of the Bower family)

Johnny Bower and Gordie Howe became friends long before they ever faced off in the NHL. They met in the 1940s, when they both spent their summers in Waskesiu. Two of the game's most famous names became pals by playing golf and fishing together.
(Courtesy of the Bower family)

Johnny was an avid golfer who worked as a pro at the club in Waskesiu, where he met Nancy. He and Gordie Howe were regulars on the course. Johnny would play the game into his 90s, when he'd join foursomes on the green to help them putt during charity tournaments. (COURTESY OF THE HOWE FAMILY)

Through the 1960–61 season, Johnny played so well he was voted a First-Team All-Star and finished second in voting for the Hart Trophy as the league's most valuable player. He earned his first Vezina Trophy, as the Leafs allowed the fewest goals against in the league. (STUDIO ALAIN BROUILLARD/ COURTESY OF THE HOCKEY HALL OF FAME)

After just two seasons with the Leafs, Johnny was a franchise star. He earned the J.P. Bickell Memorial Award as the player held in highest esteem by the team, an honour bestowed only when the directors of Maple Leaf Gardens believed it was especially warranted. Here he spends some downtime with Leafs star Frank Mahovlich. (TUROFSKY COLLECTION/COURTESY OF THE HOCKEY HALL OF FAME)

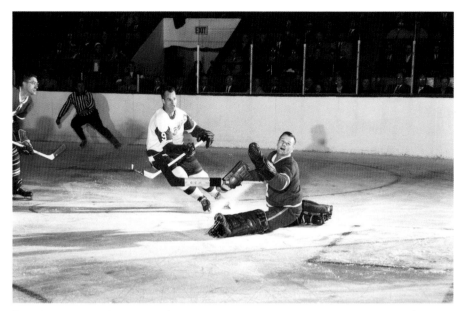

Few players in the NHL were as fiercely competitive on the ice as Johnny Bower and Gordie Howe. The pair were also alike off the ice—both earning reputations for their generosity and kindness to fans. Here they face off during a game in 1961.
(MICHAEL BURNS SR./COURTESY OF THE HOCKEY HALL OF FAME)

Johnny played in an era of great goaltenders, with only six regular spots in the NHL. Johnny and Gump Worsley had battled for the top spot in the New York Rangers' net. But despite the intense competition, Johnny and Gump became good friends. (TUROFSKY COLLECTION/COURTESY OF THE HOCKEY HALL OF FAME)

The battles on the ice were never enough to diminish the mutual respect between Johnny Bower and Gordie Howe. Both graciously addressed each other and the crowd after the Leafs beat the Red Wings to win the 1963 Stanley Cup. (TUROFSKY COLLECTION/COURTESY OF THE HOCKEY HALL OF FAME)

Roughly 60,000 fans showed up to celebrate the Leafs' Stanley Cup victory in 1962 at a parade through the streets of Toronto—and again the following two springs, as the city enjoyed three consecutive championships. (GRAPHIC ARTISTS/COURTESY OF THE HOCKEY HALL OF FAME)

During his career, Johnny became famous for his poke check—a move he used to aggressively challenge attacking shooters with his stick, forcing them to react to him while trying to score. He used it so frequently and effectively that the skill became widely known as the "Johnny Bower poke check." Johnny mastered the move after being mentored by Charlie Rayner while with the New York Rangers. (TUROFSKY COLLECTION/COURTESY OF THE HOCKEY HALL OF FAME)

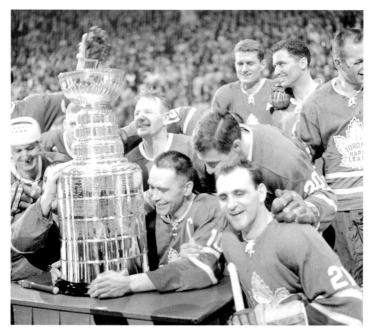

Johnny's close friend Bob Baun became the hero in the Leafs' 1964 Stanley Cup win, after scoring the winning goal on a broken leg while facing elimination in Game 6. The Leafs finished off the Red Wings in Game 7 to win a third straight Stanley Cup. Here Baun, 21, huddles next to George Armstrong, while Johnny admires the Cup next to them. (MICHAEL BURNS SR./COURTESY OF THE HOCKEY HALL OF FAME)

After the Leafs won a third straight Stanley Cup—with a second straight win over the Red Wings—Johnny shared a glass of champagne with his good friend Gordie. (MICHAEL BURNS SR./COURTESY OF THE HOCKEY HALL OF FAME)

Another year, another Stanley Cup. Johnny and John Jr. shared the jubilation of the Leafs' 1964 Stanley Cup win. While the elder enjoyed some champagne, John Jr. enjoyed some ginger ale. (MICHAEL BURNS SR./COURTESY OF THE HOCKEY HALL OF FAME)

Punch Imlach had his share of controversy with his players over the years, including with Johnny. But the two men shared a deep respect for each other. Imlach believed Johnny was the greatest athlete alive in the 1960s. (Turofsky collection/Courtesy of the Hockey Hall of Fame)

Winning the Stanley Cup and collecting Johnny's well-deserved hardware became a family affair for the Bowers through the 1960s. (Courtesy of the Bower family)

Terry Sawchuk and Johnny Bower couldn't have been more different, aside from both being exceptional goalies. They shared the Vezina Trophy in 1965—and then the Stanley Cup in 1967. They celebrated that momentous occasion in the Leafs locker room after the win.
(Graphic Artists/Courtesy of the Hockey Hall of Fame)

saves, outduelling the great Terry Sawchuk, who made 29 saves in the Red Wings goal. Toronto came from behind twice to win 4–2, earning a chance to hoist the Stanley Cup back home at Maple Leaf Gardens.

As they left the ice, the Leafs were pelted with paper cups, programs and garbage as they crossed the lobby of the Detroit Olympia to their dressing room. It had been a rough affair. Dick Duff had tossed Howe's stick into the stands and gone after Vic Stasiuk on the Red Wings bench. The ensuing melee, in which Howe gave Duff a pop in the nose, helped keep the crowd riled. An angry mob closed in as they entered the room, hurling profanity. A paper cup smacked Carl Brewer in the face and he raised his stick, ready for battle.

Red Kelly, the Canadian MP and former Lady Byng winner, stopped to beat back the taunts with a few of his own. When Imlach tried to host reporters in the hallway because the visiting dressing room was too small, the crowd kept shouting and tossing debris. One of the fans got into a small tussle with a Toronto reporter. Imlach quickly ushered the press into the tiny dressing room. "You've seen your last game," he fired back at the crowd.

Imlach's confident taunt proved prescient. Back at Carlton and Church, the Leafs took a 2–1 lead late in the third period on a pinball goal that started with a shot from rookie defenceman Kent Douglas, then was tipped by Eddie Shack past Sawchuk. It was good fortune for Johnny that Douglas was playing at all. During a team skate the day before, Johnny had snuck onto the ice without his goal pads and playfully bodychecked Douglas, knocking his right shoulder out of the socket. Douglas was able to pop it back in and played through the pain.

With Toronto up, the Red Wings frantically tried to beat Johnny and extend the series. During a mad scramble in the final minute of the game, Howe fell on top of Bower and got his skate caught in the webbing of his catcher. From the stands, Nancy yelled at Howe to get off Johnny.

"Okay . . . okay," Gordie said as he struggled, careful not to kick his friend as they manoeuvred free. Toronto's net sat wide open. Meanwhile, the puck bounced to Norm Ullman, who had a clear shot. He took a swipe at the bobbling puck, but it hit Howe in the left calf, deflecting six inches past the net. Dave Keon picked up the puck at the left boards and fired it 140 feet down the ice and into the empty Red Wings goal, for his second of the game. The crowd of 14,000 delirious fans at the Gardens roared as the puck hit the back of the net. The din continued as the clock ticked down to the final horn and the Leafs piled onto each other as back-to-back Stanley Cup champions. Garbage, programs and peanuts filled the air.

After the Red Wings and Leafs shook hands on the ice, Frank Selke Jr. asked Howe to do a live interview on *Hockey Night in Canada* that was broadcast over the speakers at the Gardens. Gordie pulled in Johnny, putting his arm around him, as the crowd gave the pair an enormous ovation.

"Fellas, I think that's just about as much tribute as we can expect tonight from this packed house," Selke said. "Are you boys just about ready to go fishing in a few weeks?"

"Well, I'm just waiting for Gordie to come out west, but first of all, I'd like to say that we certainly played a wonderful game. It could have gone either way—"

"With your help," Howe interjected, to laughter.

"I'm sure glad you didn't have too many shots on the net, Gord, because I don't know where I'd be—maybe Punch would have benched me or something." Johnny continued: "I just want to say I'm certainly glad we won the Stanley Cup again for the city of Toronto. They deserve it. They're wonderful fans. And I hope we can do it again next year. Thank you very much."

The crowd roared as Johnny skated away, and it turned into a loud mix of boos and cheers as Howe stepped in.

"Gordie," Selke said, "how about a few words on behalf of the Red Wings?"

"If I may, I'd just like to congratulate the Toronto club," he said. "And also my fellow teammates. For a team that wasn't supposed to be in the playoffs, I thought we showed up rather well." He let out a laugh, which was met with cheers from the fans, because who could not love Mr. Hockey? "I'd like to also congratulate the Toronto organization. You people up there not only have a fine hockey club, but we know personally a lot of the individuals, and in this game of hockey, I don't think there's a rotten apple in the whole barrel. So, congratulations to all."

Soon Johnny would be in the Leafs locker room, drenching himself in champagne with his teammates and clinking glasses with a proud Johnny Jr., who held up his glassful of bubbly ginger ale. Johnny would sneak a bottle over to the Detroit dressing room to give to his pal Gordie. He was staying overnight at the Bowers' house to watch his son, Mark, play in an Easter tournament held in Brampton the next day. "I wouldn't have agreed to bait his hook when we go fishing in the summer, if he hadn't of agreed to produce the giggle juice," Howe would joke.

But first Johnny had to take in the moment. The ovations weren't through. He left the ice briefly but was called back out to acknowledge the still roaring crowd, and he waved through their ovation. After so many years, Johnny was finally there—on the ice, no injuries, no doubts, no demotions to stop him.

Johnny circled again, waving to the adoring crowd. He handed his stick to a 14-year-old fan.

After nearly losing his starting job; after declarations that he was simply too old, too slow, too broken to carry on; after all of it, Johnny was a hero. He'd allowed just 10 goals in five games to win the Stanley Cup.

The season earlier had to have been bittersweet, as he watched Toronto finish off the championship from the sidelines. But not now. No, *this* was his. It was never something he'd say out loud, of course.

But somewhere inside the ageless man, a poor, rough kid named Kiszkan was realizing an impossible dream.

13

"EVERYBODY WELCOME"

ALL EYES WERE ON MR. HOCKEY IN THE FINAL MINUTE. WITH the Red Wings up 3–2, the Leafs pulled Bower from the net, hoping to tie it up with an extra attacker. Howe grabbed the puck and fired it down the ice into the empty net. The Olympia went wild. Mr. Hockey had just scored his 544th career goal, tying the all-time record set by Maurice Richard. But the referee, Frank Udvari, skated into an assault of arena debris by calling off the goal, on account of an illegal hand pass from Alex Delvecchio before Howe got the puck. Ever courteous, the Red Wings fans littered the ice with eggs and garbage, delaying the final 30 seconds of the game for an extra five minutes. When the final horn blew that evening, on October 20, 1963, there seemed little reason to note the game for posterity. But as the players headed to the dressing rooms and the fans continued to hurl their disgust at Udvari, Bower skated off the Leafs bench and collected the game puck.

Perhaps distracted by the halting of history, no one seemed to notice. In fact, Johnny appeared to be the only person in the Olympia who knew that he'd just played his 1,000th professional hockey game. Sports scribes missed the occasion; Johnny certainly hadn't pointed it out. Given that he'd played only six NHL seasons, it was difficult to fully recognize just how long Johnny's journey had been. About to turn 39, Johnny was one of the oldest players in NHL history.

A generation had passed while he played. His first professional game was a month after the Second World War had ended with the surrender of Japan, nearly two decades earlier. Now, in 1963, the American children of World War II were being shipped to Vietnam, while others marched for civil rights at home. From the steps of the Lincoln Memorial that summer, Reverend Martin Luther King declared, "I have a dream." And in another month, President John F. Kennedy would be shot dead in Dallas.

That Halloween, Johnny knelt in front of the house in Weston, handing out candy to a large pack of costumed kids from the neighbourhood. He wore a beige zip-up jacket, white shirt and skinny tie. It wasn't much of a costume. But the scars around his mouth, marking his cheeks and lining his receding hair, were perfect for the occasion. His face was creased by wrinkles too, with crow's feet at the eyes. He looked much closer to 50 than 40, which of course helped fuel the near-constant speculation in the press that, indeed, he was. But Johnny's kind eyes and apple cheeks helped mute the battle wounds.

"What are you supposed to be, little darling?" he asked a small girl wearing a curly yellow wig and a large white cardigan, pinned with a large brooch.

"An old lady," she said shyly.

"Oh! An old lady," Johnny replied. "Gee whiz! Isn't that cute."

He flashed his perfect store-bought teeth in a kind smile, sounding more like Fred Rogers (whose first children's show, *MisteRogers*, debuted on CBC that fall) than a grizzled hockey veteran who'd had all but four of his originals knocked out.

Still crouching with his basket of candy, he looked over his shoulder to one of the older children, clutching the handle of a plastic pumpkin with both hands.

"Oh, it's Susan! Oh, no!" Johnny said, tapping his forehead as though he'd been tricked. "And who are you supposed to be?"

"A hippy," Susan replied.

"A hippy?" Johnny said, scanning her from head to toe. "Well . . ."

"It's stupid," Susan said.

"You think it's stupid?" Johnny said. "Well, I think it's a nice outfit. I wouldn't want to see you be a hippy—but I think it's a nice outfit though. It's real sharp."

Johnny then turned his attention to a little girl hiding her face behind a white goalie mask, with the eyes and mouth cut out and the paint badly chipped from puck marks.

"Barbie!" he said to his youngest daughter, who was busy with a bag of candy. "What are you doing with my goal mask? I have to wear that tomorrow. In practice, that is."

Tiny Barb shook her head.

"Oh, you'd better take that off. You'll scare anybody going down the street. You know that."

She shook her head again, emphatically, holding the chin of the mask so it wouldn't fall off.

"Did you lose your tongue?" Johhny asked, gently lifting the mask. "I just want to see your face!"

She let him pull it back slowly before squeezing her eyes shut and quickly pulling it back down.

"Oh, look at that!" Johnny said. "A nice round face, just like daddy's."

The mask young Barbie had donned was the one he agreed to use in practices—and practices only. He simply refused to use the extra protection in games, even though it would have saved him a lot of pain and scars, not to mention several teeth. It wasn't an even bargain to Johnny if it meant he'd give up more goals. The mask impeded his vision. And besides, an in-practice deflection had clipped him at his hairline even with the mask, so how much better could it be?

"It's probably a good idea," he told Jim Proudfoot. "I know it's saved me lots of injuries in practices. But you can't teach an old dog new tricks."

Johnny had signed a new three-year contract with the Leafs in 1963, despite telling Imlach he wasn't sure if he'd last that long. Imlach told Johnny not to worry about that—just to come back every fall and see if he was good enough to play. If he wasn't, he wasn't, and there was nothing he could do about it. It could be viewed as an act of loyalty and kindness on the part of Imlach. And he certainly valued Bower. After his performance on the ice, who wouldn't? But Imlach also took advantage of his trust. Johnny was still making about $11,000 per season, which was less than several other players on the team. He was happy to earn an NHL salary and didn't realize how much he was being underpaid at the time. After all, at the start of his sixth season in Toronto, Johnny had earned much more than he would have made had he stayed in the AHL. At the time, each player negotiated his contract on his own. Any sight of a lawyer, an agent or even a friend at a meeting with Imlach and the player was sent away until he came back, alone, with a better sense of just how fortunate he was to be playing for the Leafs at all. The NHL before the days of a players union and expansion was the domain of the owners. Players were at the mercy of the brass. And few wielded that power as forcibly as Imlach.

But even Imlach lamented that Johnny hadn't been a tougher negotiator. "He was never hard to get to sign," he wrote in his autobiography. If Johnny had been more demanding like some of the other players, Imlach said, he likely would have gotten what he asked for. It was a hollow statement. Imlach knew what his goalie was worth and underpaid him anyway.

And that, despite the fact that less than a year earlier, the Leafs brass believed that Johnny was likely through—and once again, he had proven everybody wrong. He'd delivered them another Stanley Cup banner to prove it.

"I don't care how old you are," Imlach told Johnny. "As long as you can stop the puck, you've got the job."

But Imlach also knew he'd need to continue managing Johnny's minutes more and more. He would remain the team's starter, but Simmons was kept around to pick up about a third of the Leafs' games.

Still, the coach and general manager openly marvelled at Johnny's ability to play so well into what he believed was the goalie's 40s. Johnny once produced a birth certificate for his coach to prove his age, but having heard stories that he was overseas serving in the war in 1939, Imlach didn't buy it. (It was the stories, of course, that were actually untrue, the big fish having grown too large to contain.) Imlach claimed he'd sent Johnny away with his birth certificate, and it was never seen again.

In early January 1964, Johnny had allowed only 12 goals in his last nine games, including three shutouts. He had just come off a shutout win over Chicago and a 38-save performance in a 3–2 loss to the Rangers. At the time, Johnny was considered a favourite to win the Vezina Trophy. Toronto was tied for second with Montreal and trailing the Chicago Black Hawks by three points. The Leafs had just picked up key victories over both teams in a five-day span. But during the Leafs' 6–1 win over Montreal, Canadiens rookie John Ferguson skated hard towards the crease from the wing. Ferguson had collided with Bower earlier in the season, nearly knocking him out, and Johnny had given the rookie a stern warning not to do it again. Johnny dove forward in a poke check, taking out Ferguson's feet. Ferguson fell headfirst into the boards as the horn blew on the period. Johnny skated over to Ferguson as he lay on the ice to see if he was okay. He gave the young player a pat with his stick when he slowly got up, unhurt. As the players skated off, the crowd at the Gardens gave Johnny and Ferguson a respectful clap. Afterwards, Johnny was selected as one of the game's stars. Reporters asked Imlach what he thought of his goalie's show of sportsmanship.

"I don't know what Bower said to Ferguson, but I don't like it," Imlach said with disdain. "We are here for one thing: the win. W-I-N, in capital letters."

Later, Imlach singled out Johnny for the act of kindness in front of his teammates in the dressing room. He told Johnny that his job was to stay between the goalposts. "I don't want any prima donnas on this hockey club," he shouted. "This isn't kindergarten. We're playing here to win. You do that again and you'll be riding the buses."

When Imlach got on his goalie about the matter again the next day during practice, Johnny had had enough. He shouted at Imlach, saying he'd play the game his own way and left the ice. Imlach might have been kidding around, but he was an abrasive personality, not known for his gentle spirit or sympathetic tone. Winning really was an all-caps situation for him. And empathy for an opponent had no place in his philosophy.

Johnny stormed into the dressing room and sat, drenched in sweat, glowering as he pulled off his gear. At first, he just ignored *Globe and Mail* reporter Gord Walker, who'd witnessed his abrupt departure and wanted to speak to him. As Johnny tossed his gear, piece by piece, into the middle of the locker room floor, Walker noted that it had been a short practice.

"Talk to him," Johnny shouted at the reporter. "If you a want a [uncharacteristic expletive] story, get it from him."

Imlach walked in a few moments later and cleared the room. He and Johnny shared some heated perspectives.

Later that afternoon, the Leafs released a statement from their team doctor that said, "Johnny Bower has swelling and bruising of his left hand, particularly his left index finger. I have seen this condition three times over the past three weeks and it has not improved . . . I think it will become more chronic if he does not have a period of rest for his hand." Imlach followed that up with a statement that Johnny would be excused from practice for the next week.

It was a bogus story, although Johnny did often have his hands wrapped before playing to settle the arthritis that occasionally kicked in. No one in the press box bought it, especially considering Johnny's remarkable play leading up to the incident. Imlach, who usually had a cozy relationship with local reporters, was angry that reports of his argument with Johnny had been printed. He posted a sign in front of the team's locker room ahead of Toronto's game a few nights later against Boston.

"Until further notice," the sign read, "the Maple Leafs dressing room is out of bounds to members of the press, radio and T.V."

Milt Schmidt, the Bruins' coach, had some fun at Imlach's expense. He scrawled out a sign of his own and posted it on Boston's dressing room door: "Everybody welcome," he wrote.

It wasn't the first time Johnny and Imlach had clashed. According to Bower, he nearly quit the Leafs back in 1961, before he won the Vezina. It was one of the stories that would go down in Leafs lore—told by several parties, always placed in differing times, with differing accounts of what happened. Imlach claimed it directly followed the Ferguson incident. Either way, both men agreed that Johnny nearly left the Leafs over an astonishingly silly disagreement. In Johnny's telling, it happened after a lopsided loss on the road when Punch was in a typically foul mood. He demanded that his players be on the ice for 10 a.m. the next morning. There had been a wrestling match at the Gardens the previous night, and the floor around the players bench was littered with cigarette butts. As the team sat on the bench waiting for practice, Eddie Shack spotted an unused cigarette on the floor, Johnny claimed, and asked him to slip it into his glove for later. A cooperative chap, Johnny did just that. But as he picked it up, Imlach walked out—and Shack, that scoundrel, ratted him out as a gag: "Punch, Bower's smoking a cigarette!"

"You smoking?" Punch asked (according to Bower).

"Yeah, I'm smoking, all right," Bower said sarcastically.

"Get in that room, Bower!" Imlach scowled, or so Bower recounted. "You want to run the hockey team? I'm the coach and the manager."

The recollection comes off as a bit contrived, especially because Johnny was a regular smoker in the Leafs' bathroom. In Imlach's version (set three years later), Shack again played the rat—telling the coach that Johnny was smoking on the bench. When Imlach checked, he claimed, Johnny hid the lit cigarette in his hand. Imlach told Johnny to get on the ice but he refused, still gripping the cigarette, which was now burning his palm. Johnny said something that seemed angry to Imlach, and Imlach sent him to the locker room.

It's there that this rather ridiculous little tale finds agreement. Both men had it out, and Johnny said he was through. He stormed out of the dressing room with every intention of quitting the Leafs. According to Johnny, it was George Armstrong who talked him in off the ledge. The next morning Johnny was back at the Gardens.

"Well, I'm glad you made practice," Imlach said with a wry smile.

While that hot-tempered show cooled quickly, Johnny's clash with Imlach over helping Ferguson simmered much longer.

Johnny's banishment was a short-sighted move. The netminder was one of the most beloved members of the team. He was the focal point of team morale and good spirit. And his competitiveness was unmatched in practice. He demanded the best out of his teammates.

"John symbolizes the type of guy who can't quite make the grade in the NHL, then did make it after it seemed to be too late," Dick Duff said at the time. "And he's always been so grateful in everything he does that everybody's got a soft spot in their heart for him."

Toronto managed to beat Boston in the first game of Johnny's absence but then went into a tailspin as the goalie nursed his imaginary hand injury. The Leafs lost the next three games, including an 11–0 blowout at the hands of the last-place Bruins. The fans at

Maple Leaf Gardens jeered at Imlach throughout the brutal loss and cheered for Boston when the Bruins scored their 10th goal of the game. The *Toronto Star*'s Milt Dunnell sarcastically referred to Imlach as the Leafs' "Peerless Leader" in his column the next day, suggesting that he might have undermined the confidence of too many of his players, like Dick Duff, who had spent most of his time on the bench. Ron Stewart told the scribe: "Write something about me—so my mother will still know I'm with the team."

Poor Don Simmons had allowed 22 goals in those three straight losses. The Leafs called up Al Millar from the Denver Invaders in the Western Hockey League to replace him, but his plane was grounded by a malfunction. So, with Johnny still banished to the press box, Simmons had to face the Black Hawks in Chicago a night after the embarrassing blowout, giving credence to the claim that Bower was actually injured. But the backup played remarkably, shutting out the home team in a 2–0 win.

Toronto lost one more match before Johnny returned to the ice two weeks after his confrontation with Imlach, in a 1–1 tie with the New York Rangers. But the Leafs' dive continued. On February 12, with the team having won just two of their last 13 games, Imlach handed each of his players a copy of the bestselling self-help book *The Power of Positive Thinking* by Dr. Norman Vincent Peale as they departed for a game in Montreal. The coach was a fan of the book and had distributed it several times before. He hoped some inspirational reading might help get his team back on track. In Johnny's copy, Imlach wrote: "Best of luck Johnny, I know you can do it." It was, perhaps, as close to an apology a player would get from the "Peerless Leader." Any animosity between Johnny and his coach appeared to have been resolved.

Toronto lost against in Montreal that night. But the gift proved significant in the long run. Johnny loved the book. He read it several times. He believed it gave him a better outlook on his own abilities, and it helped him feel more at ease. Despite his midseason setback and blowup with Imlach, Johnny played exceptionally through the rest of the 1963–64 season, posting a league-best 2.11 goals-against average in 51 games played. (But the Vezina went to Montreal's Charlie Hodge, because the Habs had a lower team goals-against average.)

On February 22, after rumours had swirled through most of the season, Imlach had pulled off an enormous trade that brought star forward Andy Bathgate to the Leafs from the New York Rangers, along with Don McKenney, for Dick Duff, Bob Nevin, and prospects Arnie Brown, Bill Collins and Rod Seiling. It was a blockbuster. The Leafs had struggled all season to find the back of the net. Bathgate was exactly what they needed. He had averaged 28 goals a year in nine seasons in the league. Toronto was only three games above 500 when the deal was made. They lost only four games afterwards. Bathgate had 18 points in the final 15 games of the regular season. And even with their dreadful slump, the Leafs managed to finish third in the standings, with 78 points.

Once again, Toronto faced the Montreal Canadiens in the semifinals. The Habs, led by Jean Beliveau, had finished first overall in the regular season. The rivals split the first four games of the series before Montreal put Toronto on the brink of elimination with a 4–2 victory in Game 5. Johnny was singled out for poor play throughout the series. From their perches in the press box, some critics mused—once again—over whether Bower's reflexes were gone, or if weak vision caused him to misplay long shots.

Johnny needed to come up huge if he was going to quash doubts about his play and keep the series going. But the night before Game 6 in Toronto, he came down with the stomach flu, which kept him up most of the night. Johnny still felt the bug when he arrived at the Gardens the next day, but he didn't raise any alarms. Nothing was going to keep him out—and nothing was going to get in. Johnny stopped 25 shots in front of the home crowd in a 3–0 win, forcing a final game back at the Montreal Forum.

In the storied history of the two franchises, Game 7 in 1964 would go down as yet another epic. The Leafs pulled ahead in the first period off two goals by Keon and kept that lead until midway through the frantic third period, when Montreal finally broke Johnny's shutout. The Habs attacked desperately, relentlessly, firing 18 shots at Bower over the final frame. He robbed Ralph Backstrom on three chances and kicked aside a sure goal by Bob Rousseau off a rebound with his toe. Toronto was leading by one with 11 seconds remaining when Keon fired the puck in the empty Canadiens goal, completing the hat trick and securing the Leafs another trip to the Stanley Cup Final. Johnny made 38 saves in the 3–1 victory. As the horn sounded, Johnny tore out of his net and wrapped his arm around defenceman Bobby Baun as the rest of the exhausted Leafs rushed to join in the jubilation.

Afterwards, Imlach sang his goalie's praises. "Don't let me

hear anybody say he's too old," he said of Johnny. "He's the best in hockey, absolutely and positively."

George Armstrong shared similar sentiments about his long-time roommate—in his own way, of course. "Five letters fit that old geezer," he said. "G-R-E-A-T."

On the other side, the fourth-place Red Wings had once again defeated the Chicago Black Hawks, setting up a rematch for the Stanley Cup. Once again, Johnny would face his old fishing buddy, Howe—who hadn't scored a goal on him at all through a regular season in which Howe finally became the NHL's all-time leading scorer.

The Leafs and Red Wings, the third- and fourth-place teams in the regular season, battled through a memorable final. The teams split the first four games at Maple Leaf Gardens and the Detroit Olympia—the first three of which were decided by a single goal. But the Red Wings squeaked through with a 2–1 win in Game 5 to take the series back to Detroit with a chance to win it.

The Leafs were on the ropes for the second time in the playoffs. They'd need to find the will to keep going. This time the hero would be Bobby Baun. With Game 6 tied 3–3 late in the third period at the Olympia, Baun blocked a hard shot from Howe with his right leg, just above the ankle. Baun grimaced but kept playing. He even stayed on the ice through the next whistle before collapsing to his knees in pain. He tried to get up, but he stumbled as the puck was cleared over the glass. Baun lay writhing in front of Johnny, a hairline fracture in his right fibula. He was carried off the ice on a stretcher. But five minutes later, Baun was back on the ice. When the game went into overtime, the trainer had given him a painkiller and laced up his skate as tight as possible. Early in the extra frame, Baun blocked a Red Wings clearing attempt at the blue line and flipped a shot at Terry Sawchuk, who would have easily corralled it had the puck not hit Bill Gadsby's stick and changed direction at the last second. The puck went over Sawchuk and into the net.

Baun's heroics appeared to be enough to do the Red Wings in. Toronto took a 1–0 lead into the third period back at the Gardens in Game 7—and then scored three more on Sawchuk in the third period, to win 4–0. The puck was in the Leafs' end as the horn sounded and the Gardens rose in a raucous frenzy.

Johnny tossed his stick high in the air as his teammates charged towards him. The Toronto Maple Leafs had won the Stanley Cup for the third straight season. Once a distant dream, Bower's name was about to be etched on the Stanley Cup for a third time. And once again, his play had everything to do with it. It was a moment of elation, followed by a brief jab of pain. Just before Johnny's teammates reached him, the stick he'd tossed aloft came crashing back down on his head. It opened a giant gash. Johnny joined the handshake line while clasping his bloodied head, trying to hold the wound together. When they met in the line Howe embraced Bower, congratulating his friend for beating him, yet again. He asked if they could swap sticks. Howe's son Mark often worked in the opposing team's dressing rooms, taping sticks for the stars who came through Detroit. He'd amassed quite a collection of autographed sticks from friends of his famous dad. But Johnny Bower's was the one he really wanted. Johnny agreed to hand the lumber over in exchange for Howe's—which he said he intended to snap, for all the trouble the Northland's flat blade had given him.

As he left the ice, Bower was euphoric, despite the pain and embarrassment of his wounded skull. Just a few years earlier, he'd balked at his chance to join the Leafs. He'd have happily retired as a career minor-leaguer, unknown to history aside from the occasional tale about the best who never was. But here he was, beneath the vaulted ceiling of Maple Leaf Gardens, having won the Stanley Cup for the third straight time. And he'd marked the occasion with a fresh wound, which took seven stitches to close. It was one of his favourite scars.

While the Leafs' celebration roared on in the dressing room, John Jr. and a friend he'd brought along to the game slipped away with a few champagne glasses. They found some broken sticks and walked down a passageway into the rink. It was dark and empty. The overhead lights were down and the fans' celebration had pushed out onto Carlton. John Jr. and his friend slid carefully out of the players bench and onto the ice, lit by just a few remaining lamps. John Jr. turned the empty champagne glasses into goalposts and flipped a quarter to the ice, where it became a puck. And in the shadows, they replayed the Stanley Cup victory, calling out players and plays—every goal, every save, every moment forever fixed in their young minds. Eventually, John Jr. glanced up from the imaginary game. Johnny stood by the boards alone, watching silently. The son would never forget his father's smile when their eyes met that night.

14

THE ODD COUPLE

In the summer of 1964, the Bowers finally decided to make their stay in Toronto permanent. With the children getting older, it was becoming too difficult to pull them out of school each April and switch them between provinces to finish off the year. Nancy's sisters were still living nearby, and her mother, Esther, had come to live with them after Frank had passed away a few years earlier, in 1960. Aside from memories, there was little to hang on to in Saskatoon. Johnny kept in touch with several of his sisters but couldn't find much reason to return to the old world of John Kiszkan in Prince Albert. He rarely spoke *about* his mother, Elizabeth, let alone spoke *to* her. He'd occasionally visit with his father, James—who'd remarried and moved to a house on the same street, a couple of doors down from the one Johnny grew up in.

The Bowers decided that, after a Vezina Trophy and three Stanley Cups, they felt close enough to Toronto to make it their home—regardless of what the future might bring. Johnny had sold off his interest in the hotel in Waskesiu.

The Bowers also sold the home they owned in Saskatoon and the cottage they kept at Waskesiu Lake. It was a difficult decision, filled with heartache. Waskesiu had been the site of so many happy memories since they'd first met on the golf course and Johnny had awkwardly asked Nancy to a movie, nearly two decades back. But life was moving forward—with three growing kids and rising fame—and they knew it was time to let Waskesiu go.

But Johnny wasn't about to take his summers off. It was simply a reality of the time that most players had to find employment through the summer to support their families. George Armstrong, for example, returned to North Bay each summer to work in the city's timber yards and mines. Johnny agreed to seasonal work in sales and marketing as a celebrity employed by Borden Chemicals, selling glue.

The Bowers bought a new bungalow, at 84 Summitcrest Drive, in the Royal York Gardens region of Etobicoke, just a few minutes west of Weston. Their new home had much more space than the one they'd rented on Patika. It was a three-bedroom, with a rec room in the finished basement—which would become a museum of the hockey artifacts Johnny collected throughout his career. It was where the kids would entertain friends through the years, watching television via rabbit-ear antennas. (Much to the kids' frustration, the Bowers would be one of the last families on the block to upgrade to cable.) The house had a decent-sized back-yard, perfect for the July 1 barbecues to which they'd invite their neighbours, new and old, every year. And there was enough room beside the house for Johnny and Nancy to build a small ice pad each winter, on which Cindy could pursue her growing interest in figure skating.

One important person they didn't leave behind on Patika was their babysitter, Margot Duncan, who had become like another member of the Bower family. She'd watched the girls during home games because they were too young to go, while Nancy and John Jr. made their trips to Maple Leaf Gardens with Johnny. After Margot failed to pass her driver's permit test in her father's man-ual-shift muscle car, Johnny agreed to let her use their automatic sedan. He even took her out for a few lessons in the car, helping her master parallel parking. It likely didn't matter much. When Margot showed up to her test with Johnny Bower in tow, she'd pretty much passed already. Margot was there in the convertible with the family as they rode through the adoring throngs in the team's Stanley Cup parade up Bay Street in 1963—when the Leafs met with Toronto's new mayor Donald Summerville, who gave them tie bars to match the cufflinks they'd earned a year ear-lier. And Margot had made the same trip again in the spring of 1964 as the Leafs met with Mayor Phil Givens, who took office after Summerville died of a heart attack he suffered while playing hockey at George Bell Arena.

A young British band known as the Beatles wrote the sound-track of the era, with songs like "Please Please Me," "Love Me Do" and "She Loves You" filling the airwaves around the world. When the Beatles came to Maple Leaf Gardens in September 1964, Margot begged Johnny to see if he'd be able to secure impossible-to-get tickets to the sold-out show. Johnny had no connections in the entertainment industry. But during an interview with CHUM radio after winning the Stanley Cup, he asked the host if winning three in a row was enough for him to get his 15-year-old babysitter a couple of Beatles tickets. CHUM came through for the beloved Leaf, such was Johnny's power at the time. Margot Duncan found herself 11 rows from John, George, Ringo and Paul for the biggest concert in Canadian history. In fact, Johnny's popularity had grown so rapidly that the following year he'd even outdo the Beatles at their own chart-topping game.

But first, he'd have to deal with an unanticipated challenge: sharing the Leafs net with one of the best goalies to ever play the game.

After the 1963–64 season, Johnny was awarded the Bickell Award as the Leafs' most valuable player for the second time. Even on a team with star players like Mahovlich and Keon, there was no argument that Johnny's play had been essential to earning Toronto three straight Stanley Cups.

On the verge of 40, Johnny was still superhuman. He had just played 51 of Toronto's 70 games, posting a career-low 2.11 goals-against average and a .932 save percentage. But despite his competitive edge, he knew he wasn't going to be able to compete at the same pace for much longer.

So, heading into the intraleague waiver draft during the off-season, Imlach planned to pick up a quality goaltender to help

Bower carry the load through the regular season. He had no idea that one of the greatest goalies of an era would suddenly be available. But in the third round of the draft, the Red Wings left their three-time Vezina winner unprotected after claiming a younger netminder, George Gardner, from Boston. Able to protect only two goalies at a time, Detroit went with Roger Crozier—a talented 22-year-old prospect. Toronto had the pick right after Sawchuk was left unprotected, and Imlach quickly shouted, "Sawchuk!" It was a gift for Toronto. Executives around the league were bewildered that Sid Abel, the Red Wings' GM, had let Sawchuk go for just $20,000. Soon to turn 35, Sawchuk was still playing great hockey and had been essential to the Red Wings' back-to-back appearances in the NHL playoffs. He was, inarguably, one of the greatest goaltenders ever to play the game. The question was how much he had left to give.

The practice of using two goaltenders through a season was growing more common. Despite their combined age—which would be 75 through the season—there wasn't a more effective duo than Bower and Sawchuk.

Both men shared similar backgrounds. They were the sons of Ukrainian immigrants, who grew up in poor households—Sawchuk in Winnipeg, Bower in Prince Albert. They were both known for their legendary toughness and athletic ability. And both found unlikely opportunity for a different life through hockey. But otherwise, the two men couldn't have been more different.

After Bower and Sawchuk crossed paths in the AHL, Sawchuk went on to immediate success in the NHL—winning the Calder Trophy as rookie of the year, being named to the All-Star Team nine times, and winning three Stanley Cups—while Bower became a fixture in the minors. Sawchuk was a tormented man, noted for his difficult moods. He was often surly with fans and mostly kept to himself off the ice. He struggled with alcohol, suffered from poor health and battled depression. Johnny, meanwhile, had never met a fan he didn't stop to chat with. And, of course, his work ethic was legendary. He was genuinely upset when he allowed a goal in practice. Sawchuk, on the other hand, rarely tried to stop the puck if it wasn't in a game. He'd stand in net and wave at passing shots.

The complete opposites were a perfect tandem. Both goalies said they were happy with the move. Sawchuk felt he was going to a superior team. Johnny told Imlach that with Sawchuk, the Leafs were going to win another Stanley Cup.

When training camp opened up in Peterborough that fall, there were actually three future Hall of Fame goalies on the ice. Gerry Cheevers, then 23, was still trying to crack the NHL. He seemed like the ideal goalie for Toronto's future. But in Imlach's world, veterans always had more value than unproven kids. Cheevers would spend another season in the minors, with the Rochester Americans, before finding a different path to NHL greatness.

During training camp, Imlach said he planned to open the season with Bower as the starter, but he would flip to Sawchuk when needed. Bower had earned that, Imlach said. He also kept his number 1 sweater. Sawchuk, who had also worn 1 throughout his career, would start the season wearing 25, then switch to 24 and 30. When reporters asked him about having to change his sweater number, Sawchuk snapped back: "You don't stop pucks with numbers!"

As the season started, the goalies were given the chance to play while they were hot—and then were swapped out when they weren't playing as well. Johnny found the transition difficult because he thrived on playing time. While Sawchuk was able to go several games without playing—or to step into a game after sitting on the bench for two periods—Johnny was uneasy with the rest. At one point in the season, after Sawchuk had played a handful of games in a row, Johnny later told the story that he had jokingly offered to buy Eddie Shack a steak if he used his powerful shot in practice to put Sawchuk on the sidelines (noting that he didn't want him seriously injured, of course). Shack, being Shack, agreed. During a shooting drill he fired a shot at Sawchuk, who wasn't doing much of anything in the net. The goalie waved at the puck, which clipped his hand. Sawchuk threw his glove off. His finger was fractured, and he missed much of January 1965 with the injury.

It was a difficult year for the Leafs. Frank Mahovlich had a rough season, missing a stretch of games because of fatigue and depression, with Imlach all over him—as he constantly was. The Big M still managed to lead the Leafs with 23 goals and 51 points, despite playing only 59 games. One bright spot on the team was the play of 20-year-old rookie Ron Ellis, who tied Mahovlich for the team lead with 23 goals. Toronto would finish the season in fourth place, with 74 points. The Montreal Canadiens knocked the Leafs out in the first round of the playoffs, ending Toronto's streak of Stanley Cup victories.

But the story of the season was Bower and Sawchuk. The two Leafs goalies were nearly an even split for games played over the regular season. Despite their mediocre position in the standings, Bower and Sawchuk led the race for the Vezina late in the season. Imlach said he planned to play them in 35 games each, so they would both win the Vezina, which still honoured the goalie with the most games played on the team that allowed the fewest goals. (The antiquated rule was changed to its current iteration, given to the best goalie as voted on by GMs, in 1981.)

The Vezina decision went down to the final game of the season against Detroit. Roger Crozier had allowed just 171 for the Red Wings, playing every game of the season. The Leafs had 173 goals against—so they needed to win by three goals for the old-time duo to beat out the young stud, Crozier.

Imlach stuck with his rule of playing the hottest goaltender—and at the time, he felt it was Johnny. The Leafs coach wasn't able to maintain the perfect balance he had hoped, so Sawchuk would finish the season with two more games played. That weekend, Sawchuk declared that he'd refuse to accept the Vezina unless Bower's name was inscribed alongside his. As the Leafs and Red Wings took to the ice at the Olympia, Sawchuk was too nervous to watch the game from the sidelines. He spent the first and second periods in the dressing room, as the Leafs took a 2–0 lead. Johnny played exceptionally, turning aside everything the Red Wings fired at him while the Leafs spent a good part of the first and second period short-handed.

Sawchuk found the nerve to put on his team uniform and catch the third period from the end of the Toronto bench. Pete Stemkowski scored to make it 3–0 Toronto, which was enough to secure the trophy. Johnny continued to turn aside every chance Detroit had. In the final minute, the Red Wings even pulled Crozier in a wild attempt to get the extra goal. Dave Keon scored on the empty net with three seconds left. When the horn sounded Johnny threw his stick in the air as his team mobbed him. He and Sawchuk embraced in the midst of the celebration. Johnny made 37 saves in the 4–0 shutout to secure the Vezina.

Afterwards, Sawchuk reiterated that he wouldn't accept the trophy unless Bower's name was on it too. Johnny's 2.38 individual average was the lowest in the league for the second season in a row. Sawchuk's was 2.56. But Johnny graciously said Sawchuk deserved to have his name on the trophy alone.

"It was a team win," Johnny said after the game against Detroit. "But the Vezina belongs to Terry. He played 36 games and won more games than I did.

Sawchuk said that was "nuts."

And pretty much everyone agreed. But the situation had only ever occurred once before in league history, in the 1950–51 season when the Leafs' Al Rollins played 39 games and Turk Broda played 31—and Rollins had his name inscribed on the storied trophy. So the matter seldom came up. Bob Pulford, who was the Leafs' player representative, said he'd petition the board of governors to award the trophy to both keepers.

"The league is now forcing all teams to carry two goalkeepers, so it is only reasonable that the Vezina should be a joint award," said Pulford. "It is ridiculous that a man playing 36 games should get everything and the guy playing 34 games gets nothing."

Bower and Sawchuk would have to wait until the playoffs were over to learn the league's decision. But the pair had already decided that they'd split the $1,000 prize money, regardless. After Toronto was knocked out by the Canadiens, the netminders decided to throw a party for their teammates at the Conroy Hotel in Toronto in late April. It cost them all the prize money—about $8,000 today. "But it was worth it," Johnny said.

That June, the National Hockey League board of governors ruled that from thenceforth the Vezina Trophy would be awarded to both goaltenders if the winning team had two regular netminders, having played in 25 or more games. The change was retroactive to the previous season. Bower and Sawchuk had won the Vezina together—the first teammates to split the award. The odd couple remain etched side by side on the storied tribute to the game's great keepers.

WHAT'S GOOD FOR
THE GOOSE...

With Waskesiu behind them, Johnny and Nancy set out to find a new place to build decades of happy memories with their kids. They searched through Ontario's cottage country, hoping to find the perfect location. They came across an open plot of land on Little Bald Lake in Bobcaygeon, a small community in the Kawartha Lakes region in south central Ontario, a couple of hours north of Toronto. The waterway was fed by the Trent River and was filled with wild rice. It was perfect for fishing, Johnny thought. The sun set over the lake just to the right of the land. It was stunning, thought Nancy. They purchased the land and drew up designs for a cottage shaped like a goalie stick—a quaint bungalow that formed an L. It was a modest family cottage. Johnny later saved some extra cash by building the small boathouse himself, with the help of his kids.

Bobcaygeon replaced Waskesiu as the place where the family spent most of its time together. As soon as school let out in June, the station wagon was packed up and the Bowers were gone for the summer. They skipped out on vacations in favour of spending more days by the lake. After Johnny had barbecued up some of his famous burgers for dinner, the family always went for a long walk through the cottage streets, stopping to chat with neighbours. Afterwards, when the lake was still before dusk, Johnny would take the kids down to the dock and they'd throw in their miniature lines to see if the fish were biting. And later when the sun slowly set, John and Nancy would sit in their favourite chairs on the best spot on the hill to watch it melt into the horizon.

For several weeks during the summer, Johnny made some extra money by working with a hockey school in Haliburton. He'd wake up very early in the morning to make the hour-long drive to the arena and be gone while the kids spent the day swimming and biking with their cottage friends. Every day he'd return by late afternoon, in time to fire up the grill, take a family stroll, spend some time on the dock and watch the sun set with Nancy. When training camp opened in Peterborough, Johnny would spend the week with the Leafs and then make the trip back to Bobcaygeon to stretch out a couple more weekends with Nancy and the kids.

And that fall in Peterborough, Johnny needed the weekend serenity of cottage life with his family.

Changes were coming. It was inevitable. Allowing the fewest

goals against in the entire league was great, but it meant little if you didn't score. In that department, Toronto wasn't terrible—but with 204 goals scored, they were in the middle of the pack in 1964–65—and that wasn't good enough to win a Stanley Cup.

The Leafs were able to protect only two goalies in the intraleague draft that spring, and Imlach decided to protect Bower and Sawchuk, leaving Gerry Cheevers and Don Simmons exposed. The Rangers picked up old-reliable Simmons, while the Boston Bruins quickly swept in to claim Cheevers.

Over the summer, Imlach traded for 35-year-old defence-man and future Hall of Famer Marcel Pronovost—sending Andy Bathgate and Billy Harris to the Red Wings. Several other minor-leaguers were swapped in the eight-player deal. After 16 NHL seasons, Pronovost was still one of the best defencemen in the league, so the move had Johnny's stamp of approval.

It also helped fill an unexpected hole.

Carl Brewer, one of the Leafs' key defencemen, was at odds about his future with the team heading into training camp that fall. Imlach's abrasive coaching style didn't sit well with Brewer, just as it created conflicts with other players like Mahovlich and Mike Walton. Brewer's defensive partner and roommate, Bobby Baun, was in the midst of his own conflict with Imlach and was holding out for a fair contract. Brewer had advised Baun to take a stand and walk out. The unrest was spreading. Rumours spread that other players would hold out for better contracts too. Bob Pulford was one of them. Eddie Shack also refused to sign, after being told he'd be demoted to Rochester that season. Around the league, players started to discuss their salaries—trying to gauge just how much the league had screwed them.

All of this added to the growing tensions. Brewer wasn't looking for more money—he just wasn't happy. He struggled with stress and anxiety, and he'd entered training camp that fall uncertain if he wanted to play hockey at all. He thought he might have a more fulfilling life as a schoolteacher.

Brewer seemed distracted during an exhibition match against the Bruins at the Peterborough Memorial Arena. In the first period, he carelessly cleared a puck from the corner to the front of the Leafs goal. A Bruins forward fired the unexpected scoring opportunity at Johnny. The puck nearly smacked him in the face but missed and went back into the corner. Brewer picked it up again—and again, he passed it to the front of his own goal, where another Bruin took a free shot. What happened next is the stuff of Toronto Maple Leafs legend, but here's a common version of the story:

Imlach shouted at Brewer after the play, and the defenceman snapped back at his coach as he left the ice. Johnny was also furious with Brewer and tore into him during the intermission.

"I need all the help I can get," Johnny shouted. "And I don't need you throwing the puck out in front of me."

"Don't take your old-man frustrations out on me," Brewer shot back.

Johnny's age was fair game in the dressing room. Players constantly jabbed him about it and he didn't mind. But this time his temper boiled over. He jumped up from the bench in the dressing room. "I may be old," he yelled. "But I'll be in this league a lot longer than you will."

Now Brewer and Johnny were both on their feet, hurling insults back and forth. Brewer was furious, his rage clearly reaching well beyond the disagreement with Johnny. At some point, he grabbed an orange from a nearby table and threw it at Johnny, missing him by a fraction.

Imlach walked in the room a few moments later and gave his players hell because they were playing terribly.

"If any of you don't want to play," he shouted, "stay in the room."

All the players got up to leave for the second period except for Brewer, who was still steaming. He and the coach shared some harsh words when everyone left, which culminated in Imlach's telling Brewer to take his uniform off if he didn't want to play. He did just that. Imlach went back to the bench, and Brewer got undressed and left the Leafs locker room.

The issue between Johnny and Brewer quickly dissolved. Neither player held a grudge and they remained friends. The disagreement was just part of the game, Johnny later said. He'd had it out at times with players like Tim Horton too.

"Johnny is a fierce competitor," Brewer told sportswriter Red Burnett afterwards. "I never gave his criticism a second thought."

But Brewer's dissatisfaction with the Leafs didn't dissipate. Before the end of camp, he announced that he was retiring for personal reasons. His departure was huge news. About to turn 27, Brewer was a three-time all-star and was considered to be one of the most talented young defencemen in the game. He was also aggressive, having led the league twice in penalty minutes. He'd go on to play for Canada's national team for a time, then briefly in the International Hockey League, before heading overseas to play and coach in Helsinki. Brewer would eventually return to the NHL in 1969–70, after Imlach had traded his rights to the Detroit Red Wings—where he'd rejoin his former Leafs teammates and friends, Mahovlich and Baun.

With Baun still holding out for a better contract, Brewer's departure was devastating for the Leafs. The ownership was getting antsy. Stafford Smythe, who had his share of conflict with Imlach, told the *Toronto Star*'s Milt Dunnell that his priority was to sell tickets and hockey on television. With players like Brewer and Baun out, that task was much harder. "Let me say this. There is no such thing as a salary budget. Punch has the authority to sign players for what he thinks they're worth. But it is up to him to sign the players. His job depends on it."

Just three days after the season opened, Baun signed a new one-year deal that gave him an $8,000 raise, pushing his salary over $20,000—nearly double what Bower made. Baun was one of the leaders among the players fighting to get their fair share out of the game, and he would later become the first president of the NHL Players' Association. He always knew his friend was making much less than he was worth and encouraged him to take a stand, but Johnny rarely looked to cause a problem when it came to asking for his salary.

After the tumultuous training camp, the Leafs pushed ahead without Brewer. Pronovost was slotted with Baun on defence; Tim

Horton and Allan Stanley were the other pair, with Kent Douglas serving as a fifth.

During the season opener, Imlach appeared on *Hockey Night in Canada* with an optimistic declaration, despite the troubles of training camp. "We only loaned the Cup to the Canadiens for a year," he told broadcaster Ward Cornell.

But it was a silent night in Toronto. On the ice, Bobby Hull scored a hat trick on Bower as the Leafs lost 4–0 to the Chicago Black Hawks. Bing Crosby, the famous entertainer, was at Maple Leaf Gardens watching the game. He was rumoured to be interested in investing in a new franchise in San Francisco, with the NHL opening up to expansion in a couple of seasons. But the "White Christmas" crooner wouldn't be the only holiday star to grace the Gardens that year.

Toronto won only three of its first 10 games to start the 1964–65 season, but Chip Young, a producer from CBC, provided some reason for cheer when he brought his idea for a children's Christmas song to the Leafs, hoping to have one of the players sing the track on an upcoming album. Known for playing Santa Claus at the Leafs' Christmas parties, Johnny was unanimously volunteered by his snickering peers. After Young explained that all the proceeds from the recording would raise money for charity, Johnny, ever the cheerful sport, agreed. He wasn't exactly a rookie. Johnny had briefly sung in his school choir as a boy in Prince Albert. And he was known to hold a tune while singing in the shower or along with the radio in the car. He was a fan of country music but also enjoyed singing along to Nat King Cole songs. He brought a rough recording of Young's song home with him from the rink and played it for Nancy and John Jr.

It was called "Honky the Christmas Goose." It told the story of a goose named Honky who *got so fat that he was no use—til he learned how to blow his nose, honk! The way a goose nose blows.* It was nonsensical but catchy. And Johnny was a fan of hokey humour. He was a regular corny-joke comedian at home.

"You know, this is cute," Nancy said, then jabbed: "If only you knew how to sing."

"I know," Johnny said. "That's a big problem."

The song was meant to be recorded with a group of young backup singers. Young thought it would be a great idea to have John Jr. sing along with his dad on the track. The Bowers played the song on a tape recorder at home for a week, while Johnny and John Jr. practised. Johnny would sing along as Nancy coached.

"No, you're off key!" she'd say to Johnny—and they'd start right back into it again. Johnny tried to help his voice by drinking tea and honey, concerned it would become hoarse ahead of his musical debut.

On a chilly Tuesday in early November, Johnny and John Jr. drove to the CBC studios, not far from the Gardens. Young introduced them to a small group of young teenagers who would be backup singers on the album. When they got into the studio to start recording just after 5 p.m., Johnny started to sing his part and all of the lights went out. In fact, power had failed across the entire eastern seaboard. A hydroelectric power station near Niagara Falls had malfunctioned, causing a massive chain reaction across the power grid, wiping out electricity across the northeastern United States, including New York City. More than 30 million people across nearly 81,000 square miles were left without power, for up to 13 hours in some areas.

"I open my mouth and the power fails all the way to Miami," Johnny later exaggerated.

Johnny, John Jr. and the crew of ragtag adolescent singers stuck it out as the power flickered for intermittent periods before cutting out again. It took nearly five hours for Johnny Bower, Little John and the Rinky Dinks—as they would soon be known—to record "Honky the Christmas Goose" and a B-side track, "Banjo the Mule."

In fact, Johnny had decent singing chops. His gentle, steady voice was perfect for the children's song. He hit each note perfectly (after all those takes). Johnny carried the first verse, while singing along with the Rinky Dinks through the chorus—and then little John took over the second verse, with a soft soprano solo. It was a delightful, catchy performance.

A month later, Johnny sat at a table at the Eaton's department store, a block away from Maple Leaf Gardens, as fans lined up to buy a copy of the holiday season's biggest hit. (He grabbed a stack of the Beatles' latest album from a nearby table and hid them under his chair, to help boost the "Honky" sales.) The record was an enormous success. Johnny's popularity at the time certainly had a lot to do with it. The record sold 21,000 copies in the first week it was released and almost 40,000 records through the holiday season, which made it the biggest-selling Canadian record ever at the time. It hit number 29 on the CHUM charts in Toronto and was ranked ahead of Frank Sinatra's "A Very Good Year" in the *Toronto Telegram*'s Hot 100 list.

For all of the song's success, Johnny wouldn't make a penny off the track. That was part of the deal he wanted, with all the proceeds going to charity. And while Johnny politely declined Young's request to record more children's songs, he'd never be able to fully retire from his musical career. "Honky the Christmas Goose" became a near-constant request at events he would attend, and the song would become a holiday staple in the Bower home for decades to come.

JOHNNY'S BILLBOARD HIT was about the only gift the Leafs would receive that year. His teammates hummed the tune in the showers. But Toronto hovered in fourth place for most of the season before pushing into third in the second half. In February, Johnny missed several games after straining his groin. In the practice before his scheduled return, he was struck just above his right eye by a shot from Eddie Shack that deflected off a stick. Johnny's face mask was lying on top of the net behind him. The cut required 26 stiches to close—10 internally and 16 on the surface—and put Johnny out of action for another two games. Sawchuk was also out with a leg injury at the time. As both veteran goalies missed time through the season, Toronto had Bruce Gamble, Al Smith and Gary Smith tend goal at various times.

Toronto sat in the middle of the standings as the season wound down, while Montreal surged ahead of the pack, comfortably in first.

Johnny stopped 34 shots at the Montreal Forum to help Toronto to a 2–0 victory over the Habs in late March. But a week later, his performance was forgotten as the Canadiens won 3–1—securing themselves a first-place finish in the regular season. Imlach hated to lose to Montreal and especially despised handing them first place overall. He punched a door in the Leafs dressing room. Then he turned his ire on his goalie.

"You blew two," Imlach told Johnny.

"I'll bet the second one wasn't over the line," Johnny protested, referring to a goal by Gilles Tremblay that had just squeaked in.

"You're paid to stop shots, not bet on them," Imlach replied. "I'd bet, but I don't want to take your money."

But the coach's criticism didn't cut deeply. Johnny had played admirably throughout his 41st year. In 35 games, he posted a 2.26 goals-against average and a .930 save percentage, leading the NHL in both categories. It was a busy season for the old man. He not only became a music star but also tried his hand as coach.

The Leafs were stuck in third place heading into the last game of the season against the Red Wings in Detroit. The result meant nothing in the standings, so Imlach decided he'd put on a bizarre show. Two games earlier, in Boston, Imlach had alternated Bower and Sawchuk every five minutes throughout a 3–1 loss to the Bruins. This time, Imlach took his goalie shuffling a step further. Johnny started the game and played the entire first period, without allowing a goal. Then Johnny, who had been suffering from the flu, was replaced by Sawchuk for the second period. The Leafs were leading 2–1 when Bruce Gamble—who had been watching the game from the press box—came out to play the third period for Toronto. As though the three-goalie shuffle wasn't bizarre enough, Johnny returned to the bench in his street clothes to coach the third period. Imlach sat in a nearby seat in the stands and watched as a spectator. The rules indicated that a team could dress three goalies only if one was unfit to play.

"Bower's sick. Got the flu," Imlach said with a mischievous smile when the *Globe and Mail*'s Paul Rimstead approached him in the stands to find out what was going on. "Sawchuk felt a little pull in his groin and we don't want to take any chances, so I declared an emergency situation."

It was the first time three goalies had ever been used by one team in a game. It was also Johnny's coaching debut. It didn't go well. Under his guidance, the Leafs blew a two-goal lead as the Wings scored a pair 42 seconds apart to tie the game at three.

The powerhouse Montreal Canadiens swept Toronto in the playoffs en route to winning the Stanley Cup. Still battling the flu, Johnny missed the first two games, but his return for the final two did nothing to slow the slaughter. The Canadiens—with a mix of speed, finesse, scoring and muscle—were just too good for the decrepit Leafs. In the fourth game, in one of the more colourful coaching displays in NHL history, Imlach laced up a pair of skates in the locker room and walked into the hall, threatening to go on the ice to confront the refs, who he thought were blowing the game. The theatrics did little to rally the Leafs. They fell in four straight. Following the disappointing sweep, it seemed inevitable that the dynasty was over. The tensions that had mounted in training camp still festered. The team was old and broken. Critics charged that the Leafs needed to get faster and younger. Imlach doubled down on his allegiance to veterans, saying that talk of youth was nonsense—especially when old Allan Stanley and Johnny had been, in his view, the team's best players. Johnny broke the disappointing loss to Montreal down to the simple calculus of hockey: "We didn't score enough goals and they got too many."

With his three-year contract with Toronto done, it wasn't clear what Johnny's future with the Leafs would be.

"I don't know where I'll be next season," he said after the loss to Montreal. "I'm too unhappy to think about it."

Heading into the 1966–67 season, the NHL was reaching the start of a fundamental shift in power dynamics, as players continued to catch on to the idea that they actually deserved more than the share they received. The league that had long belonged to an old patriarchy was moving towards a new order where players had something to say about their position in the game. The strictly enforced hierarchies and traditions of professional hockey were shifting rapidly. A lawyer named Alan Eagleson, who'd negotiated young Bobby Orr's first contract with the Boston Bruins, was stirring up trouble for the old guard as players started to get organized. Soon Eagleson would become the first executive director of the newly formed National Hockey League Players' Association. (And years later, he'd be exposed for bilking the players he had claimed to protect as ruthlessly as any owner ever had.)

At training camp that fall, Bob Baun's relationship with Imlach soured even further when the coach found a group of young players lined up outside Baun's door, looking for contract advice. Imlach would later get back at Baun by nailing him to the bench. It was in that tumultuous climate that captain George Armstrong approached his roommate and suggested he should ask for a raise.

"How much money are you getting?" he asked Johnny.

At the time, Bower was still making $11,000—just $1,000 more than he'd initially signed for nearly a decade earlier.

"Eleven thousand?" Armstrong said, astonished. He told Johnny that most of the other guys on the team were making between $15,000 and $18,000. As the best goalie in the league, Armstrong argued, Johnny should have been making close to $20,000. Johnny argued that he was in his early 40s and probably didn't deserve that much. But Armstrong urged him to ask for a raise when he went to sign his contract for the upcoming season. Reluctantly, Johnny did.

The first time he went into Imlach's office and asked for a $10,000 increase, the coach got up, opened the door and told him to get out. He added that at Johnny's age, he should be happy to be playing the game at all. But Armstrong convinced Johnny not to back down. He went back to Imlach's office and said he wouldn't sign without an increase.

"Johnny, this is your last chance," Imlach said. "Either sign or I'll send you down to the minors."

"Can I think about it?" Johnny asked.

"Well, don't think about it too long," Imlach replied.

Once again, Armstrong had to convince his friend to not give in. He assured Johnny that there was no way Imlach would send a goalie like him to the minors.

Johnny worked up the courage to return. This time he came with a plan. He told Imlach that Nancy was pregnant and that he needed the extra money to provide for his growing family. Nancy, of course, wasn't pregnant. Imlach was unmoved regardless. Then, King Clancy walked into the office and asked why they were arguing. Johnny told him he needed a raise.

"How much do you want?" Clancy asked.

"I'm asking for $10,000," Johnny said. "I have to be up there with the other veterans."

"Ten thousand," Clancy replied. "We can't give you that, we're on a budget. Frank Mahovlich isn't even making that."

Clancy was lying, of course. Mahovlich made $32,000 a year. Sawchuk made $18,500.

Clancy offered Johnny a $5,000 raise instead. Imlach, Johnny later recalled, nearly fell off his chair. "You're not getting $5,000!" he yelled. "You're not getting anything!"

But Johnny happily signed to his $5,000 bump, realizing only later that he'd likely been had by Imlach and Clancy's good cop–bad cop routine. The pay bump was long overdue. It was the first significant raise that arguably the best goaltender in the NHL had received in nearly a decade. But it still left Johnny below the team average. And it came at a time when the near-dynasty he'd backed was breaking down.

More and more, Johnny's seemingly immortal body was giving in to the grind of age. He was at the top of a long line of Leafs who seemed closer to the comforts of retirement than having another shot at a Stanley Cup. The roster had seven regular players over 35.

Most critics had written off the Leafs heading into the season. It looked like the near-dynasty days were over for Toronto. The league would double in size in just a year, with an expansion draft sure to take a chunk out of the roster. The team that won three Stanley Cups would need to break apart eventually. The near-dynasty had one last, unlikely, chance.

THE OLD FELLOWS
ATHLETIC CLUB

JOHNNY SLUMPED DOWN ON THE BENCH IN THE LEAFS LOCKER room, dripping with sweat. He took an exhausted sip from a soft drink as his teammates filed into the room, tapping his pads in congratulations as they passed him. Steam rose from his soaked gear and his scarred, weathered face. Johnny had just held the Black Hawks to a 2–2 tie in front of nearly 20,000 wild fans in the smoke-filled Chicago Stadium. The madhouse had gasped when Johnny made a remarkable save on Bobby Hull. The effort was all the more impressive because it was his first game in net after missing a month with muscle spasms in his lower back.

Johnny unstrapped his goal pads and stripped down to his drenched undergarments. Then he absentmindedly reached back in his stall for a plastic case and popped it open. It was empty. His teeth were missing. Was it another prank? Johnny looked around for a moment, confused, before locating his dentures in the last place he'd left them—his mouth. Usually Johnny popped his teeth out before going on the ice. It was against club rules to play with plates. For starters, if a puck hit a player in the mouth, he could choke on a broken piece (which, technically, could happen with real teeth too). The team also refused to cover a new set if they were broken during a game. Johnny figured he'd forgotten to take them out. "I guess I was a bit excited before the game," he told Louis Cauz, a young sportswriter with the *Globe and Mail*, as he got up and headed to the showers.

Johnny had recently turned 42, but after yet another show of his goalmouth heroics, Cauz noted, he looked at least a decade older. He had been sidelined with a dislocated finger and a groin pull during the team's exhibition games, after trying to hide the injuries in training camp because he was worried about competition for his job. That was followed early in the season by back troubles. But Johnny insisted he wasn't breaking down.

"I'll just keep playing as long as my reflexes are good," Johnny said. "The doctor recently told me I have the body of a 25-year-old man. I feel great, so what are you going to do?"

Imlach backed him up.

"As far as I'm concerned, Bower can play in the NHL forever," he claimed.

But forever was fading fast. Injuries plagued Johnny through-out the season. In fact, injuries plagued the entire team. Ahead of the season, the Leafs had looked like a pile a of broken toys. Bob Baun had a broken thumb. Brian Conacher had a sprained wrist. Allan Stanley had a bashed-up right knee. Imlach limited his practices to shooting drills because he was afraid to lose more players to injury in a scrimmage. That summer Sawchuk had spinal surgery. By early December he was sidelined with severe back pain that would keep him out of the lineup until February.

Once again, the Leafs would need to use five different goalies throughout the season, with Bruce Gamble playing nearly a third of the games for Toronto, while Al Smith and Gary Smith filled in the holes.

After missing three games with torn shoulder ligaments in December, Johnny returned in back-to-back games against the Bruins, with a 2–0 win on Christmas Eve in Toronto and a 4–2 win on Christmas Day in Boston. But a few days later Johnny stretched out his blocker to turn aside a blistering shot from Frank Mahovlich in practice. There were seven thousand young fans on hand to watch the Leafs' training session over the holidays. The crowd broke out into a loud ovation as Johnny made the save. The puck caught him under the blocker. Johnny shook his hand for a few seconds to chase away the sharp pain and went back to practice. Afterwards, as he tried to sign his name for autograph seekers, his little finger jutted out at an awkward angle and his hand was too swollen to grip the pen.

"Well, I blocked the shot anyway," he chuckled.

A couple of hours later at Toronto Western Hospital, Johnny was told that he'd broken his little finger and a knuckle. The fractures would cost him another month on the injured list.

Toronto was in third place at the midseason mark, and 11 different Maple Leafs had missed a combined total of 68 games since the start of the season. Things only got worse from there. In early January, Toronto slipped into a month-long slump that threatened to derail the entire season, losing 10 straight games. Then, in February, Imlach was admitted to the hospital, suffering from exhaustion. It looked like things couldn't get any worse. Toronto lacked goal scoring. It lacked youth and speed. The team had several erratic, difficult personalities, creating fissures in the dressing room. There was tension in practice, and several fights broke out on the ice.

But Imlach's departure seemed to be a turning point for Toronto. King Clancy stepped in to coach in Imlach's absence, and his easygoing approach seemed to lift the team's spirits. The Leafs won eight games with Clancy on the bench. In early March, Johnny was again forced to the sidelines for a couple of weeks after straining his knee while attempting his signature poke check. But he was back in time to close out the regular season, with the Leafs somehow finishing in third place, just behind the Montreal Canadiens.

There was a sense of something ending in the Leafs locker room that spring, a collective acknowledgement among the players that it was the last act of something special. They were a close team, in a way that is hard to comprehend by the standards of modern hockey. Sure, there were many bickering battles of big and eccentric personalities, but that was part of their charm. Eleven players on the roster had been brought up through the Leafs' development system, having played junior hockey with either the Toronto Marlboros or St. Mike's. Each of them had only ever played pro hockey for the Leafs. Armstrong and Horton had been Leafs regulars for 15 years. Allan Stanley had been Horton's defence partner for nearly a decade.

Four of the players had played together on the Red Wings' 1955 championship team and had been with Toronto for at least two seasons: Sawchuk, Red Kelly, Marcel Pronovost and Larry Hillman. Eddie Shack had been with the Leafs for six years, even though he hadn't come up through the Leafs' system. Everything they were was about to break apart with the upcoming expansion of the NHL. The 1967 playoffs would be their stand.

"I think deep down that everybody in that Maple Leafs dressing room knew we were part of something special," Johnny recalled decades later. "And we were enjoying a ride together that most of us would never take again as teammates."

THE LEAFS LOOKED like an easy match for the first-place Chicago Black Hawks, who finished first overall in the regular season with 94 points—19 more than the Leafs. Toronto entered the playoffs looking tragically similar to the team that had been swept a season earlier by Montreal. After the pathetic 10-game spiral that winter, every team in the league knew how beatable the geriatric Leafs were. Even Johnny and the Leafs knew they were the underdogs. They were broken and tired. They were almost done. The Leafs lacked youth, speed and healthy bodies. But they had experience. And they had desperation. This was their final shot together. And there was no way in hell they were going to quit now.

If they were going to make any sort of run, it would depend on Johnny—one of the best playoff performers in the league. But once again, an injury almost kept him out.

Wearing a brown goalie mask for protection, Johnny shuffled between his posts in practice at the Peterborough Memorial Arena, squaring up for shot after shot, before the Leafs' first match against the Black Hawks. "I only hope that nobody gets hurt," Imlach said before starting the first drill of the scrimmage-free practice. With about 12 minutes remaining, Pete Stemkowski fired a hard shot at Johnny. He lifted his little finger off the paddle of his stick as he stretched to make a blocker save. The impact slammed the finger back against the wooden shaft. Johnny felt a familiar sharp pain. He flipped off his mask and skated out of the net, holding his right hand. "Oh, my God!" he shouted. Blood dripped down the same small finger and knuckle he'd broken at the start of the season. "Damn, damn, damn!" he said as trainer Bobby Haggert led him to the dressing room. "Damn, damn, damn!"

The broken digit put Johnny on the sidelines through the first four games of the series against Chicago, so Sawchuk was in goal as the Leafs split two apiece with the Black Hawks. Imlach decided to put Johnny back between the pipes for Game 5, but he looked unsettled as the first period ended with the teams tied at two. The Leafs caught their breath, sitting around with untied skates, with cold damp towels draped over their heads. Some sucked on orange slices to regain some energy.

"You look a little shaky," Imlach asked Johnny, chomping his gum nervously. "Are you?"

Johnny hadn't felt right since the puck dropped.

"I'm a little shook," he admitted.

Imlach thought for a moment.

"You want me to make a change?" he asked.

It was entirely up to Johnny. The Leafs' starting position through the playoffs was his to take. But Johnny knew he wasn't playing as well as he could. The game was too important for a show of individual pride.

"Well," Johnny said, "there's a lot at stake."

Sawchuk started the second period. Early on, Bobby Hull took a slap shot that clipped him on the left shoulder. It was already blue from several bruises earned in practice. Sawchuk went down hard. The Leafs players circled anxiously as trainer Bobby Haggert rushed across the ice to tend to the fallen goalie. Pierre Pilote, the Black Hawks' captain, passed by with a quick taunt. "How do you feel, Terry?" he said. "You should have let it go. It might have been a goal."

Haggert asked Sawchuk if he thought he could continue.

"I stopped the shot, didn't I?" Sawchuk replied as he slowly got to his feet and picked up his gloves.

The Leafs goalie stopped several more too. He kicked out 36 more shots—including several booming slap shots—offering one of the best performances of the season, as the Leafs won 4–2. Johnny watched from the sidelines as his counterpart, Ukey, played the hero. Sawchuk held off the Black Hawks again in Game 6 as the Leafs completed the upset and earned a spot in the Stanley Cup Final. Their hated rival, the Montreal Canadiens, was already waiting for them. Once again, the Leafs went into the series as the underdog. The Habs were viewed as the superior team, even though Montreal and Toronto both posted 32 wins during the regular season. Their roster boasted veteran stars like Jean Beliveau and Henri Richard—along with future stars like 23-year-old Yvan Cournoyer and 21-year-old rookie Rogie Vachon in goal. Montreal had won the Cup in '65 and '66, and with Chicago out they looked likely to match the Leafs' streak of the early '60s by winning their third championship in a row. Montreal had been undefeated through the final 11 games of the regular season and then beat the Rangers in four straight games to reach the Stanley Cup Final.

The Canadiens crushed Toronto 6–2 in the opening game at the Forum. Sawchuk was pulled after the second period. Johnny seemed to have his old form back as he finished off the third. In practice the next day, he continued to work himself back into game shape. A *Globe and Mail* columnist observed that Johnny made every save in practice "as though it was the last period and the score was tied, in the last game for the championship of the universe."

Imlach went with his intergalactic hero in Game 2. Johnny always played well at the Forum and he continued the tradition, blanking the Habs on every opportunity. He carried a shutout into the third. Less than a minute in he dove for a loose puck and took a whack in the face from John Ferguson's stick. Blood poured from Johnny's nose. He tried to dab out the bleeding with his glove. Haggert came running across the ice to tend to him.

"You want to come to the bench?" he asked.

But once again, a Leafs goalie was having none of Haggert's efforts to take him out.

"I'm hot!" Johnny said. "Just leave me alone. Don't bother me!"

He stayed hot right to the end, stopping 31 shots to complete the shutout in a 3–0 victory—while enduring another tap to the head from Ferguson late in the game. Afterwards, Johnny sat in the Leafs dressing room next to Sawchuk, pulling off his pads. There was a noticeable gash across the bridge of his nose. Reporters inquired about the injury.

"Nothing serious," Johnny said. "It's like Punch Imlach says, a hurting nose doesn't hurt anybody. Right, Terry?"

"Not unless you get knocked out," Sawchuk said with a smile.

Later, Johnny said he'd finally agree to wear a mask during games in the upcoming season, something he'd managed to avoid through 22 years of pro hockey. Curved sticks were making the shots too unpredictable, he said. He probably should have put a rush on that decision. With his nose still swollen two days later during a Leafs practice in Toronto, Frank Mahovlich fired a puck off Johnny's chin—opening yet another gaping cut. Johnny, once again, took a trip to the hospital to get stitched up.

But Johnny's battered face didn't bother him as he took to the ice for Game 3 back in Toronto. In fact, the scarred goalie put on one of the best performances ever witnessed at Maple Leaf Gardens. Game 3 was a netminding battle between the 42-year-old veteran and Rogie Vachon, who was half Johnny's age. They exchanged one unbelievable stop after another, as both teams pressed for the winner in the tied third period. Dave Keon hit the post with one second to go, nearly winning it for Toronto.

In the first overtime period, Cournoyer cut in with open ice behind Larry Hillman—and Johnny dove out with a daring all-or-nothing poke check to knock the puck off his stick. He knew that if he missed, Cournoyer would go right by him and have an open net for the game-winner. He would have looked reckless and foolish. Instead, he kept the game alive. The fans in Maple Leaf Gardens breathlessly watched as both teams had chance after chance through the extra time. Johnny made 20 saves in overtime before Bob Pulford finally scored for Toronto halfway through the second overtime period just before midnight. It was an enormous goal, giving the exhausted Leafs a 3–1 victory to lead the series by a game. Vachon stopped 51 in the loss. Johnny played the hero, turning aside an incredible 60 for the Leafs.

In the locker room afterwards, Johnny dressed quickly. He collected John Jr., who was sitting in his stall, and hurried out the door without speaking to the press so he could be home and in bed by 1 a.m. Imlach had already declared him the starter for Game 4, and Johnny was focused on doing whatever he could to keep his hot streak going. But Johnny couldn't get to sleep when he climbed into bed. He tried to read for a while, but he couldn't get the game out of his mind. He played it over and over—obsessing over the small mistakes he'd made and what he needed to do to fix them. He didn't doze off until after 3:30 a.m. When he finally fell asleep, he had a nightmare about Henri Richard scoring on him and that the Canadiens had actually won the game.

When he woke up the next morning, the *Toronto Star*'s front-page headline confirmed reality: "Bower is the world's best," it read, quoting an excited proclamation from Imlach.

"Johnny Bower has to be the world's greatest athlete," the coach had declared after his goalie's remarkable performance in the nearly 90-minute win. "Bower is the oldest guy, playing the toughest position of all in the fastest game there is. Sure, he's amazing. Name me somebody in any sport who compares with him."

Perhaps trying to get out of his own head, Johnny was tired but relaxed when he arrived at the Leafs' skate that morning. It was a light practice and most of the players didn't dress in full gear. Johnny didn't even take off his rayon sports jacket. He skated around holding a player's stick, calling for passes in front of the net. George Armstrong circled the ice in trousers, a white dress shirt and a tie. As Dave Keon left the ice, Johnny called out, "Hey, Davey, I'll take your stick. I can't shoot with this one." Keon stopped as he opened the door to the Leafs bench and handed his stick over to the goalie.

In the dressing room, Imlach was still singing Johnny's praises.

"Bower hasn't lost any of his eyesight or quick reflexes that make him a great NHL goalie despite his 42 years," he said. "I don't believe in age. Ability is what counts to me, age doesn't mean a thing. If his eyes and reflexes are good he could [be playing] at 60 years old."

When he came off the ice, Johnny was in a philosophical mood. After the best performance of his life, he reflected on his long career.

"Probably my greatest thrill was to get another chance. After all I was 32 or 33 and most people figured I was washed up. I'd had my fling earlier, but it didn't last."

He listed all the great goalies he just couldn't best, who had kept him out of the league: Sawchuk, Turk Broda, Harry Lumley, Bill Durnan, Al Rollins, Jacques Plante and Glenn Hall. Bower also hinted at his future. He talked of pushing off retirement—*and who could blame him after making 60 saves?*—saying he would definitely keep playing if he was picked up by one of the new expansion teams in the coming draft. But, typically, he shrugged off reporters' praise for his performance the night before.

"When a goalie gets hot, he's hot," Johnny said. "When he's cold, he's cold. Last night the puck was bouncing for me. A couple of times it hit the goalpost. The goalposts are a goalie's friend. Sometimes that's all he has behind him to help."

But if luck had been a factor, Johnny had used it all up on those 60 saves. As he took shots in the pregame warm-up the next night at Maple Leaf Gardens, he reached to make a routine save and felt a bad strain in his left leg. It was bad enough that he couldn't hold his crouch. When the Leafs returned to the ice for the opening faceoff, Sawchuk was unexpectedly in net. The last-minute switch appeared to throw the entire team off—especially Sawchuk, who was mediocre as Toronto lost 6–2 in front of the disappointed home crowd. The Leafs dressing room was sullen after the game. King Clancy tried to lighten the mood.

"What is this? You'd think it was a wake! It's not the end of the world for God's sake," Clancy told the press. "We just didn't play good. And you reporters should like that. It's a short story."

Johnny had left the Gardens before the game ended, avoiding prying questions from the press. He had an ice pack affixed to his left thigh. He'd allowed just two goals on 93 shots in the previous seven periods. He hoped his pulled muscle might heal in time for him to get another chance in goal, but it seemed unlikely.

"If Johnny Bower returns in this series, the Toronto club's staff of physicians will be a sure-pop cinch to win the 1967 Nobel Prize for medicine," wrote the *Globe and Mail*'s Jim Coleman. "Observing Bower's limp, I can tell you what would happen to him if he was a horse on a well-supervised track. The track vet would issue orders to have Bower humanely destroyed."

Johnny didn't travel with the team as the series headed to Montreal tied at two. Instead he stayed behind in Toronto, trying to rehabilitate his leg. Al Smith was on the bench for the Leafs while they played Game 5. Johnny watched on television as Sawchuk returned to form, beating the Habs 4–1 at the Forum.

He missed another practice the day before Game 6, and it looked as though the Leafs' physicians would miss out on that Nobel Prize. But Imlach wasn't about to put his wounded goalie down. With a chance to win the Stanley Cup at Maple Leaf Gardens, Imlach told Johnny he was dressing for the game regardless of his injury. Imlach was loyal to the players who had gotten the Leafs this far. There was no way in his mind that Johnny wasn't going to be part of it. But he knew he'd be useless if something happened to Sawchuk, so Smith was on hand, waiting in the locker room in case of an emergency. If Johnny had to go in, he was to drop down on the first play and say he was injured, so Smith could enter the game.

Heavy rain pounded the streets of Toronto on a warm afternoon on May 2, 1967. By evening the glare of street lamps danced in the puddles on Carlton Street. People moved quickly along, shuffling and hurried. They paid a face value of $7.00, $6.00, $4.50 or $2.50 for seats. Some standing-room spots were available high in the stands for $1.50.

It was the last game this group would play together in Toronto. Some were sure to retire. Others were sure to be picked up in the expansion draft. Down in the Leafs dressing room, Imlach pulled his old stunt of piling cash in the middle of the room as an incentive for his players. This time it was $3,000 in one-dollar bills. It was a reminder of the cash bonus that each player would receive for winning the Stanley Cup. (They'd already earned a bonus of $750 each for finishing third in the regular season and $1,500 for winning the first round of the playoffs.)

Bobby Haggert had to strap Johnny's pads on for him before the game because he couldn't reach over to pull the straps himself. All three goalies were on the ice for the Leafs' warm-up. As planned, Johnny watched from the bench as the game started. His old friend Gump Worsley was in goal for Montreal, having replaced Vachon for the third period of Game 5. Worsley had spent most of the season injured and hadn't started a game in nearly two months.

Once again, Johnny's counterpart was masterful in the Leafs goal. While Bower had been the hero of Games 2 and 3, Sawchuk was everything in Game 6. Several times, he made two, sometimes three saves in a row as the Canadiens desperately tried to bring the series back to Montreal for Game 7. Dick Duff, who had scored the winner for the Leafs in 1962 but was now playing for the Canadiens, managed to get one by Sawchuk. But it was all the Habs could find. Toronto led 2–1 in the final minute of the game. Imlach put out a line of old, battered veterans to hold off Montreal's final push as they lined up for a faceoff beside Sawchuk. Horton, 37, took his defensive position while his partner, Allan Stanley, 41, was in the circle against Jean Beliveau—in line with Imlach's custom of having defencemen take faceoffs in their zone. Stanley crashed into Beliveau off the draw, and Red Kelly, 39, swept in to pick up the loose puck. Kelly passed the puck ahead to Bob Pulford, a spightly 31. Pulford took two strides and flipped a backhand pass across the ice to 37-year-old Armstrong. The Leafs captain—the 15-year team veteran—carried the puck over centre ice, as the Canadiens' Ralph Backstrom backpedalled, and flipped the puck into the empty Montreal net.

When the final horn sounded and the cheers and debris rained down from the vaulted heights of the Gardens, Johnny was the first off the bench. He skated into Sawchuk with an enormous hug. Uke had made 40 saves to win Game 6, but both goalies would enter Leafs lore as the tandem that led Toronto to its last Stanley Cup. Even the Canadiens admitted they were undone by the Leafs' unbeatable goaltending.

Only 30 seconds after the Leafs collided in jubilation, both teams were shaking hands at centre ice. Toronto was led by Pronovost, Kelly and Johnny. Sawchuk left the ice before league president Clarence Campbell presented the Cup. Bob Baun was close behind him.

Armstrong skated over to accept the trophy, with his young son Brian close behind him. They lifted the Cup together. It was the 11th time a Toronto Maple Leafs captain had hoisted the storied mug.

At the same time, Sawchuk sat in the Leafs dressing room. He gripped a Coke in both hands, his head sunk forward. He was silent. The back operation in the off-season had nearly knocked him out before the season started. He'd considered heading home during training camp. Countless other troubles weighed heavy in his life. After a few moments, dripping in sweat, he looked up with bloodshot eyes. "My greatest thrill," he said quietly. "My absolute greatest."

Champagne filled the air as the rest of the Leafs entered the room, spraying and cheering and dancing. Team executives, reporters, friends and family filed in behind them. Conn Smythe met Imlach in the middle of the room, near a large bucket filled with beer. Each man held a glass of champagne in his left hand. They clasped their right hands and clinked their glasses.

"I told you you'd be a great coach if you'd go with young guys," Smythe said.

"The Old Fellows Athletic Club played pretty good though, wouldn't you say?" Imlach replied with a smile.

"If you'd lost the game, I'd be mad at you," Smythe said.

"So would I," said Imlach.

They parted ways, with Imlach making the rounds of reporters, continuing his praise for the Old Fellows Athletic Club, who he just knew wouldn't let him down.

"It's tremendous that they should win it in the final year before they change the rules," he said, referring to the league's upcoming expansion.

Soon the Stanley Cup overflowed with champagne. Jim Pappin and Mike Walton hoisted up Imlach and carried him to the showers as the room cheered. Outside, thousands of rowdy fans on Carlton Street revelled in the rain, celebrating yet other Stanley Cup victory in Toronto.

Johnny grabbed two bottles of champagne. He wanted to bring them home to celebrate with Nancy, so they could open them the next time the Leafs won the Stanley Cup. He hid the bottles behind his wooden stall. He and Sawchuk sat there, side by side. Both of their bodies were marked with fresh dark bruises, their faces lined with old scars and recent wounds. They each took deep, slow drags from their cigarettes. And the last Stanley Cup celebration in Toronto—for more than half a century, at least—danced on around them.

17

THE LAST PARADE

MORE THAN 60,000 PEOPLE SHOWED UP FOR THE PARADE three days after the Toronto Maple Leafs last won the Stanley Cup. The streets surrounding City Hall flooded with fans for the fourth time in six seasons. A motorcade of 20 convertibles left Maple Leaf Gardens at 4 p.m. that afternoon on what was starting to seem like a routine trip. The cars made a triumphant tour down Church Street to Wellington and Bay to City Hall. A marching band escorted the Leafs up Bay Street to the civic square. They were greeted by mayor William Dennison, who was the fourth Toronto mayor to be part of the celebration since 1962.

Johnny and his veteran cohort of Tim Horton, Allan Stanley, Larry Hillman, Red Kelly, George Armstrong, Frank Mahovlich, Bob Pulford, Eddie Shack and Dave Keon had all been part of the previous three championships that decade. As had Bobby Baun,

Growing up a Bower never seemed odd to John Jr., Cindy or Barbara, despite their father's fame. Johnny and Nancy worked hard to keep their kids grounded, humble and ready to work for everything they'd later achieve in life. And despite the busy schedule of NHL life, the Bowers always made room for family time. Pictured on the dock, from left to right: Cindy, John Jr. and Barbara. At Toronto City Hall: Cindy beside Nancy, Barbara in the middle and John Jr. in front of Johnny.

(Both photos courtesy of the Bower family)

John Jr. was a regular at Maple Leaf Gardens growing up. After games, he'd join the Leafs in the locker room and sit in his father's stall, just like another member of the team. And he got closer to the Stanley Cup—this time in 1963—than most kids his age could ever dream. (Turofsky collection/Courtesy of the Hockey Hall of Fame)

After spending so many summers in Waskesiu, the Bowers decided it was time to find a summer retreat that was closer to Toronto. They found the perfect piece of land on Little Bald Lake, near Bobcaygeon, and built a family getaway that housed decades of memories. (COURTESY OF THE BOWER FAMILY)

There were few tasks that Johnny was willing to let others do for him. Always a handyman, Johnny preferred to do the work himself. (COURTESY OF THE BOWER FAMILY)

Johnny wasn't just a Hall of Famer on the ice. He was a legendary grandfather too. Each summer the grandkids spent time at the family cottage on Little Bald Lake, where they passed the days swimming, going into town for ice cream and spotting bears at the local dump with their grandfather. Here Johnny shares a laugh with Alison, Dale, Staci and Kelly. Alison and Staci are Cindy's daughters. Barbara's daughters are Dale and Kelly. (COURTESY OF STACI SUDEYKO-SWITCH)

Johnny adjusts the goalie sticks above the garage of the bungalow he and Nancy shared in Mississauga. The garage was one of Johnny's favourite places to putter. He kept a box of Milk-Bone dog treats nearby to hand out to passing pups. (Courtesy of Staci Sudeyko-Switch)

Nancy and Johnny spend some quality time with their great granddaughter, Harper Rose Switch. (Courtesy of Staci Sudeyko-Switch)

There was nothing Johnny loved more than spending time with his family. And to his delight, that family just continued to grow through the decades. Here Johnny and Nancy are joined by their entire family to celebrate his 90th birthday, including grandkids and their partners. John Jr. is in the front row on the left, next to Johnny. Cindy stands behind John Jr., and Barbara stands in the middle, far right, wearing a poppy. (Courtesy of the Bower family)

Despite being spread out across the country, the Bower family remained as close as ever. Here John Jr. stands next to Nancy, while Cindy and Barbara (far right) stand beside their father. (COURTESY OF THE BOWER FAMILY)

Anne Batting is Johnny's only surviving sibling. When Johnny was a star with the Toronto Maple Leafs, she made sure her 10 kids watched their uncle every Saturday night on *Hockey Night in Canada*. (COURTESY OF THE BATTING FAMILY)

Johnny remained lifelong friends with Bob Ochs, after they met during his first season with the Cleveland Barons. As far away as Johnny's career took him, he never lost touch with his old friend who first took care of him in Cleveland. (Courtesy of the Ochs family)

Johnny Bower and Gordie Howe, two of the most famous names in hockey, shared a mutual respect on the ice and a lifelong friendship off it. When Howe passed away in 2016, Johnny made the long journey to Detroit to honour his old fishing buddy. (Michael Gelfand / Courtesy of the Toronto Maple Leafs)

There was a time when it looked like Johnny Bower would remain a career minor-leaguer. Now it's difficult to imagine a time when he wasn't a Toronto Maple Leaf. Today he's one of the few players honoured with a statue on Legends Row outside of Scotiabank Arena. (Courtesy of the Toronto Maple Leafs)

Throughout Johnny's career, Nancy held the household together. She cared for the kids while Johnny was on the road, making sure they kept up with school and made it to practices, and dishing out the discipline when needed. She was the matriarch who allowed the Bower family to flourish. (Courtesy of Paul Patksou)

After so many years of memories, it broke Johnny's and Nancy's hearts to have to give up the family cottage on Little Bald Lake when it became too much for the fiercely independent Johnny to maintain on his own. They shared one last moment, enjoying the view, before saying goodbye. (Courtesy of the Bower family)

Johnny turned 93 on November 8, 2017. In the final month of his life, he attended several events with fans, watched hockey and spent time with his family—all the things he loved most. Here Johnny and Nancy celebrate his 93rd with their good friend Father Mark Curtis and his wife, Rita. (Courtesy of Father Mark Curtis)

Long after his playing days were over, Johnny remained a fixture within the Toronto Maple Leafs organization and in the hearts of hockey fans. His saying that it was "a privilege, not a right" to have worn the Leafs sweater is now painted in the team's locker room.

who skipped the parade celebrations because he'd been benched through the final and his relationship with the franchise was deeply fractured. While all the recent additions to the roster would receive new Stanley Cup rings, the repeat victors would only get another diamond for the ring they already had. That would always be a sore point for Johnny. But one gift that he'd make frequent use of in later years was a lifetime pass to Maple Leaf Gardens, in the shape of a gold medallion.

As the massive crowd roared for the unlikely Stanley Cup champions, the old-timers were a vision of the battered and broken. Ten of those old folks would become members of the Hockey Hall of Fame. While it wasn't clear then, the 1967 Leafs would be remembered and revered as if they were the knights of Conn Smythe's round table. It wasn't just the last stand. It would be a turning point for a franchise that would spin and sputter for decades. The '67 Leafs were the last victors of a storied franchise, the last champions of a historic era. The following season the NHL would double in size, placing six brand new franchises in the same division. The league would spread its farthest borders from the Midwest all the way out to southern California. While several of the old Leafs would linger for a while in the new world, it wouldn't be long before they'd fade away.

But in September 1967, a looming demise was the furthest thing from the defending Stanley Cup champions' minds. Johnny, in particular, was much more concerned about what he was going to tell Nancy when she saw the rainbow paint job on her car. He'd been walking up to the eighth hole at the Kawartha Golf and

Country Club for the Leafs' annual golf tournament at the start of training camp when he'd heard the mischievous holler of his coach.

"John, they delivered your car!" Imlach shouted.

Johnny looked down the fairway, where Imlach was pointing. He tossed his golf club high in the air. The convertible he'd driven to camp was parked on the course. It had been white when he last saw it. Now it was a psychedelic medley of red, green, blue, black, orange, fuchsia, yellow and pink stripes—with Maple Leafs decals on the doors, trunk and engine hood. Johnny had made the mistake of driving Nancy's car to camp. She'd wanted it painted black. When Johnny asked his teammates if anyone knew a good place to get a paint job, he should have noticed that his coach had seemed a bit too eager to help out.

"Give me $50 and I'll get the job done here for you," Imlach said.

The gag had the entire Leafs team in hysterics. Armstrong made Johnny drive the convertible through downtown Peterborough to show off the new look. "We're heading for Yorkville," Armstrong told the *Globe and Mail*. "We're a couple of hippies."

You'd think that, entering his 23rd season of professional hockey, Johnny might have earned a pass on the pranks, but the 42-year-old was apparently still a prime target. Later in training camp, Armstrong teasingly tossed a pail at Johnny's feet as he was leaving the ice after practice, indicating that he was to pick up the pucks—a sacrilege in the order of hockey. In the dressing room afterwards, Johnny stood on a scale to be weighed by trainer Bobby Haggert. He squinted his eyes and peered forward to see the numbers. "What's it say?" he asked. Imlach overhead him.

"What's it say?" he mocked. "Did you hear what that old gentleman said? Bower, I'd better get you an eye doctor. No, on second thought, I'd better not. It's too much of a risk."

Johnny objected that the glare from an overhead light had obscured his view, but Imlach just continued to laugh. It was all in jest, but throughout camp there had been real speculation in the press that the Leafs netminder might finally have tipped past his prime. Toronto had lost much of its roster to the expansion draft, including Johnny's goaltending partner, Sawchuk, who was selected by the Los Angeles Kings with the first overall pick. Imlach had left Sawchuk unprotected but had made sure no team could take Bower. Imlach still believed his ageless goalie had some time left. Others weren't so sure.

"I see we protected our 47-year-old goalie," Stafford Smythe quipped after the draft.

Sawchuk was just one of the veterans the Leafs lost, as they were able to protect only 11 skaters. Red Kelly retired and became the Kings' first head coach. Bob Baun went to the Oakland Seals. Along with Johnny, old hands like Allan Stanley, George Armstrong, Tim Horton and Marcel Pronovost remained. Dave Keon, the Conn Smythe winner, was still in his prime. As were Frank Mahovlich and Bob Pulford. Meanwhile a host of young players like Ron Ellis, Mike Walton and Pete Stemkowski were to be the key cogs on the team.

Throughout camp, Johnny had been average. Not bad; good, even. But when you're about to turn 43 years old—on the cusp of being able to collect your players pension—anything less than spectacular is sure to get the doubters talking. But Johnny himself said the rumours of his demise were premature. He'd played 27 games through an injury-riddled season during the Leafs' miracle Cup run. And he'd posted a 2.65 goals-against average and a .925 save percentage while doing it. Johnny felt healthier than he had the year before and predicted he was good for at least 45 games, in tandem with 29-year-old Bruce Gamble. At the very least, Johnny would be less likely to lose time with a face injury.

After playing his entire life without one, Johnny had promised to finally wear a mask that season. He'd worked on a special design with one of his neighbours on Summitcrest, a young dentist named Richard Bell—who, Johnny said, had actually tragically died that summer. They had been working on making the nose smaller so Johnny could see the puck better beneath him when Bell passed away. The mask was made of fibreglass. Johnny hated wearing it. The sweat pads in the helmet were soaked after every practice. Whenever he wore it, sweat rolled down his face and into his eyes. Then he struggled to locate distant shots and to see the puck in scrambles around his net. During an exhibition game against the Rochester Americans, he made a stick save without even reacting because he hadn't seen the shot. When the puck hit him he was visibly startled, and the crowd broke out laughing. Johnny came out for the second period without the mask. He managed to put off the shielded visage for another year.

For all his teasing, Imlach also showed Johnny some moments of good faith. Just before his goalie turned 43, he finally handed him a raise without grinding him down in negotiations. After

Johnny pulled off a spectacular shutout win over the Montreal Canadiens in early November, Imlach walked up to him in the dressing room, told him he was getting a raise and made the gesture of tearing up a piece of paper. Johnny didn't believe it at first. "He was probably only kidding," he said while combing his hair in the dressing room mirror a few minutes later. But Imlach confirmed that he meant what he said, adding that only players over 40 get the opportunity to get a raise during the season. He made good on his promise, bumping Johnny up to $25,000 a year. It was, of course, long overdue. Imlach's sudden bout of generosity followed years of underpaying one of the best goalies of the era.

A week later, Johnny and Armstrong both slept in at the hotel where the Leafs were staying. The entire team had already checked in to their flight home from Minnesota when the two veterans were woken by a frantic call from King Clancy. "I guess that'll cost us $25," Bower complained later, already seeing his raise heading back to the team. But, aside from oversleeping, Bower's play once again showed little sign of age through the 1967–68 season. In fact, he was selected as a midseason all-star by the league's coaches. And true to his preseason prediction, he'd play 43 games in a season that had been extended to 74 with expansion. It was more games than he'd managed in each of the previous three seasons. Still, reporters were on him about his future.

"Some guys are always asking me if this is my last year, and I always give them the same answer," Johnny said in early February, shortly after returning from an elbow injury that put him on the sidelines for a couple of weeks. "This *is* my last year . . . It's a joke. I don't know when I'll retire."

But after a decent start to the season, Johnny started to slip in the second half. He was booed after a poor performance in a 5–1 loss to the St. Louis Blues at home—a game in which the blame could just have easily fallen on the Leafs' lacklustre defence. But Johnny was an easy target. He'd recently been yanked after a bad showing in Chicago and allowed a couple of particularly soft goals against the Blues. The jeers grew when the public address announcer informed the Gardens that Johnny would be appearing at a milk store the following week to sign autographs and talk hockey. The fans then mockingly cheered for Johnny as he easily collected a fluttering puck. After the game, Blues manager Lynn Patrick called the display from the Leafs fans disgraceful. The backlash was tough on Johnny's family too. John Jr., now in high school, faced taunts every time his father played a bad game or let in a bad goal.

Through that first year of expansion, Toronto played in the East Division, made up of all the Original Six teams. With a mediocre record, the Leafs languished at the bottom of the division entering the final stretch of the season. They'd ultimately miss the playoffs. In early March, Imlach decided to clean house. He pulled off a trade that made Johnny think the general manager had lost his mind. The Leafs sent Frank Mahovlich, Pete Stemkowski, Garry Unger and the rights to Carl Brewer to the Red Wings for Norm Ullman, Paul Henderson, Floyd Smith and minor-leaguer Doug Barrie. Mahovlich, who had an embattled relationship with

Imlach, learned about the trade when a reporter called him with the news. Johnny was angry that Imlach had traded Mahovlich. He later said he was ready to quit the team. He went into Imlach's office and told him exactly how he felt.

"You traded my best player," he said.

"*Your* best player?" Imlach shouted at him.

"That's right," Johnny said. "You traded my best left winger. He's our best goal scorer."

"You just play goal," Imlach said, having had enough of Johnny's insurrection. "Don't worry about anybody else."

Johnny shut up after that. He had his own problems to worry about. He'd been playing well but knew his time was coming to an end. Despite a few poor showings—and the mindless taunts of the mob—Johnny had rebounded to piece together a fine season. He finished the Leafs' losing campaign with a 2.26 goals-against average and a sparkling .934 save percentage. He and Gamble would finish second in the race for the Vezina, behind Montreal, with just 176 goals against—despite the Leafs' finishing the season in fifth. Still, near the end of the year, Johnny made it known he was winding down, telling reporters he felt Bruce Gamble had earned the number one spot in goal for the upcoming season, but that he'd back him up if another goalie wasn't ready to take his spot.

The following season, more than a dozen players from the Stanley Cup–winning roster were gone. The Leafs were moving into a new generation, with long-standing players like Bower, Armstrong and Horton staying on. The team brought in 37-year-old veteran

Pierre Pilote on defence, while giving 20-year-old prospect Rick Ley a shot. They also gave a spot to a 26-year-old minor-league journeyman named Pat Quinn.

As Johnny turned 44, it was becoming more and more apparent that his body and vision just couldn't keep up with a game that was growing increasingly faster and more unpredictable. He'd finally relented to Imlach's pestering and agreed to wear a mask during games that year, but it never felt comfortable. And on the ice, he just wasn't the same. Johnny was booed again by the home crowd at Maple Leaf Gardens early in January 1969. He'd come in to replace Gamble in the third period against the Oakland Seals. Johnny had knocked the puck off the leg of teammate Mike Pelyk for a fluky own-goal, and the Gardens let him have it. Afterwards, Johnny said he had no problem with the booing fans.

"They paid their $5, or whatever it costs to get in here nowadays, and they have the privilege," he said. "Don't forget, they pay my salary and they can do whatever they want."

The Leafs barely squeaked into the playoffs in the spring of 1969, meeting the second-place Boston Bruins in the first round. Both teams had clashed through the regular season—especially Bruins star Bobby Orr and Pat Quinn. The rookie Irishman quickly became Boston's biggest enemy when he knocked out Orr with a devastating hit in the first game of the series. The play nearly caused a riot at Boston Garden. The Bruins were routing the Leafs at the time. Orr had to be carried off the ice on a stretcher. Johnny came in to relieve Gamble in the third period and spent much of his time chatting with Bruins goalie Ed Johnston while their teammates brawled through the final frame. The Leafs dropped the next two fight-filled games. Johnny took over for Gamble again partway through the third game, making 28 saves in relief and earning the game's second star in a close 4–3 loss. He was one of the only bright spots on the outmatched roster. For his efforts, Johnny was given the start in Game 4 at home in Toronto. He wore a mask in both playoff games, finally relenting to the changing times. At 44 years, four months and 28 days old, he was the oldest to ever play in an NHL playoff game. He played brilliantly, stopping 28 shots—including a sprawling stick save on Ed Westfall. He also survived a collision with Derek Sanderson, who ran the net. Sanderson was protected from a fuming Quinn by the referee. Despite the shakeup, Johnny played true to form, keeping the outclassed Leafs in it to the very end. But the Bruins were just too much. Toronto lost 3–2 and was eliminated.

It was the last playoff hockey game Johnny ever played.

18

TIME

THE DEMOLITION STARTED WITH PUNCH. THE SAME EVENING of the Leafs' violent and embarrassing end at the hands of the Boston Bruins, the architect of the franchise's happy decade was fired by Stafford Smythe. For all of the clashes he'd had with his players and the missteps he made near the end of his run, Imlach would remain a revered figure within the organization. His firing was undoubtably the beginning of a new era, and Johnny knew he was quickly becoming a relic. When he heard that Imlach was gone, Johnny immediately announced his retirement.

Jim Gregory, a 34-year-old coach and manager who had worked within the Leafs organization before taking a head coaching job with the Vancouver Canucks of the Western Hockey league, was brought back to Toronto to replace Imlach as general manager. Gregory would have a successful run at the helm of the

Leafs—introducing talents like Darryl Sittler, Lanny McDonald and Borje Salming—while dealing with the difficult reign of infamously burdensome owner Harold Ballard (who'd spend time in the early '70s in prison after being convicted of fraud). One of Gregory's first moves was to bring in John McLellan as head coach. McLellan had been coaching the Tulsa Oilers, the Leafs' minor-league affiliate in the Central Hockey League. He was also the player who had broken Johnny's face with a shot that took out most of his teeth when he was playing for the Pittsburgh Hornets.

That August, Johnny spent time touring with the Canadian Armed Forces and instructing in hockey schools in Germany along with Armstrong and Marcel Pronovost. Despite announcing his retirement, Johnny was convinced to return by the persistent George Armstrong—who reminded him that he was now making pretty decent cash for an old man and likely wouldn't have the chance again. (Armstrong himself would hold out at the start of the season, even though the Leafs wanted their 39-year-old captain to return.) Johnny's salary of $25,000 was equivalent to about $215,000 today. It was by no means the millions that players would make in a matter of decades, but it was a sum that the frugal Bower couldn't ignore. Gregory had spoken with Johnny several times over the summer and was insistent that he was still a valuable member of the franchise.

"Everyone I've talked to in the building believes John deserves an opportunity to remain in hockey," Gregory told the *Globe and Mail*'s Lou Cauz, while he wrote out letters in the summer inviting the players to training camp. "I think we owe it to him and besides

I still think he can do the job in one way or another . . . There are a lot of people around who still think John can play. We'll see."

The Canadian national team certainly still had faith in hockey's oldest player. Hockey Canada expressed interest in having Johnny join the team as soon as he announced that he might be done with the Leafs. But that September, Johnny hinted that even though he'd agreed to return to Toronto it was unlikely fans would eventually see him in a Team Canada sweater. "If I was 10 years younger, I'd be very thrilled," he said. "But I'm not a young man anymore. I wouldn't want to find myself in the position of playing for Canada and having a bad game. Imagine, a bad game against Russia and a 45-year-old in net." Even though he was returning for one more season, Johnny knew this was his final tour. He expressed his interest in coaching and planned to help the organization scout its younger goalies. The Leafs would carry three goalies through the season: Bruce Gamble, Marv Edwards and Bower. Of the group, he knew he'd be number three, and for a workhorse like him, that just wouldn't cut it. "I may get in a game or two. Or I may not," he said during training camp. "If I do get in I won't be sharp. You can't be sharp unless you're playing regularly.

As expected, Johnny was effectively number three behind his two younger counterparts and didn't see any game action early in the regular season. True to his reputation, though, Johnny continued to outwork both in practice. And he was still as tough as ever. During a practice in late October, the face mask Johnny's neighbour had designed for him was shattered by a shot from Norm Ullman. Everyone on the ice stopped as Johnny fell hard to the ice.

The puck hit him right in the nose, and the broken fibreglass fragments left him with several cuts on his face. After a few moments he got up and skated, dazed, to the bench. "If I hadn't of been wearing that mask, I'd be in Honolulu," he said.

When he turned 45 just over a week later, Johnny was old enough to start collecting his NHL pension. He spoke with league president Clarence Campbell to see when he could start picking up his cheques, but Campbell laughed and informed him he wasn't eligible because he was still an active player. Of course, at the time, "active player" was really just a technicality. Johnny worked a lot with Marv Edwards, an NHL rookie at age 34, and gave both goalies playing ahead of him tips on how to handle opposing players.

Johnny didn't get an opportunity to play until December 10, against the Canadiens in Montreal. It was the first time he'd played since an intrasquad charity game at the start of October. Johnny played well through the first two periods and the Leafs led 3–2 at the end of the second. But things fell apart in the third. Johnny felt sluggish, allowing three goals. The Habs scored an empty-net goal to beat the Leafs 6–3 in what would be the final game of his career.

It was a disappointing end. Without any real game action, Johnny didn't feel like himself. He wasn't able to just jump in cold, like Terry Sawchuk had been. A three-goalie system would never work for him. A couple of weeks later, just before the new year, Johnny suffered a knee injury in practice. He knew it was bad and tried to push on. But that evening, the pain was so bad he couldn't sleep. Nancy took him to Toronto General Hospital, where he'd become something of a regular over the years. Coincidentally, both Cindy and Barbara Bower were having their tonsils out at the same time. The doctor informed him he'd torn ligaments in his right knee. He was put in a cast from his ankle to his thigh. It was the first time in his career that he'd needed one. Edwards was also injured at the time, and the last-place Leafs had planned to use Johnny in several games to give Bruce Gamble a rest.

Over the next month, Johnny desperately hoped his knee would heal. When he was able to remove the cast, he put himself through a relentless regimen of rehabilitation drills, trying to work his knee back into playing form. He was used to his body recovering quickly, but this time it just wasn't happening. The ageless one had broken down. Although he didn't want to admit it, he was having a diffi-cult time seeing long shots in practices. The Leafs had even sent him to an eye doctor and he'd started wearing glasses. Even if his leg healed, he knew his vision was a huge liability. There was no way he could play the way he once had. Still, he trained relentlessly through February and into March. He did all sorts of drills that focused on quick starts and stops, trying to build up strength. But nothing worked. One day in March, he drove home from practice, parked the car in the driveway and walked into the house to Nancy. "I can't go on any longer," he said.

Nancy worried about what her husband would do if he wasn't going down to the rink every Saturday night to strap on his pads and play in front of the fans at Maple Leaf Gardens. Even though he wouldn't be able to play the game, Nancy knew her husband could never leave it.

The Leafs announced a press conference for March 20, 1970, at Maple Leaf Gardens. They served cheese sandwiches and cold beer. Then Johnny Bower came in and told reporters that his long career was finally over.

"When hockey is no longer fun," he said, "it's time to quit."

Jim Gregory made sure to point out that with Johnny's official retirement he wouldn't be allowed to play for at least two years, hinting that the goalie just might change his mind.

"And in two years he will be 39," Gregory joked. "He just told me today that he's 37."

On the topic of mythical birthdates, disbelieving reporters in the room pressed Johnny to finally reveal his true age now that he was retired.

"If you don't know by now," he said, "you never will."

Gregory told reporters that Johnny would take on a new position as a goaltending coach and scout with the team. While he was still wearing his cast, Johnny had travelled to Phoenix to help the goaltenders on one of the Leafs' minor-league affiliate teams. It was a unique job in an era where it was unusual for a team to have more than one coach, let alone specialists for specific positions. Although goalie coaches would become commonplace in the coming decades, Johnny would be one of the first.

It was as close to playing as he could get. And even at that, Johnny wasn't quite ready to give it up. When a curator from the Hockey Hall of Fame asked if he could acquire his skates to put on display, Johnny told him he could have one pair but that he'd still need the other for practice.

The morning after announcing his retirement, Johnny was back on the ice at the Leafs' practice, competing as though it was a Stanley Cup Final.

Bob Baun sits at his kitchen table in his house east of Toronto, telling stories about his old friend Johnny. It's the kind of life that requires time to sit and reminisce, he says—time to slow down and remember someone unlike anyone he'd ever met. "He was a sweetheart," Baun says. "He didn't have a mean bone in his body."

One story, in particular, makes him laugh as hard at 81 years old as it did all those decades earlier. It happened shortly after Baun had recovered from the broken neck that ended his career in 1972. He joined a few of his old Leafs teammates, including George Armstrong and Johnny Bower, on a trip to run a series of hockey schools in Canada's northern communities. After visiting Yellowknife, they flew in a small Twin Otter plane to a remote lake to go fishing. The old Leafs stood on big boulders on the shore of the lake, casting out their reels. Armstrong snuck behind a large rock, out of sight. "John! John!" he yelled. "I've got a big one! Come help!" Johnny dropped his rod and scrambled over the rocks as quickly he could, nearly falling as he did. When he got to Armstrong, he was holding the tiniest fish in his hand.

"Aww," he said to Johnny, "too small."

And he tossed it back into the lake.

Johnny stood there, shaking his head. "You turkey," he said.

Baun is laughing as he tells it now.

"If you just had a camera at that time to see John's face," he says. "And Chief just looked at him! 'Aww, too small . . .'"

He misses those days. He misses the time spent among friends, joking and laughing in those carefree moments in a locker room or on the side of a remote lake. The game was a business. It was fun, but it was employment. It was the teammates that made it worthwhile—they were in it together. A brotherhood, like his old captain once said. And among them all, Baun says, there was no one like Johnny. No one who could maintain the same sense of kindness, of gentleness, of friendship within the rough macho veneer of a hockey team the way Johnny Bower could.

A few days earlier, Baun says, he'd watched as the world reacted to the sudden death of a beloved television celebrity. He saw the tears of that man's colleagues as they spoke about him on television after news of his death—how they talked about how he'd transcended shallow fame, how he'd connected with them personally and how he seemed to connect with every stranger he met. He could tell it had been a special life because of how raw, how visceral, the reaction was.

"They're not false tears. They're genuine," Baun says, and he pauses. "They're missing *their* Johnny Bower."

A tear slides down the right side of his face. He collects himself as it falls.

"I'm sorry," he says.

He's been thinking a lot about Johnny lately. He's been thinking about how Johnny used to bring instant coffee on road trips. How his teammates never quite believed his age. How marvellous he was to play in front of. The magic he wielded game after game. He's been thinking about Johnny's friendship—during those years together in Leafs sweaters and through the decades since. He's been thinking about the example Johnny showed of a life well lived—one full of gratitude and appreciation, through it all.

Like a lot of older players, Baun has felt blessed by the love still shown from fans that come to chat and line up for autographs. But Johnny, he says, loved it more than any of them. The last time they saw each other was at a card signing in early December 2017. The lineup to meet Johnny was enormous. "John, we can't do this," Baun had told his 93-year-old friend, knowing it could take hours. But Johnny remained until the very last fan.

And the fans waited to meet Johnny because he transcended fame in a way few other players had.

"John, how he gave . . . how you depict that isn't easy," Baun says. "He had the biggest heart of all."

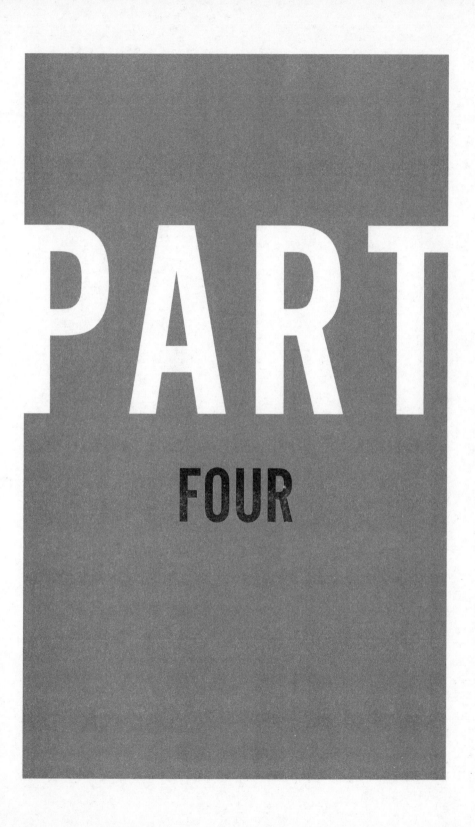

PART

FOUR

19

THE EXTRAORDINARY ORDINARY

CINDY SUDEYKO AND BARBARA BOWER SIT AT A CORNER TABLE at a Tim Hortons in Georgetown, Ontario, a quaint suburb west of Toronto, remembering all the moments, big and small, that formed the extraordinary ordinariness of what it was like to grow up a Bower. The coffee shop named after their father's teammate was a favourite hangout for their parents in old age. They were regulars at the Tims near their home in Mississauga, where they'd have a coffee, watching the busy rush in and out. They were a long way from Waskesiu, but some things just never changed. Those fragments of time found within a busy life, simply spent enjoying a cup of coffee, chatting with strangers and watching the world go by, were part of who they were. The Bower sisters are often asked what it was like to grow up with such a famous father and such a famous name. It was hard to explain because it seemed so perfectly unexceptional to them.

"Well, he was our dad," says Barb, now nearing 60 with two grown daughters of her own. "He was just like any other dad—except whenever he went anywhere, he was well known . . . It was just part of our life. It's what happened."

They sat beside him in the convertible year after year as thousands of wild fans clapped and cheered. They waved to the TV cameras that captured their family entering Maple Leaf Gardens for their holiday skate. They saw the lines of people waiting to get their copy of "Honky the Christmas Goose" signed. And they waited patiently when autograph seekers surrounded them anytime they went out as a family. They knew it wasn't normal, although it seemed to be. Their father's fame didn't define their childhood. While Johnny was away on road trips, Nancy worked hard to maintain the routines of their everyday lives. And when he came home, it was just like any other father who'd been away on a business trip—although his job was televised and kids at school were interested in how he did.

They lived by rules familiar to most: If you wanted a car, you got a part-time job . . . Respect everything and everyone . . . Family is number one, always. And while the sisters admit there was a certain Cleaver-ness to life as a Bower—the worst phrase the children ever heard their father say was "for frick's sake," and use of the word *stupid* was strictly prohibited—they insisted they had their warts, just like any family. Like the time Cindy punched Barbara in the eye because she thought she was cheating during a card game. Or when Cindy would hide under her little sister's bed and then jump out to scare the bejesus out of her. When it came to discipline for such malicious behaviour, the task usually fell to Nancy. With John away on road trips for so much of the season, Nancy had to keep all three kids in line without him there. They knew not to mess with her. Because of his absence, John was able to play the teddy bear more often. Both were loving, kind and devoted parents. But Nancy ran the house.

Johnny was, frankly, a bit of a softie. It was he who drove his son to the breeder to pick out the family dog, a beagle puppy. They chose the biggest of the litter. The two Johns, father and son, decided the family needed another—and so the Bower's family pet was "Big John." And it was Bower who laughed, delighted, when the feisty little pup ripped around the cottage or leaped over the backyard fence on Summitcrest Drive. Nancy thought it funny too, when she'd call out for dinner and just had to shout the name John to have all three males come running. Big John became part of the family, as any dog does—packed tight in the car on trips to the cottage, curled up for warmth on stormy nights, protecting the household from all the menacing squirrels and cats. When he passed away in his early teens, it was Nancy who declared he'd never be replaced because it hurt so much to lose him. "That's the end of it," she said. "No more." After Big John, the Bowers would never raise another pet.

When Johnny retired from the Maple Leafs, he was far from done with hockey. He treated his responsibilities with the franchise with his typical all-in commitment, but without the taxing travel schedule of professional hockey, Johnny was able to settle into life beyond the rigours of the game for the first time since returning from the Second World War. Johnny still went on some coast-to-coast scouting trips that would take him away for a couple of weeks at a time. Nancy was grateful he was able to keep his mind in the game and his attention on the Leafs as he adjusted to his retirement. As a scout, Johnny found a few promising talents, like Errol Thompson, whom he first saw as a 19-year-old playing senior hockey in Charlottetown, P.E.I., shortly after Johnny hung up his blades. Thompson was overweight and playing hockey well below his ability, but Johnny felt he had the makings of a future George Armstrong. Johnny pushed for the Leafs to draft him in the second round in the spring of 1970. "You just put your job on the line," Stafford Smythe told Johnny as they sat at the Leafs' table at the draft. But Johnny's first recommendation as a scout turned out all right. Thompson went on to play six seasons with the Leafs and scored 43 goals on a line with Lanny McDonald and Darryl Sittler in 1975.

The 1970s were a tumultuous time for the Leafs franchise, mainly because owner Harold Ballard had tightened his grip on the team. A couple of years into his career as a scout, before the 1975 season, Johnny saw Ballard walking down the hall at Maple Leaf Gardens and said hello. Ballard turned around sharply and asked Johnny where he had been. He explained that he'd been away for several days scouting junior hockey players. The owner then asked if the Leafs were going to be able to get all the good players he'd spotted on the trip. But Johnny informed Ballard that under the draft rules other teams would have the ability to select the players as well. This fact, for some reason, rankled Ballard.

"You know, I'm sick and tired of you guys," Ballard said. "You scouts told me how good Lanny McDonald was. For two years, I've paid him a good salary and he's done nothing for me."

Johnny objected, saying McDonald had just graduated from junior hockey and simply needed a couple of years to develop. In fact, McDonald had put up 30 and 44 points in his first two NHL seasons—and the future Hall of Famer would score 37 goals and 93 points in 1975–76. But Ballard was having none of it.

"I'm not waiting two years," he shouted. "I'm in a business here and I can't do that. You know, all you scouts, all you do is give me a headache. I've got a notion to fire everybody. In fact—you're fired."

Johnny took the bizarre dismissal seriously. He went to his office and started packing up his things, heartbroken that his career with the Leafs had ended in such an ignominious way. In the office at Maple Leaf Gardens, Johnny sat next to his old friend George Armstrong, who had retired the year after him but had also continued to work in the Leafs organization. Armstrong asked why he was packing up his things. Bower told him he'd been fired—and Armstrong started to laugh.

"This isn't funny, George," Bower said.

Armstrong told him to put his stuff back on his desk, go home and relax, and come back the next morning. Johnny thought he was crazy, but Armstrong insisted. That night, Johnny could barely sleep, stressing about having just lost his job. The next morning, he returned to the Gardens, just as Armstrong told him to. He saw Ballard shuffling towards him and worried about what was going to happen.

"Good morning, John," Ballard said. "How are you?"

He'd completely forgotten about firing Johnny the day before. Relieved but shocked, Johnny asked Armstrong why he'd found the whole thing so funny the day before.

"You really want to know?" Armstrong said with laugh. "He's fired me six times."

While Johnny continued to spend a lot of time at the Gardens and on scouting trips through the 1970s, he was also able to spend more time in the stands watching his kids. Cindy had become a competitive figure skater, while John Jr. was a talented defenceman. Through their early years in sports, most of the trips to practices and games were taken care of by Nancy, as Bower was either on the road or at his own practices. When he was about 10 years old, John Jr. had played goal for a recreational team in Etobicoke. Most of the team's games at the time were still played at an outdoor rink, and with two goalies on the team, John Jr. would spend half of his time standing in the freezing cold, working the door on the bench. He didn't share his father's ability to withstand the frigid temperatures and decided he'd rather play out, where he'd get more playing time and therefore be much warmer. Johnny wasn't bothered by his young son's move to defence. In fact, he seemed a little bit relieved. No one could know the toll that position took on a person better than Johnny and his cohort of NHL goalies through the 1950s and 1960s.

John Jr. excelled as a defenceman, playing rep hockey in the Toronto Marlboros system and then going on to play Junior A for Royal York and Downsview. Just about every night, Johnny would be out watching junior hockey at some rink in the Toronto area, scouting for the Leafs. But as he sat on the bench, waiting for his next shift, John Jr. often scanned the crowd, looking to see if his father was there. It was difficult for Johnny to walk into a rink without quickly becoming the centre of attention. So when he did make it to John Jr.'s games, Johnny would often stand at the top of the stands, behind the fans watching the game. Whenever he was able, Johnny would try to make it for at least the third period. John Jr. would find his father at the back of the stands, with the same smile he'd worn that night at the Gardens, watching his son play on the empty ice after the Leafs had won the Cup.

Although John Jr. would be drafted by the Washington Capitals, it was Cindy who'd actually find a lasting career in ice sports. She was a competitive figure skater through her teenage years, with Nancy taking her to most of her practices and events. But as with John Jr., whenever Bower was able, he'd find his seat in the rink and he'd catch her eye with his smile. Later on, Cindy would become a renowned skating instructor who taught high-level hockey players how to improve their strides. Sometimes she'd invite her father to come out to her training sessions. "This is my dad," she'd say, as the players stood there dumbfounded. They'd circle around Johnny and he'd tell stories, while the clock ticked down on their hour-long ice time. It was hard to get any work in whenever he showed up.

Through those years in the 1970s, the Bower family continued to spend every summer up at the cottage on Little Bald Lake, just outside of Bobcaygeon. As soon as school was out they were in the car, heading to the lake. With the Bower kids in their teenage years, the cottage became a gathering place for them and their friends, so the three-bedroom bungalow always seemed full. Even though the kids were older and often had friends in tow, the Bower family traditions remained much the same. There was tubing, water ski-ing, swimming and fishing. There were after-dinner walks, sunsets on the dock, evening campfires—and spooky games of nighttime hide-and-seek. When they were older they were allowed to take the boat out themselves, but they had to be back by dark. If they were out too late, the spotlight would flash on from the dock and Johnny would find them on the black water. "Shut the light out!" Barb would shout. "I'm like four minutes late! Shut the light out!"

Decades later, looking back, they'd remember the late-night talks around the dinner table with family and friends—over a game of cards or a board game. Games of euchre and crib were particu-larly competitive. Sometimes they'd be there at the table for hours without any of them realizing. (Especially as they got older and shared a bottle of wine.) The Bowers gabbed about the news, about what was happening at school or in college. And as his family sat together, talking into the night, Johnny often just sat there quietly, taking in the moment. "He was a great listener and he was a great observer," says Barb. "But when he spoke, everybody listened."

Sometimes there were wild adventures. Like the time the tor-nado ripped through and left them huddled together as a family in the corner of the cottage, while the A-frame ceiling shook and the windows rattled in the furious wind and rain. They'd seen the storm coming in off the water and frantically tried to secure what they could and make sure everyone was inside. Cindy and Barb believed the cottage would blow down. They'd never been more terrified. Barb clung to Big John, the beagle, while they all waited it out, huddled together. Nancy was scared too; she hated storms. Johnny tried to settle his family down, making sure they'd be okay. But at the same time, he carefully watched the large tree outside that could have crashed through the ceiling if the tornado swept through. It shook and bent in the wind but stayed rooted and strong.

When the tornado had passed, the Bowers went outside to survey the damage. The lake was completely silent. It looked like a disaster zone. Several of the cottages had been almost levelled. Others were partially smashed by fallen trees. Someone's boat had been swept clear across the lake. The deck at a neighbour's cottage was uprooted and flipped back against the house. Somehow, though, the Bowers' bungalow had stood through the storm. When it was over, they set out to make sure their neighbours were all right. The terrified residents of Little Bald Lake slowly emerged, realizing just how powerful the tornado had been. Those with the least damage quickly mobilized. The Bowers invited one small family whose place was severally damaged to come stay with them. That wouldn't be enough for Johnny, though. He had to do something. He went down to his workshop, grabbed his chainsaw and fired it up. He spent the afternoon and most of the next week chopping up the trees that had fallen through roofs and blocked the road, so the small cottage community could begin piecing their paradise back together again.

While that one had been the worst, storms were common in the area—and the community was used to leaning on each other whenever it got particularly bad. Thanksgiving was an enormous holiday for the Bowers, complete with epic meals of so much food that the fully gorged kids would lie under the table afterwards, amazed that they'd managed to eat as much as they had. But one year, a storm knocked out the power on the lake while families that had come up to enjoy the holiday were in the middle of cooking their turkey dinners. With the electricity gone for a day at least, Nancy opened the oven door and pulled out her half-cooked turkey. It looked like that Thanksgiving meal was ruined, until she and Johnny came up with some old-time Waskesiu ingenuity. Johnny jerry-rigged a stand in the coal-fuelled fireplace so they could cook the turkey on the open flame. It was a cold and stormy autumn afternoon. With no other source of heat, the Bowers huddled close around the fireplace to stay warm while their turkey slowly baked. Soon, neighbours without fireplaces were knocking on their door, hoping to borrow the flame. Between a few working barbecues and the Bowers' fireplace, a communal Thanksgiving dinner slowly came together. When the turkey was finally ready, they all crowded around the massive solid pine table inside the Bowers' cottage by candlelight, sharing what they'd managed to salvage from their own kitchens. Of all the Thanksgivings the Bowers would have up at the cottage—a tradition that would last decades—the most memorable would always be the one without power, when all of Little Bald Lake crowded around their table in the flickering light to share some fireplace-cooked turkey.

Over the years, Johnny kept finding new projects at the cottage. He'd replaced the old flat roof with the A-frame himself. He built the dock, the boathouse and the closed-in-porch with some assistance from his kids, whom he let be little helpers. Nothing ever went to waste. Sometimes when there were extra scraps of wood, he'd show the girls how to build something of their own, like a birdhouse. He was careful to show them just the right way to piece it all together, even though he didn't have a written plan. They'd sit out on the grass for hours, fiddling with the small projects. Johnny's own childhood had been far from idyllic, but he took the best parts of it and made sure to pass those experiences on to his own children.

Being handy was much more than just a hobby for Johnny. It was a fundamental part of his life. As a boy, he had learned how to take mere scraps and turn them into something with a real purpose. The art of resourcefulness had been passed down from his father, who'd carved out a life in a new world when he was still a teen. There was a direct line between hockey's hardest-working goalie and the drive of a young man who had nothing to his name but set out to make his own way in a new, strange world. He'd learned a new language, changed his name, built a home out of logs, tamed wild land in the summers and survived the harsh winters in the middle of nowhere. James Kiszkan had left an indelible mark on his son. Johnny's relentless work on and off the ice mirrored his father's daily grind at the Pat Burns Meat Company.

James worked at that meat factory, earning a menial wage, for more than four decades. After his marriage to Betty Jacobson fell apart, he eventually fell in love with a woman named Polly Bodnarchuk. She had also been born in Ukraine before coming to Canada in 1901. She'd lived in Elaine Lake, about two hours north of Prince Albert, before moving to the town when they married in 1945. James lived in the same house at 526 Sixteenth Street until the mid-1950s, when he and Polly moved to another house, down the block but on the same street. They attended the Holy Trinity Greek Orthodox Church on the east side of town, James having put Sacred Heart behind him. Polly died suddenly in 1971, at the age of 78. James stayed on Sixteenth Street for a few more years, until he had to move to a nursing home in the mid-1970s. His grandchildren who still lived in Prince Albert took care of him through those final years. He'd outlived all three of his brothers, Peter, John and Mike. In early October 1978, James sat in a chair outside of his nursing home, smoking a cigarette. His health was failing. As he sat there, James told a relative who had come to check on him that he could hear his mother calling him. He died late that night, on October 5, 1978, at the age of 87.

Although he wasn't able to visit his father often, Johnny held a lifelong affinity for him. He kept a portrait of his dad in his bedroom, along with the photographs he'd collected from his youth. But his relationship with his mother was always strained. Betty Jacobson and Mike Dupay married sometime after 1945, and they lived in the east end of Prince Albert. Despite his close relationship with Nancy's family—in particular his mother-in law, Esther, whom he called Essie—Johnny rarely spoke to his family about the specifics of his childhood, aside from the tall tales he'd tell the kids. Nancy didn't want to pry into something that might make him feel uneasy. She met Betty Jacobson only twice. Johnny seemed uncomfortable to Nancy when they stopped by to visit with Betty.

"We just went in and saw her and spent maybe half an hour visiting," she says. "And then he was up and 'Let's go.'"

Betty Dupay, as she was then known, died in February 1965, when she was 75. When she died, the Bower family didn't attend the funeral—although Johnny may have on his own. It was difficult to remember the specifics, decades later. But there was no doubt that Bower's relationship with his mother wasn't as close as the one she had with some of her daughters, like Anne—who would remember her as a sharp-witted, funny and loving woman.

Bower's relationship with his younger brother Mike was also a difficult one. The two were different in many ways, from their demeanour to their physical appearance. Mike had a dark complexion and brown hair, while Johnny was blond and fair. In the one photo that shows them both together as boys, Bower tilts his head slightly to the side, a slight grin pushing up his round cheeks, while Mike, a bit shorter and wearing an oversized tie, hangs his head forward and looks to be scowling. A single photo doesn't reveal much, but it certainly fits the narrative of both boys as they grew into adults chasing their own lives. While rumours of the younger Kiszkan's alleged illegal exploits and time spent in prison likely grew and expanded with time, one person who actually knew him—Mike Kvasnak, the nephew who calls bullshit—says he was simply a man who wanted to have his own life and keep it to himself. By all accounts, Mike was a nice, shy kid. He loved peanut butter and candy, always sharing it with his siblings when he managed to get his hands on some. He once sent Anne a photo of Johnny in his hockey sweater, in an advertisement for a shaving company.

The idea that Mike was some sort of criminal mastermind—as the local legends suggest—seems laughable to those who knew him. But he was a kid who grew up in a desperate time who, it seems, likely resorted to desperate measures.

Mike left the city shortly after his time in the Prince Albert penitentiary, his sister Anne said. He drifted in and out of their lives, rarely keeping in touch. It wasn't overly unusual for a large family to lose touch, especially with the geography between them as they each went off to live their own lives. Like his older brother, Mike would change his name. Two public records from 1953 and 1955 show a Mike Joseph Kiszkan trying to change his last name to Dermac in Regina. According to family, he moved to Alberta and was married for a time to a woman named Lecaira. But the marriage fizzled and they separated without having any children. When Betty (Jacobson) Dupay died, in 1965, her obituary mentioned her two sons, "Johnny Bower of Toronto and Mike Kishkan of Winnipeg." Mike returned to Prince Albert for Betty's funeral, which was one of the few times any of the Kiszkan relatives had seen him in later years—and many would never see him again. A couple of times during Johnny's career with the Leafs, Mike had shown up at the arena after a practice. Johnny would go home and tell Nancy they'd chatted. She never met his brother. Johnny rarely spoke of him, except to make it clear he felt hurt by the way Mike had decided to conduct his life. It was another area of his past that was clearly a sore point, so she didn't want to press him further.

When their stepmother, Polly Kiszkan, died in 1971, Mike was listed in the obituary as still living in Winnipeg. But seven years later, when James passed away, Mike was living in Toronto. It was sometime in the 1970s that he disappeared. Years later, one of Bower's nephews, Fred Buchy, had a friend who was a police detective look into his whereabouts. He learned that Mike had changed his last name to Risko and was living in Toronto. They even found a phone number for him. They thought about reaching out, but Johnny and his sister, Betty Buchy, decided it was best to respect Mike's desire to have no contact with his family or his past.

Years later, the family spoke of Mike in the past tense, as though he'd passed away—believing he had. Anne Batting, his only sibling left, says she's certain that Mike's gone. Although, if he did die, it's not clear when or where. In later years, several write-ups and videos about Johnny's life would mistakenly report that the iconic Leafs goalie was the only son in a family of nine. The two Kiszkan brothers followed vastly different paths through life, starting in the same place but creating their own identity. One impossible to forget—the other lost in anonymity.

20

DUSK

JOHNNY SITS LOW IN HIS CROUCH, HIS HELMET-LESS BUZZ
cut well below the crossbar. His right leather pad is bent slightly
more than the left—bracing to push off. His catcher is turned
so the mitt faces the net, an unorthodox quirk of Johnny's old-
school style. The white boards, blurry in the background, are
made of wood panels. The crease is square and faded under layers
of skate marks. The image carries a blue-grey tint, which gives it
the feeling of a dream. The print is one of 1,967. Bower signed
each one with a silver pen. Produced sometime in the late 1980s,
the print is just another part of the memorabilia machine that
would capitalize on Johnny's legacy as he entered his senior years.
Unlike many famous players, Johnny's fame didn't seem to dissipate with time. His legend only grew as he worked as a Leafs
scout and goalie coach for two decades, before "officially" retiring

from the organization in 1990—at 65 years old, as though he were just another regular working man.

That regular working man had been inducted into the Hockey Hall of Fame 14 years earlier, in 1976. The honour was the greatest thrill of his career, next to winning the Stanley Cup. When he received the news that he'd be forever remembered with the game's most prestigious honour, Johnny broke down and cried. "I was just dumbfounded," he wrote in his autobiography. It was, in many ways, the beginning of Bower's third act. He'd played more games in the minors than most goalies play in their entire career. And he'd somehow found his way to the NHL when many goalies would be retiring. Once there, he became the best of a generation.

Debate would always swirl about the greatest of the era. It was certainly never a title that Bower would claim for himself. Not with goalies like Terry Sawchuk, Glenn Hall, Jacques Plante and Gump Worsley around. By the flawed measure of goals-against average alone, Bower was near the top of that list. When factoring in an adjusted save percentage for the era, as hockey historian Iain Fyffe did, Bower consistently topped the other contenders over a 10-year period from 1955–56 through to 1964–65. Over that time (of which of course, he was still in the minors for the first three seasons), Johnny never posted an adjusted save percentage below .906. When applying a weighted save percentage that factors in minutes played over an entire 10-year period, Johnny's .914 mark beat each of Plante, Hall, Worsley and Sawchuk. In fact, Johnny posted the best adjusted save percentage in the NHL in all but two seasons between 1959–60 and 1964–65. (Along with

Worsley, Bower missed tying Hall for the top spot in 1963 by one one-thousandth of a point). Add in the fact that Johnny was the oldest player in the league through the majority of his NHL career, and it's hard to argue that he wasn't the best goalie of his time. In fact, there's a strong case to be made—as Punch Imlach did—that he was the best athlete of the era as well.

Decades after he'd finished playing, Johnny passed on his legacy in the game first-hand through a goalie school that operated in the Toronto area for several years. Young netminders as young as six up to the junior ranks came out to learn the position from one of the best to ever play it. Even though the way goaltenders played the game had changed dramatically, evolving from the traditional stand-up school to the butterfly style, Johnny remained relevant. He understood the changes but also the unmoving foundations of the position—the angles, the reflexes, the read on each play before it happens. Few had Bower's instincts. And a generation of goalies came to listen to a legend pass on his wisdom. Among them was a talented young player with an unorthodox style that relied entirely on athleticism. His name was Curtis Joseph—and soon, he'd star in the same net that Johnny once had. In his own way, Joseph would pass on Bower's legacy to a future generation of goalies who watched him play with awe.

But that was only part of what would keep Johnny's legend going. It was also the stories of thousands of fans who'd watched his remarkable feats first-hand and then met the superhuman workingman they'd marvelled at from afar. The legend was built not only on Johnny's miraculous feats but also on the character he exemplified. Through the 1980s and 1990s, Johnny would sign autographs for hours, taking photos and interacting with adoring fans. He would take the time to show each person that he was like them. It was how he supplemented his income after a career of making far less than he should have. Being a legend was a full-time job, and Johnny treated it with nearly the same commitment he'd given in his playing days. But it wasn't all for monetary gain. Johnny attached himself to charities, rarely saying no to appearances that would benefit one of the many, many causes he supported. He went to SickKids hospital several times each year, a cause that was deeply close to his heart. He almost never denied the many requests he received to appear at minor-league hockey banquets or to drop a puck at a tournament. In later years, he'd regularly visit the veterans care facility at Sunnybrook Hospital in Toronto. He'd do so much work in his community that he'd be named the honorary chief of the regional police department in Peel, an enormous suburban area west of Toronto where he and Nancy moved in retirement.

In all the ways he gave back to a world that had taken him well beyond his dreams, Johnny remained a constant while other stars naturally began to fade. Many of the fans who adored him never sat in the wooden seats of Maple Leaf Gardens through the glory days of the 1960s. They never counted down the final seconds to a Stanley Cup win or felt the rush of a roaring crowd as it poured onto Carlton Street. But the halcyon prints on their walls . . . the photos next to a grinning icon . . . that careful, perfectly symmetrical signature on a hockey card, practised and practised so it would be legible—all of those relics, and the memories they carried, were part of the collective, ever-growing memory of who Johnny Bower was. The ageless one remained a present-day fixture from the past—a memory for those who lived it, a legend for those who didn't. He gave life to the faint cheers of the old Gardens on Carlton Street. You could feel the first-period chill, hear that organ song, smell the popcorn in the lobby. Johnny became a living memory, a boy who found his dream and passed it on.

And as Bower settled into his life as a full-time hockey legend, he soon became a full-time grandpa legend too. As the family grew larger, the cottage near Bobcaygeon remained a constant source of memories. John Jr. and his wife had two boys. Cindy had two daughters—and Barb did too. Suddenly, it seemed, the Bower family had more than doubled in size. No longer able to fit the whole crew in a three-bedroom bungalow, Bower went to work building two new cabins on the property. He called them "Cozy Cabin One" and "Cozy Cabin Two."

Each summer throughout their youth, Barb's and Cindy's daughters would spend about a month with their grandparents at the cottage. And Johnny took every opportunity he could to take the grandkids out on an adventure. They would go hunting for frogs in the reeds or go fishing off the dock. He'd teach them how to drive on a side road. He'd work the pedals while they slowly steered. (They were never supposed to tell their grandmother, but Nancy always knew.) And every once in a while, Johnny would take them down to the dump, where still-useful items were lined up out front for sale. Johnny would barter with the manager for the best deals. He was able to pick up some old bikes for the cottage that way.

Sometimes, after their dumpsite bargain hunting, they'd drive a little farther in, where they could sometimes spot bears scavenging for food. He'd pile the kids into his truck and drive into downtown Bobcaygeon to get ice cream or pick up some goodies at the bakery. Then they'd sit on a bench at the marina and watch the boats come in and out while Johnny told them stories about growing up in Prince Albert—like the time he and his friends took some horses out on a trail, except his horse ran off and he had to walk five miles back into town along the train tracks. The tales always seemed just a little too tall to be true, but he enthralled them with his storytelling. Each one had a moral—some underlying message about the importance of hard work, perseverance or kindness.

They'd be interrupted every time by passing strangers who recognized Johnny and stopped to shake his hand and ask for an autograph. He was gracious with each one. For the girls, it was just part of life with their grandfather. It was part of his existence as an old hockey legend. He was every bit a grandfather but a celebrity too. If he took them to a game, he'd disappear for a half-hour with a simple trip to the concession stand or the washroom. There was no way he could pass by the countless people who wanted to say hello. Signing his name became habitual, almost a given in any interaction. He rarely left the house without a few sharpies and small pictures to sign.

Once when he took his granddaughter Staci to a Toronto Raptors game, a trip to the concession turned into another marathon greeting session. When he finally returned to his seat, he'd forgotten that he'd planned to get a hot dog. But he did have a new stuffed Raptor doll for Staci, which he'd signed for her. It was an odd thing to do, to sign a professional signature on an item for your grandchild. But that action had become automatic. And the full signature was the only way Johnny would write out his name, in that perfectly legible cursive that adorns the memorabilia in the homes of so many hockey fans. Even when the grandkids had a birthday, he would sign their cards "Johnny Bower"—while Nancy would add, "Love Grandma and Grandpa."

Johnny often found ways to give his grandkids small gifts, even though—as they noticed with age—he'd rarely spent more than $20 on a pair of jeans. One gift, in particular, would always stick with his grandson Bruce.

When they were up at the cottage, Johnny often went out fishing with John Jr. and his two grandsons after dinner. The four Bower men would pile into the boat and head out, searching the reefs and drop-offs of Little Bald Lake for walleye, bass and muskie until sunset. They talked the language of boys in a boat—about school, about the sports they played, about the Leafs, about the chores that needed doing, about projects they dreamed of starting.

Back on shore, the boys worked alongside their grandfather and father, working away to repair the dock, the roof, the boat-house and whatever else was needed to keep that treasured place functioning. The boys learned how to keep a house from falling down. They learned that every nail could be used more than once and that even the bent ones could be hammered back into working form. Johnny kept a jar for the nails he'd pulled from old projects and refurbished for future use. He fastened it to the wall above the workbench he built in the boathouse, along with all the old nuts and bolts he'd salvaged.

One day when Bruce was about 13 years old, he was in the boathouse with his grandfather and noticed a fishing rod he hadn't seen before hanging from the rafters.

"What kind of rod is that?" he asked his grandfather.

"Well," Johnny said, looking up. "That's a fly rod."

He climbed up and pulled it down to show his grandson how to use it. He found some poppers to tie to the line, which bass would take. They went out to the dock, and Johnny spent the afternoon showing his grandson how to fly-fish. Bruce fell in love with the sport right away.

"You can borrow the rod whenever you want, Bruce," Johnny told his grandson. "You just have to take care of it."

When he was old enough to drive the boat, Bruce would always wake up at sunrise to go fishing. Each morning, he'd stop by the boathouse and pick up the fly rod. He practised and practised his technique until he finally felt the tug of a catch, and he was hooked.

Years later, when he was a grown man with kids of his own, Bruce had become an avid fly-fisher. He'd travel all over the country, mastering his craft—learning everything he could take in about how to get better. "That's one thing with fly fishing, you never stop learning," Bruce says, echoing his grandfather, who often said the same thing about the sport he played. "I'm still learning."

And although he's accumulated quite a collection of gear over the years, his prized rod remains the grey one with the Scientific

Anglers reel that his grandfather pulled down from the rafters in that boathouse nearly three decades ago.

"It works fine, and that's one thing my grandfather always taught me," Bruce says with a laugh. "If it's not busted, and it works fine, why get a new one?"

The Bower cottage lasted through nearly four decades of summer adventures, wild storms and packed Thanksgiving dinners. It held the imaginations of the three Bower kids, and it did the same for their children—until they too were grown and busy with charting their own paths. Trips to Bobcaygeon became less and less frequent with each new season. The work that had once seemed routine became more and more difficult to get done as Johnny pushed into his 80s—though he'd never admit it. Despite his age, Johnny tried to operate as he always had. He shunned offers of help. He wanted to mow the grass, tend to the garden and fix all the cracks and leaks that constantly plagued the old goalie-stick-shaped bungalow. Nancy and the kids tried to tell Bower that he needed to slow down and pass some of the tasks on to hired help. He continued to press forward, believing he could do it himself. He broke several bones that way—like the time he slipped off the roof and onto the outdoor shower he'd built beside the house, cracking several ribs in the fall. He had Nancy wrap his torso tight and tried to get right back out on the roof before his grandkids stopped him.

Johnny was so used to being ageless that he wasn't sure how to handle time's inevitable victory. He was frustrated that his body struggled to do what it always could—or to heal as quickly as it always had. In the early 2000s, heart surgery forced Bower to slow down much more than he wanted. Even though he relented, it soon became apparent that the cottage had become an untenable burden, despite all the joyful memories it carried. As long as his heart was beating, Johnny would always try to maintain the property himself—and that reality now ran the very real possibility of being what could actually kill him.

The decision to sell the cottage in 2010 was one of the hardest that Johnny and Nancy ever had to make. It had been their extension of Waskesiu, the place where they had met and built their lives. It was their own private paradise, where they'd withstood vicious storms and ill-timed power outages and come away with a lifetime of memories. Nancy didn't want to lose it. She tried to convince Johnny that he could hire people to take care of the garden, the lawn, the weeding and all the other endless upkeep of cottage life. But he refused to hand over the cottage maintenance needs to an outside source. And with Cozy Cabins One and Two being vacant more and more often, it was difficult to justify the place. Johnny and Nancy both felt empty and broken when they officially sold the cottage. It was difficult to clear out the property and prepare to hand the keys over to another family. They kept busy on that last day, distracting themselves with the endless to-do list that comes with any move. But before sunset, they took a moment to sit on the picnic table that faced out over Little Bald Lake. Johnny put his arm around Nancy. With tears in their eyes, side by side, they watched the sun slowly set, one last time.

"IT WAS A PRIVILEGE"

Johnny woke up early, put on his best suit and tie, and made sure he was ready for his ride. It was three and a half hours from his bungalow in Mississauga, Ontario, to the Cathedral of the Most Blessed Sacrament in Detroit, Michigan. It was a long haul for a 91-year-old man—even one who was famous for his longevity. But an old friend was leaving and Johnny wasn't going to miss his goodbye. It was June 15, 2016, and Mr. Hockey had died.

Pat Boutette left his house in London, Ontario, at the break of dawn to drive a couple of hours east to pick up Johnny, whom he first met when he joined the Leafs as a rookie in 1975, when Johnny worked as an assistant coach for Red Kelly, who'd taken over as the bench boss. Sometimes in practice, Johnny would still put on his pads and take shots from the new generation of Leafs whenever they needed a spare goalie. Now that he was retired, no one could force him to wear a mask. He'd have played every day if they'd let him, Boutette recalled. Johnny still had the reflexes to match his undying competitive streak. Boutette felt a great affinity for Johnny, and the two had remained in touch over the years. Recently, they'd been chatting and Howe's failing health had come up. Johnny hadn't been able to see his old fishing friend as much as usual in recent years, since Howe had begun a battle with dementia and suffered a stroke. Johnny had struggled with the effects of old age himself. He'd lived as healthily as he could after a scare with his heart, but he'd refused to slow down when it came to chores around the yard or making public appearances. With his failing eyesight, however, he was unable to continue driving. So Boutette told Johnny that if Howe passed away they'd travel down to Detroit for the memorial service together. Mark Howe had called Boutette to let him know his father wasn't in good shape two days before he died. Boutette called up Johnny and told him to be ready. Picking up his old coach would tack on an extra four hours of driving for Boutette, but that was a small price to pay for some extra time with a 91-year-old icon.

Johnny was waiting when Boutette pulled up in his Ford F-150 at around 7:30 a.m. He shuffled out the front door of his suburban bungalow, marked with two crossed goalie sticks beneath the street number. It was the place he and Nancy had decided to make their last home together after the stairs in a townhome they'd downsized to had become too difficult to navigate.

On the long drive to Detroit, Johnny told Boutette stories about those long-ago days back in Waskesiu, when Howe would come help him work the grill at the restaurant, and when they'd spend early mornings sitting fishing together out on the lake. Hockey had bound them. They'd both been the best in their time and were athletic enough to play well beyond the years that lesser athletes could sustain. They were both beloved by fans in a way that transcended generations—much like baseball's Ruth, DiMaggio, Williams or Mantle, although Stan Musial was probably a more apt comparison to their personas.

But hockey wasn't all that joined them. Like Gordie, Johnny was adored by so many not only because of what he'd done but also because of who he was while doing it—and who he remained long after. Gordie and Johnny were both outsized talents with astonishing humility. They were country boys from Saskatchewan who never abandoned their simple roots, despite the fame they achieved. And for both, family was everything. Gordie had found his love in Colleen, who became the fire behind the Howe brand after he was taken advantage of for years. Much like Nancy, she kept the family going while Gordie played. She was Howe's world, and when Colleen was overcome by Pick's disease and her memories faded away, he clung to her as tightly as he ever had. He took her skating on the Rideau Canal and bought her favourite birthday cake. He sang to her, danced with her and held her close—and while her memory clouded over and faded away, she remembered Gordie until the day she died. He'd fallen into a depression when she left, from which he was eventually lifted only when he returned to greeting fans and signing autographs. Being Mr. Hockey brought him back for a time.

It wasn't hard to imagine Johnny falling in the same way had he lost Nancy first. She was the force behind his life. He loved her madly, through seven decades. They still danced together in the kitchen and watched Leafs game side by side in matching chairs in their living room. They went for coffee dates to Tim Hortons and knew the staff by name at their local Swiss Chalet. They filled their life with time spent with their kids and grandkids—and, eventually, tiny little great grandkids too. Just as Johnny had treated his children's children to ice cream trips to town and frog-hunting adventures by the lakeshore, Gordie would take his grandkids for long walks along the beach. They called him "Peepaw." And when they grew tired he'd scoop them up in his hulking arms and carry them home to Colleen, whom they called "Honey." In the course of their lives, Johnny and Gordie had traced remarkably similar paths to the kind of men they'd become.

Between his stories, Johnny stared out the window and silently watched the countryside pass by. It was a grey, rainy morning when they crossed the border into Detroit. When they arrived at the church, they entered a side door off the parking lot to avoid the mob of reporters that stood out front, trying to get comments from generations of hockey stars who had come to pay tribute to one of the game's greatest players. Inside the cathedral, Johnny and Boutette were seated on the right side of the altar, in a private area shielded from most of the church. Johnny sat next to his good friend Walter Gretzky and his son Wayne. He was quietly emotional as he watched the service, while Howe's youngest son, Murray, shared the lessons he'd learned in life from his father.

When it was over—after he'd said his personal, final good-bye to his old friend—Johnny wanted to leave as quickly as possible. Out front, reporters strained to try to get a word from the passing stars, but once again Johnny slipped out a side door and climbed into Boutette's truck. He just didn't have it in him that day to play the gracious, smiling hero. Boutette and Johnny crossed back into Canada and stopped to grab a hamburger in Windsor. It was a special occasion, Johnny told Boutette, so he'd put $20 in his pocket to buy lunch. They passed the rest of the journey telling old stories about the game, and life and Howe. They arrived back in Mississauga around 7 p.m., passing Johnny Bower Park, a playground that backed onto a small pond a couple of doors from his house. Every morning, Johnny walked over to the park that carried his name after the local community pushed to honour their famous neighbour. There, around the monkey bars and slide, he'd bend over to pick up the pieces of litter that had been left behind in the bustle of the busy families that passed through each day. After all, the park was named for him—and so, he believed, it was his duty to keep it tidy.

Along with the park beside his home and the street sign of Patika Avenue, where he and Nancy had raised their kids, Johnny's name had been affixed to many places across the city of Toronto. It also adorned the atrium of a new arena in Prince Albert. And it hung high in the rafters of Air Canada Centre, where his image and number hung alongside the Leafs' most revered names. A statue of Johnny was unveiled in front of Air Canada Centre in 2014 as part of Legends Row—a hockey bench holding the Leafs' all-time greats. He bore each new honour with a sense of responsibility, so grateful that he seemed determined to continue to earn it. Even as he'd tipped into his 90s, Johnny was a near-constant presence at Air Canada Centre. Every so often a spotlight would shine on the Leafs' alumni box and find Bower, to the delight of thousands of fans, most of whom had never seen him play live. But they knew who he was and they knew what he meant. It was impossible not to.

Johnny would wait by the door at his house, watching through the window for the driver the Leafs would send to bring him to the games. "Driver's late again," he'd often complain out loud. When the car finally pulled up, he'd grab his favourite blue cap with the white logo and fit it firmly on his head. He'd journey down the Queen Elizabeth Way, onto the Gardiner Expressway, where the spotlights from Air Canada Centre would punctuate the Toronto city skyline beneath the CN Tower. When he arrived beneath the arena, Drew Rogers would be waiting for him.

Rogers was in charge of alumni relations for the Leafs, organizing all the former team stars who came out to support Maple Leaf Sports and Entertainment at corporate and charity functions. Despite the fact that Rogers was only in his early 30s, he and Johnny had become good friends over the years. They always bantered back and forth. He'd call Johnny up and say, "How's my favourite goalie in the world, Terry Sawchuk . . ." And Johnny would laugh every time. One year, during a home game around his birthday, Johnny was wary of a big fuss being made. Rogers had to come up with an excuse for Johnny to interact with fans on camera during a stoppage in play. When he appeared on the big screen, the entire Air Canada Centre sang happy birthday to him.

Johnny stood there red-faced—duped by Rogers again. Another time, Rogers and Nancy both gave Johnny a hard time when he finished near the top of a fan poll to determine the all-time greatest Leafs. "Turk Broda would have had my vote!" Nancy jabbed.

When Johnny would arrive at Air Canada Centre for the half-dozen or so games he attended each year, he would often stop in the hallway near the visitor's locker room, marvelling at the young players' athleticism. Then he'd make his way towards the elevator in the Toronto Raptors' locker room, which usually took a while because he stopped to shake so many hands and take so many photographs. "All the girls loved him," Rogers says. Johnny suffered from a sore shoulder, and when fans came up to say hi they often gave him a loving pat on the arm. He'd never say anything, but as soon as the elevator would close, he'd clutch his shoulder, clench his teeth and let out a loud, painful sigh. Even in his old age, Johnny's body took a beating. When they finally made it to the Leafs' alumni box upstairs, Johnny would settle into the same spot every time. It was known as "Johnny's corner." The box had two rows of seats, with a standing-room area behind it. Johnny didn't like to take up a seat that guests could be sitting in, so he always insisted that he stand. But the layout of the box meant that a bench was needed for anyone behind the seats to stand on if they wanted to see the game. For Johnny to see, he actually needed two benches stacked on top of each other. Even though it scared everyone around him, Johnny would climb up on the benches—nearly two feet off the ground—and watch the game from there. And unlike others in the box, Johnny was there to *watch* the game.

He wanted to see how the team was doing and how the goalies played. At the Leafs' home opener on October 7, 2017, Bower told Rogers how bad he felt for New York Rangers goalie Henrik Lundqvist, who allowed several goals in what would be an 8–5 loss to the Leafs.

A month later, on November 8, Johnny's closest friends gathered to celebrate his 93rd birthday at a large Chinese restaurant in Toronto's west end. Several of his old teammates, including Frank Mahovlich, Bob Baun, Dick Duff and Ron Ellis, were there. Johnny wore a black dress shirt and a grey sport coat with a small Maple Leafs pin on his lapel. He stood with his head hung forward, his chin almost to his chest, while the room sang happy birthday to him. Johnny slowly lifted his right arm to his eyes and wiped away the tears that welled beneath his silver-rimmed glasses. He shook his head slowly. It was the first time Baun had seen his old friend be that emotional in public.

But Johnny's soft side was well known to his family. He was prone to tearing up around Nancy and the kids over the slightest gesture of kindness. "Oh, it would kill him to have to punish his kids," his daughter Cindy says. He was a gentle person too, Nancy says—it didn't matter if he was interacting with a child or an animal. He maintained a number of bird feeders in the backyard and always fed the squirrels that ran by (unless they tried to steal the birdseed—then he shooed them off). He gave names to the regulars. Johnny also kept a box of Milk-Bone dog treats in his garage that he would give out to dogs as they passed by on walks. Neighbourhood dogs would reflexively drag their owners towards

Johnny and Nancy's home. He was always puttering around the garage—would have lived there, if he could, his daughters say. If he was out in the yard and saw a dog out for a walk around the pond behind the house, he'd make sure he was out front waiting with a treat when the dog and its owner came back up the sidewalk.

Even at 93, Johnny was in great health for his age. When he'd had heart surgery 17 years earlier, the doctor told him he was certain he'd have another 20 years. Now it looked as if that was an understatement. Johnny still made as many as five appearances at charity events some weeks. He was by far the most active and engaged alumni the Leafs had. "He was easily the most involved in the community out of any guy who has ever worn the jersey," Rogers said. A couple of nights after his birthday, Johnny once again waited for the driver to pick him up and take him to Air Canada Centre. The Leafs were playing the Boston Bruins, and Johnny watched intently from his double-stacked benches. As usual, Johnny left the game five minutes before the end of the third period, as he always did to avoid the crowds that would consume him if he left with the masses. This time the Leafs trailed 2–1. He hated leaving early, knowing he might miss something important. That evening, on November 10, no one thought much of Johnny's departure. He would be back; of course, he would—he always was. Through the last five decades, there was nothing more constant with the Leafs than the knowledge that Johnny Bower would be there. He took the elevator down to the main floor with Rogers, and as they walked beneath the stands, James van Riemsdyk scored to tie the game for the Leafs with less than a minute to go. Johnny heard the faint cheers of the fans above him before he climbed into the car and left the arena, heading into the night. He was listening on the car radio as Patrick Marleau scored the winning goal for Toronto in overtime.

Ten days before Christmas—shortly after attending another event where he met with fans—Nancy noticed that Johnny was battling a nagging cough. He didn't complain about it. He never would. And he didn't seem to be in pain—although, he wouldn't let on about that, either. But the cough was starting to get worse, more forceful. "He shook with it," Nancy says. It wasn't going away. He seemed lethargic during the day, falling asleep on the sofa when Cindy came to visit. Later, he woke up in the middle of the night and wasn't able to stop coughing, his body shaking. A day later, he wasn't himself, and Nancy called an ambulance. Johnny went to Credit Valley Hospital and was diagnosed with pneumonia on December 18. A day later, he started to do a bit better, no doubt trying his best not to have to miss an appearance at the Leafs' centennial celebration that evening, for which he'd been selected as the seventh-greatest Leaf of all time. The nurses who came in to care for him marvelled at his strength despite his age. Up to the last couple of years, Johnny had remained active, still walking fairways when he golfed, until he started to have trouble breathing. Even then, he'd often sneak out to his park and practise chipping over the walkway. His physical strength hardly wavered. "He had arms and legs of steel," Nancy says.

But even Superman was mortal. And despite his brief turn-around, Johnny's pneumonia settled in, and as Christmas neared, the family was told it didn't look good. He was fading in and out of consciousness now. The family invited one of their close friends, Father Mark Curtis, to come to visit Johnny in his hospital room. Johnny loved to attend the Christmas concerts put on by the Anglican priest, who was famous for his singing. Father Mark held Johnny's hand and placed his other hand gently on his head. When he heard his voice, Johnny opened his eyes. As he sat beside Johnny, Father Mark sang "O Holy Night." Johnny smiled slightly, tears welling in his eyes. Then he closed them, falling back into his dreams. By Christmas Eve, John Jr. had arrived from Calgary, Alberta, joining Nancy, Cindy and Barbara at his bedside. Johnny had been unconscious all day, but when his son arrived and held his father's hand, he opened his eyes and said, "John."

"He knew we were all there," says Cindy.

On Christmas Day, they sat next to him while he slept. He never opened his eyes, but he seemed restful with them near. They chatted to him as though he could hear, recalling old, happy stories. They played some of his favourite songs, including one final rendition of "Honky the Christmas Goose." Nancy sat beside him, with her hand cradling Johnny's head, talking him through to the end. She and Barbara stayed Christmas evening and slept overnight in the hospital room, next to him. Nancy held Johnny through the night. Shortly after four in the morning, still holding tight, Nancy felt him slip away.

IN THE DAYS that followed Johnny's death, the family was flooded with tributes to his legendary life. Letters and cards arrived at the house from people across Canada and the United States, telling stories of what he had meant to them. There were stories of the people he'd met in person, or those he'd taken the time to write to. One person wrote in about the time he and Johnny had shared a grilled cheese sandwich. Another about the time he sat next to Johnny as they both got their hair cut. There were stories of the impact he had on the charities and causes he gave his time to, from veterans to sick children. A small memorial appeared at Johnny Bower Park with pictures of all the dogs who used to come and get treats from him, with letters from their owners, placed inside a cookie jar next to candles.

A private funeral was held, where Johnny's old teammates came to pay their last respects. They sat together in a row, remembering the tough old man who used to lie about his age, who was always fun to pull pranks on and who was one of the kindest friends they'd ever had. Armstrong said it felt like he'd lost a brother. Baun said the world just wasn't the same without Bower in it. At the memorial, Father Mark sang "Danny Boy," one of Johnny's favourite songs. Barbara spoke about the kind of dad her father was. And Ron Ellis shared stories about the humility and honour Johnny had carried throughout his life. He shared a phrase that he'd learned Johnny had told his grandkids about his time as a Maple Leaf. "It was a privilege, not a right," he said. Johnny's words were later painted above the players' stalls in the Leafs locker room.

In early January, a larger celebration of Johnny's life was held at Air Canada Centre, attended by the game's dignitaries. Gary Bettman, the NHL commissioner, and Bill Daly, the deputy commissioner, attended. Lou Lamoriello, the boy who shared his mother's delicious Italian cooking with Bower, was there too, representing the Leafs as the team's general manager. "Your dad *is* the Maple Leafs sweater," Lamoriello told Cindy Bower. The room was filled with former teammates, staff, scouts and coaches who'd experienced the glory years of the 1960s alongside Johnny. Legends from later eras, like Doug Gilmour and Darryl Sittler, came to pay their respects—because for them, Johnny was still, in his own endless way, a part of their teams too. Even Yvan Cournoyer, of the rival Montreal Canadiens that fell to Toronto in '67, came out to honour Johnny. Dave Keon, speaking about what he had meant to the Leafs through those four Stanley Cups, said, "Johnny was our soul."

Later, before the Leafs played the Tampa Bay Lightning, four generations of the Bower family were welcomed to the ice, led by Nancy, while a video tribute to his legendary life played on the scoreboard screen overhead. Everyone in the arena froze, watching the story unfold. Johnny's name was one of the few that overcame the amnesia of time. Like Richard and Beliveau, Gretzky and Orr. Like Howe. But Johnny's long echo had been all the more remarkable because he'd spent so much of his time on course towards being forgotten. More than a decade in the minors and yet ovations at every appearance, regardless.

Watching the broadcast from her nursing home in Castlegar, B.C., Anne Batting said, "That's my brother" when a shot of Johnny's picture and retired number was shown hanging in the rafters. She was eating beet borscht, a Ukrainian treat she and her siblings enjoyed as kids, to remember him. She scoffed when a video tribute to Johnny's life said that he was "the second of nine children, no brothers, eight sisters." Once again, the story was wrong. And once again, "Mikey" had been forgotten. Even in Johnny's death, the details were hazy.

The tribute showed fragments of Bower's legendary life, from his speech standing next to Gordie Howe after winning the Stanley Cup, to his beloved appearances as Santa Claus, to him still driving a golf ball in his 90s. "Along the way, Johnny has made more appearances in the community than any Leafs player in history," the narrator, Joe Bowen, said. "And he most certainly holds the record for standing ovations at the Air Canada Centre."

When it was over, it was time for another. The thousands stood, cheering and clapping one final time for Johnny. As she looked around the arena while her husband's life was celebrated, Nancy was grateful for the show of love. But she felt empty too. It was 70 years, gone just like that. "Is it really true?" she thought. Nancy shook her head and wiped a tear from beneath her glasses. The ovation carried on as Johnny's image appeared across the entire surface of ice, falling across his family. It was him in old age, wearing a grey jacket with a Leafs crest, his arms stretched out, acknowledging the crowd. Then Nancy heard the familiar words drifting from the stands.

"Go Leafs go . . ."

It rose slowly.

"Go Leafs go . . ."

And Nancy could feel Johnny saying it too. She clapped her hands, hard. And then, once more, for him.

"Go Leafs go," she said.

EPILOGUE
NO BEGINNING, NO END

INSIDE THE HOME MARKED BY CROSSED HOCKEY STICKS, Johnny Bower's life is laid out in layers. There is no beginning, middle or end. Just the pieces of his world he chose to display. Photos of his family line the fireplace mantel, with grandkids and great grandkids taking up the fridge. A picture of James Kiszkan in old age hangs in the bedroom. On the wall in the living room there is a photograph of Nancy embracing John as they laugh in front of his statue at Air Canada Centre. One of Johnny holding his goalie stick as he stands in the spotlight, looking to the ice, taken when his sweater was officially retired by the Leafs and he pinched himself, right then and there, just to see if it was true. And there is a photo of Johnny and Nancy, seven decades as one, standing in the same living room, wearing Leafs sweaters as they cheer with hands high in the air after watching a Toronto win.

Out back, past the sunroom where he kept the plaques celebrating his biggest fish, several bird feeders sit empty. Nancy shakes her head at the thought of her husband's commitment to the hobby.

"We've got three birdhouses out there and you wonder why we've got the mice," she says. "Come spring they're underneath that shed and you wonder why they're under there. Because the big can of birdseed's in the shed. But I couldn't convince him not to feed the birds."

Nancy has lived two months without him. Spring will be the first new season with him gone. She laughs softly, looking out at the grass peeking through the patches of melting snow.

"It took a long time for him to agree to have somebody cut this lawn," she says. He was 91 before he'd reluctantly hire a caretaker. "I used to kid him, 'It's not your goal net.' Come on."

But he liked to keep his yard and to putter around the house, she says. The garage was his favourite spot. He was in there just a few months earlier when someone stopped by in a U-Haul and asked him to sign their kitchen table. The house is filled with memories like that—remarkable moments that just became a normal part of life as a Bower. Nancy has filled a box with letters and cards she's managed to respond to. She has another one full of letters and cards that still need a reply. One letter from the Patterson family makes special note of Bower's small acts of kindness, with a photo of Rusty the goldendoodle looking into the camera with big brown eyes. She might keep that one for her scrapbook, which is almost finished—filled with stories and photos that she cut out of the papers when he passed, along with letters and cards of meaningful note.

The basement is a museum, filled with relics. There are photos and tribute paintings from each of the Stanley Cup wins. Newspaper cartoons from way back to his days in Cleveland. A photograph of him and Terry Sawchuk, smiling and crouching side by side. A picture of Bower with his old friend from the Barons, Bob Ochs. A plaque from his induction to the Cleveland Barons Hall of Fame.

"Oh, this is a favourite of mine," Nancy says, pointing to a large sketch of Johnny in a checkered suit, reading from a storybook titled *Johnny Bower, Cleveland Barons Star Goalie*—the story of his minor-league legend. "Look at that suit!" she says, pointing. "Holy cow."

The first pads, blocker and catcher he wore as a Leaf are framed in a display case. A model replica of Maple Leaf Gardens sits up high on a shelf. At the bar in the corner is an old bottle of wine with his image on it. There's a Molson Canadian can with his likeness too. On the wall behind hangs a cartoon drawing of George Armstrong shooting arrows at Bower instead of pucks. "Chief, I don't think other goaltenders practice like this," a sweating Bower is saying, with several arrows stuck in his pads. It's signed, "Happy birthday, to a very special guy, with best wishes and our love, the Armstrongs." It was drawn by George's daughter, Betty-Ann, Nancy says. She looks around for the last bottle of the champagne Johnny had taken from the locker room when the Leafs won in 1967. They'd planned to open it when Toronto won its next Cup, but in the midst of this long drought, they sipped the first at their 50th wedding anniversary. There's still one left, somewhere there, waiting for a reason to toast.

But the artifacts reach back further still. By the bar, the pads he wore when he played for the Vernon Military All-Stars sit in a glass case. A photo of the team, with each player's name carefully written on the back, hangs on the wall down the hall. Near it is another old black and white photograph—this one of the M&C Warhawks. He sits in the centre of the photograph in a striped sweater, holding the provincial championship trophy.

"He's just a boy," Nancy says. "And that's when John's name was still Kiszkan . . . I can't give you any information on that."

All these years and she's still not quite certain why her husband became a Bower. When they first met, he didn't say anything about it at all. Eventually when she did ask, he said he'd just thought of changing the name on a whim because it sounded good. It was easier for the press, he said. But Nancy never bought the story that it was because others struggled with Kiszkan. "It's an easy name," she says. Still, Nancy didn't question it. There was no reason to. "He was Bower when I met him," she says. And together, they made that mean something entirely their own.

In Johnny's workshop in the basement behind the row of photos, his tools are laid out where he'd placed them last—and reused jars hold nuts, bolts and refurbished nails that he used to hold their house together. He fiddled around in there right to the end, Nancy says. Always trying to fix whatever he could. Above his workbench, Johnny had posted several more photographs of the two of them together. Heading up the stairs from the basement, Nancy points out the framed photograph of a sunset at the cottage, and another from the lake. "And that's the prairies," she says, pointing at the fields of golden wheat, dotted with grain elevators, in the painting at the top of the stairs.

At the front door, on the way out, Johnny's favourite blue and white Leafs cap hangs on the coat rack, where he'd left it. A short drive away, the names of those once loved and lost mark row upon row of headstones at Glen Oaks cemetery. A narrow road weaves through the graves, leading to a mausoleum that overlooks a small pond lined with trees. Inside, white marbled walls hold tributes to hundreds more lives. On the far edge of one of the rows, closest to the window, a bronze chest sits behind the glass. A blue and white fly-fishing lure rests beside it, tied by a grandson who still dreams about casting out his reel next to his grandfather on the dock. In unadorned lettering, the chest is engraved "John W Bower." There are no dates. No beginning, no end—just a name, and everything it carries.

ACKNOWLEDGEMEMTS

Several years ago, I spoke with Johnny Bower for a story I was writing for *Sportsnet* magazine about the greatest Maple Leafs of all time. It was an enormous privilege for me to speak with him. As I wrote for *Sportsnet* then, I belong to a different generation than most Johnny Bower fans. I'm too young to have sat in the wooden seats of Maple Leaf Gardens through the glory years of the 1960s. I've never counted down the final seconds to a Stanley Cup win or felt the rush of a roaring crowd as it poured onto Carlton Street. But Johnny meant something to me, all the same.

When I was a kid, my aunt gave me a framed painting of Johnny Bower, a limited-edition print, number 968 of 1,967. He signed it personally in silver ink—"To Danny"—immediately making it my most prized piece of art. The silver frame had a light blue trim to match the blue-grey tint of the painting. It carried the feeling of a dream. That painting hung on the wall of my bedroom, on top of the airplane wallpaper, next to the plaques and team photos of my minor-hockey career, when my goalie pads were brown like his. The painting came with me when I went away to university and to every apartment I've lived in since. I never saw Johnny play live, but I imagined the chill at Maple Leaf Gardens and the smell of popcorn in the lobby. I could hear the cheers of fans who have become mothers and fathers, grandparents and ghosts. Johnny's painting tied me to something I wanted deeply to be a part of. Dreams beget dreams; they're passed on.

And so, Johnny transcended time in a way that few athletes, few people, ever do. He held—he holds—a unique place in our hearts and minds. I don't mean to belabour the point. But it's important to me that I thank the legend in the painting that hung on the wall of my childhood bedroom—the one who helped inspire the pursuit of some sort of a dream, regardless of where it wound up.

Thank you to the Bower family. I am indebted to you for your graciousness and trust. The marvellous Nancy Bower was generous, kind, funny and strong throughout our many meetings. Cindy, Barbara and John Jr. were patient with my many requests and so helpful in sharing the legacy of a beloved father who had recently passed. Thank you for the honour of telling his story. I hope it reflects what he meant to you and to the people who cherished him.

Thank you to the many family members, teammates and friends

who took the time to share their stories about Johnny. And thank you, too, to the writers and historians who generously shared their insights and research with me. To the newspaper and magazine writers who came before, preserving the details that keep moments alive. To the Prince Albert Historical Society—to Ken Guedo—for your selfless help in maintaining the history of your great city and its stories. I can't thank you enough.

Thank you to Paul Patskou, a peerless researcher and fact checker, without whom a book like this wouldn't be possible.

To Sportsnet, for granting me the time needed to pursue this project. And to my colleagues there, whose work inspires and challenges me every day.

To my agent, Rick Broadhead, a friend and constant support. I couldn't ask to work with anyone better.

Thank you to Patricia MacDonald for your thorough copyedits and to Lloyd Davis for your critical eye on the proofread.

Thank you to the team at HarperCollins for believing in me as a storyteller and giving me an opportunity I couldn't have dreamed of. As always, it has been a pleasure to work with you. To Jim Gifford, to Noelle Zitzer, and to the entire group who has put up with me on several projects now. And to Kate Cassaday, a tireless and brilliant editor: Thank you for championing this project and for your invaluable eye for a story. And for embracing my 4 a.m. chapter submissions, long after they were due. A project like this could never happen without someone like you guiding it and believing in it.

Thank you to my family and friends, who always support me. To Jayme, my inspiration—for our life together and all its crazy adventures. To Mom, Jenna and Jai, for all of your love. Thank you to Auntie B, who years ago gave me a painting that hung on my wall and made this book possible.

And to my father, Rick Robson. Because of you; always for you.

SOURCES

Stories of Johnny Bower's life have been well documented, ever since he started playing professional hockey back in 1945—and even more so after he joined the Toronto Maple Leafs in 1958. The focus of this biography was to recount many of the familiar tales that helped build the legend of an extraordinary athlete, while providing unique insights into the kind of man—the friend, husband and father—Johnny was. To do that, it was imperative that the sources at the heart of this story be those who knew and loved the man best. For that reason, I'm so grateful for the gracious support of the Bower family in piecing this book together. Interviews with Johnny's wife, Nancy, and his children, Cindy, Barbara and John Jr., are central to the narrative. Further interviews with several of Johnny's grandchildren helped shape a vision of a grandfather in his later years. And interviews with several of Johnny's relatives who've done research on the family's history were key to piecing together details of his youth. In that regard, Johnny's 99-year-old sister, Anne, was remarkably helpful. As were her children, Harold Batting and Susan Batting. Anne's accounts of life in Prince Albert provided colour to a distant memory.

As details tend to shift with the passage of time, sorting through the specifics of Johnny's early life was a particular challenge. I have relied on dates and facts uncovered in primary documents as much as possible. Johnny's military records, requested from Library and Archives Canada by his family, were essential to tracing Johnny's journeys during the war. This narrative also leans heavily on records preserved by Sacred Heart Cathedral in Prince Albert, the Prince Albert Historical Society, the Prince Albert Public Library, the Saskatchewan Provincial Archives, the Saskatchewan Genealogical Society, the Saskatchewan Sports Hall of Fame, the Vernon Museum, the Toronto Public Library, Library and Archives Canada, *Hockey Night in Canada* and the Hockey Hall of Fame. For online research, ancestry.com, newspapers.com, hockey-reference.com and the Toronto Public Library were all very helpful. Ken Guedo of the Prince Albert Historical Society was particularly generous and helpful in providing a sensory understanding of the place where Johnny lived his early life. Subsequent research completed and generously provided by John Chaput, Tom Hawthorn, Eric Zweig, Stephen Smith, Greg Oliver, Bambi Lafferty and Forrest Pass was incredibly helpful. Author and historian Tim Cook provided helpful guidance in understanding military history. The vast collection of content collected and curated by Paul Patskou was invaluable, as is the case for so many projects that centre on hockey history.

Interviews with Johnny's teammates and friends provided a sense of how Johnny was viewed within the brotherhood of hockey players. Discussions with George Armstrong, Bob Baun, Ron Ellis, Red Kelly, Dick Duff, Bob Nevin, Mark Howe and Lou Lamoriello, among many other former NHL players and executives, helped provide a multidimensional view of Johnny as a player. The book is further indebted to conversations with Johnny's friends from throughout his life, from Bob Ochs, with whom he started a lifelong friendship during his first season with the Barons, to Drew Rogers of the Toronto Maple Leafs Alumni Association, who built a strong bond with Johnny despite the six-decade gap in age.

Several books offered a historical perspective and details that helped round out this narrative. Each of the following provided context and content for this book: *The China Wall*, by Johnny Bower with Bob Duff; *'67: The Maple Leafs, Their Sensational Victory, and the End of an Empire*, by Damien Cox and Gord Stellick; *The Toronto Maple Leafs: The Complete Oral History*, by Eric Zweig; *Forest Prairie Edge: Place History in Saskatchewan*, by Merle Massie; *Sawchuk: The Troubles and Triumphs of the World's Greatest Goalie*, by David Dupuis; *Lowering the Boom: The Bobby Baun Story*, by Bobby Baun with Anne Logan; *Heaven and Hell in the NHL*, by Punch Imlach with Scott Young; *Hockey Is a Battle*, by Punch Imlach with Scott Young; *Pal Hal*, by Dick Beddoes; *Leafs '65: The Lost Toronto Maple Leafs Photographs*, by Stephen Brunt; *Forgotten Glory: The Story of Cleveland Barons Hockey*, by Gene Kiczek; *High Sticks and*

Hat Tricks: A History of Hockey in Cleveland, by Gene Kiczek; *Maple Leafs Legends*, by Mike Leonetti; *Canada's Army: Waging War and Keeping the Peace*, by Jack Granatstein; *Maple Leaf Empire: Canada, Britain, and Two World Wars*, by Jonathan F. Vance.

The historical records from newspapers and magazines throughout Johnny's career were essential to providing on-the-spot accounts of what transpired. This book reflects the hard work of newspaper journalists to capture a sense of time and place, preserving it for the future. The following publications were vital to this research: the *Toronto Star*, the *Globe and Mail*, the *Toronto Telegram*, the Cleveland *Plain Dealer*, the *Cleveland Daily News*, the *Prince Albert Daily Herald*, the *Vernon News*, *The Hockey News*, *Hockey Illustrated*, *Blueline* magazine, *Maple Leaf Gardens Official Programme and Sports Magazine* and *Hockey Pictorial*. Sportswriters like Dick Beddoes and Scott Young of the *Globe and Mail* and Jim Proudfoot, Milt Dunnell and Red Burnett of the *Toronto Star* wrote the kind of stories that give life to players beyond the game. I'm indebted to their work and their example. I'm also indebted to Frank Orr and Louis Cauz, both young writers with the *Toronto Star* and *Globe and Mail*, respectively, who covered the later years of Johnny's career. As had their older colleagues, Orr and Cauz wrote rich accounts of the people within the game, as opposed to the minutiae of the game itself. Both sat down with me to discuss their memories of covering Johnny and the Leafs, providing rich, first-hand context on the era from a journalistic perspective. Their work and their time were both a gift.

Prologue: Ledgers in the Closet

The details of Johnny's early years have always been vague, beyond the few, often humorous, stories he told about growing up poor in Prince Albert. The mystery of his birthdate followed him throughout his career, adding to the mystique of his life. To find the earliest account possible of Johnny's life, I travelled with Ken Guedo, of the Prince Albert Historical Society, to Sacred Heart Cathedral— which was the only parish in Prince Albert around the time Johnny could have been born. There, inside a closet, were stacks of ledgers that held the truth about when Johnny's parents had been married and when each of his siblings had been born. With the kind help of the staff at Sacred Heart, we were able to piece together these details, which help set a timeline for Johnny's childhood.

Chapter 1: Branches

The Prince Albert Historical Society has done a remarkable job of preserving the history of one of Saskatchewan's great towns. Ken Guedo, who is a volunteer, took me on a tour of Prince Albert to help me piece together the geography of Johnny's youth. James Kiszkan's homestead was located through Cummins maps of the area, which recorded the land grants. Addresses were located through Henderson's Directories, which indicate who lived at each home. James Kiszkan's journey to Canada was followed through documents obtained by Bambi Lafferty, a relative of Bower's—as well as Forrest Pass, a distant relative and an expert historian, who had spent considerable time tracing his family tree and uncovering the history of the Kiszkan family. Homestead files provided by the Saskatchewan Genealogical Society revealed the details of James Kiszkan's move to the Prince Albert area, what he owned and what he would have needed to do to survive. Further context about homesteading in the Prince Albert area came from *Forest Prairie Edge: Place History in Saskatchewan*, by Merle Massie—in particular chapter 4: "A Pleasant and Plentiful Country."

Memories of Kiszkan family life were provided through interviews with Anne Batting, Johnny's only surviving sibling, as well as other close relatives who requested that they not be named. Details were also taken from interviews Johnny had done about his childhood over the years, including a lengthy one with me for an article in *Sportsnet* magazine. Past interviews with John Chaput and Roland Harris were also very helpful, as was a feature on Johnny's life by Paul Rimstead in the *Winnipeg Free Press* from 1967. Recollections from Cindy Sudeyko and Barbara Bower, Johnny's daughters, provided details of the stories he told his family about his childhood, including the one about his friend getting stuck in a coal chute. Johnny's autobiography, *The China Wall*, written with Bob Duff, gave further first-hand recollections of his childhood.

Chapter 2: Best as a Butcher

The first newspaper accounts of Johnny Kiszkan are found in the *Prince Albert Daily Herald*. The paper is not available online, so the help of Ken Guedo in scouring the paper's microfiche at the Prince Albert Historical Society was essential. Ken uncovered these early references to young Johnny. Further references to hockey in Prince Albert in this chapter were all taken from the *Prince Albert Daily Herald*.

Details about the Canadian war effort were provided by Veterans Affairs Canada, as well as *Canada's Army* by Jack Granatstein and *Maple Leaf Empire* by Jonathan F. Vance. Chapter 6 of *Canada's Army*—"McNaughton's Army: The Long Wait"—was particularly helpful in creating a sense of the feeling and circumstances in Canada leading up to the war. Chapter 5 of *Maple Leaf Empire*—"A New Generation in the Old Country"—gave further details and interesting specifics about young Canadians who volunteered to fight. The details of Johnny's journey to war are outlined in his military records, which were obtained by his daughter, Barbara Bower. They added context to the stories Johnny had told through the years about his time at war, especially about his continual fibbing about his age. These documents also provided a detailed timeline for Johnny's whereabouts during the war.

The Vernon Museum supplied context and details about life in the town during the Second World War. The *Vernon News*, accessed on microfiche from Library and Archives Canada in Ottawa, offered further accounts of the era as well as specific details about Johnny's hockey career while he was training for war. *Rookie* magazine, published in the Vernon Military Camp, was provided by the Vernon Museum.

Chapter 3: Warhawk

Details about Johnny's departure for England, his time spent in training and his subsequent trips to the hospital were found in his military records. Vance's *Maple Leaf Empire* once again provided details and context about Canadians posted in England, including the appendix to the book, which provides a guide for Canadian soldiers there. Johnny's own recollections of his time in the war are outlined in *The China Wall*, although there are several discrepancies within the timeline found in his autobiography and the information provided within his military documents. In regard to Johnny's bout with arthritis, in his autobiography Johnny indicates that when he got older and started playing hockey for a living, he got used to the pain. He said his fingers throbbed constantly, but that was just the way it was. Bobby Haggert, the Leafs' trainer, would bandage up his fingers, especially his middle fingers, before he played.

In regard to Johnny's departure from England, his records give two accounts that appear to interpret the same information differently. While his service record suggests he was back in Regina on January 9, his discharge interview in February suggests he returned on January 1, meaning he would have been travelling at sea during Christmas. There are, however, several mistakes in his discharge interview—including listing his birthdate as November 8, 1921, and his enlistment as November 16, 1942, both of which are false. I defer to the more direct and consistently accurate files here. John Chaput and Eric Zweig first drew my attention to the newspaper accounts of Johnny playing hockey for an all-star team in Prince Albert on January 22, 1944, just a couple of weeks after his return. Details of Johnny's intentions after the war were outlined in his military records. The *Prince Albert Daily Herald* provided accounts of his time with the M&C Warhawks.

Chapter 4: Baron

There is a chance that Johnny was at the Cleveland Barons' training camp in September 1944, as one newspaper record states that he attended in Windsor, Ontario—but there is no subsequent record of that visit. He very well may have been invited after his performance with the Warhawks. Most accounts indicate that the Barons' interest—or at least serious interest—followed Johnny's season of junior hockey with the Prince Albert Black Hawks. Details of Johnny's signing with the Barons came from *The China Wall*, as well as interviews with Roland Harris, John Chaput and Ken Newans. Johnny's crossing into Michigan for training camp was recorded in border crossing records from the time. In that document, Johnny lists his address as 466 9th Street East, Prince Albert—which at the time was the address for Cherry's Northern Insurance. It was a large two-story red-brick house, so it is possible that Johnny was renting a room there. At the border, Johnny told customs officers that he was heading for the Delta Chi Fraternity House in Ann Arbor.

The story of Johnny's isolation on the Barons team came from a later feature in *Hockey Pictorial*. Johnny's name change is legally recorded, with the record available through the Saskatchewan Genealogical Society. Accounts of Johnny's early days with the Barons were taken from reports in the Cleveland *Plain Dealer*, the *Cleveland News* and *Forgotten Glory: The Story of Cleveland Barons Hockey*, by Gene Kiczek. Details were also provided by Bob Ochs, Johnny's lifelong friend whom he met during his rookie season in Cleveland. Reports of Johnny's swap to the Providence Reds were uncovered with the generous help of Lloyd Davis, Bob Duff and Ralph Slate, members of the Society for International Hockey Research. I visited Anne Batting at her long-term-care home in Castlegar, B.C., along with her son, Harold Batting, and daughter, Susan Batting. Over two days, Anne told the story of her life with Johnny and her family.

Chapter 5: What's in a Name?

I spoke with Johnny's nephew Mike Kvasnak a couple of times. First, over the phone in a lengthy interview. Second, in person, while visiting Prince Albert to conduct research for this book. He is a delightfully colourful man, full of great stories—and yes, quick to call out bullshit.

Insight into the stories Johnny told about his own name change came from interviews with Johnny's friends, interviews he had done with other journalists, and stories that had been shared several times in features about Johnny's life. Many stories have also been told about Johnny's brother, Michael. In this case, I defer to Anne Batting's account of her brother's life as she is his only remaining sibling and the most authoritative source on the matter.

Chapter 6: Standing Close

The story of when Johnny met Nancy is based on the version Nancy herself told me during our interviews and that which Johnny recounted for his book, *The China Wall*. The descriptions of the Brain family came directly from Nancy Bower as well. Reports about Johnny's time with the Barons came from *Forgotten Glory:*

The Story of Cleveland Barons Hockey, by Gene Kiczek, the *Cleveland News*, and the Cleveland *Plain Dealer*. Details about Cleveland as a city at the time came from clevelandhistorical.org.

Chapter 7: China Wall

Nancy Bower told me the story of waiting for Johnny to return from Pittsburgh after he was struck in the face with a puck, losing most of his teeth. She expressed her dismay that the team hadn't given him proper care before returning him home—and of waking up next to a pillow covered in blood in the middle of the night, while he was downstairs trying to tend to his own wounds.

The story of how Johnny came to be known as the China Wall was described in his autobiography, *The China Wall*. Johnny's musings over the possibility of finally making it to the NHL came from a *Blueline* magazine feature. Details of Johnny and Nancy's time working with Ken and Jean Turnbull came from Johnny's own recollections as well as a publication called *Waskesiu Memories*, a local history of the area that includes a passage by Ken and Jean Turnbull. Other details about Waskesiu were taken from the same publication.

Johnny's first-hand account of being called up to the Rangers came from *The China Wall*. The version of Johnny's story about learning the poke check from Charlie Rayner came from his interview with Roland Harris in 1985. Nancy Bower expressed her feelings about New York City to me during our interviews. Johnny's feelings about his family, relayed during the birth of his first son, were sentiments repeated by his immediate family and stated by him several times.

Chapter 8: Minors Consolation

The Bower family's journey through the mountains en route to Vancouver was described to me by Nancy Bower. Johnny's recollections of why he was demoted from the Rangers were described by him in his autobiography and several articles. A *Blueline* magazine feature from 1958, when Johnny had joined the Leafs, tells the story of him being at odds with his teammates at times, suggesting that might be the reason he'd taken so long to reach the NHL on a full-time basis. Johnny's feelings about being sent to Vancouver were shared with Roland Harris in their 1985 interview, a transcript of which is on file in the Hockey Hall of Fame archives.

The story of the Bower family meeting and interacting with the Lamoriello family was told to me by Lou Lamoriello in an interview for this book and was also told briefly in Johnny's book, *The China Wall*. The autobiography also told the story of the Boston Bruins considering a trade for Johnny and of the Leafs pursuing him. In-season action came from various newspaper articles, mostly from the *Cleveland News* and the Cleveland *Plain Dealer*. The final section about Nancy and Cindy was taken from our in-person interview at the Bower home.

Chapter 9: Brothers

George Armstrong graciously took the time to speak to me about his good friend Johnny, what he meant to him and what he misses most. Accounts of Johnny's initial concerns about joining the Leafs were documented in several interviews he did, as well as in his autobiography.

Details of the transaction were outlined in the Cleveland *Plain Dealer* and *Cleveland News*. Reports from the *Toronto Star*'s Red Burnett were also very helpful on Johnny's early days with the Leafs. Bob Baun provided context for how he and other teammates saw Johnny—largely as a talented veteran minor-leaguer, with a dubious future because of his age.

The best description of the time and place in which Johnny entered the franchise is found in Damien Cox and Gord Stellick's book '67. They discuss a team in a time of transition. Soon the Leafs would lose their long-time prestigious high school affiliate in St. Mike's, which had been a draw for so many working-class Catholic families in Ontario, offering their children a quality, conservative education away from the mines and farmlands of the rural parts of the province. Other NHL franchises would soon become more aggressive in their efforts to sign Ontario talent, offering higher signing bonuses and other perks. In 1960, the Leafs would pass on an opportunity to sign 12-year-old Bobby Orr, while the Bruins signed him two years later. At the same time, the NHL was moving towards ending the sponsorship of amateur teams and developing a draft that would give all teams better access to young players. By 1969, the NHL's rights system would change completely with the creation of the universal amateur draft—ushering in an era of futility at Maple Leaf Gardens.

Nancy Bower's transition to life in Toronto was shared in a feature written by Margaret Scott in the Leafs' official program and also recounted to me during our interviews. Articles from the *Toronto Telegram*, *Toronto Star* and *Globe and Mail* helped fill in the details about how Johnny's performance on the ice was viewed through his first season with the Leafs. Stories about Johnny being teased came from each of his old teammates interviewed for this book, most notably from Dick Duff, Bob Baun and George Armstrong.

Chapter 10: Grand Old Man

Johnny's humility surrounding whether Diefenbaker would remember him was shared in a *Hockey News* article in November 1959. A short feature in the *Toronto Telegram* in March 1960 told the story of Johnny's postgame waves to Esther Brain. The story was also told in *The China Wall*. Johnny's advice to Frank Mahovlich was shared in a *Toronto Telegram* story by Fred Cederberg in March 1960. Details about Johnny's fitness regimen were shared by Nancy, Cindy and Barbara. The family's investment in a Waskesiu hotel was mentioned in *The Hockey News* in December 1960 and discussed in *The China Wall*. Scott Young of the *Globe and Mail* captured the fun postgame interviews with Johnny and Gump Worsley after the Leafs beat the Rangers in February 1961.

Chapter 11: Champions

The Bower family's babysitter and long-time family friend, Margot Duncan, shared specific details about the family's life on Patika Avenue, as did all three of the Bower children, Barbara, Cindy and John Jr. Details of the reach of *Hockey Night in Canada* at the time were discussed in a paper by Richard Cavanaugh on the development of sports broadcasting in Canada, published in the *Canadian Journal of Communication* in 1992. The interaction between John

Jr. and his father after hockey games at the Gardens was first told by the *Toronto Star*'s Milt Dunnell in December 1961. My interview with John Jr. filled in the rest of the details. The anecdote about John Jr. celebrating the Allan Stanley Cup came from Johnny's own recollections in his foreword to the book *Diary of a Dynasty: 1957–1967*, by Kevin Shea, with Paul Patskou, Roly Harris and Paul Bruno. Various newspaper accounts helped fill in the details about the first Stanley Cup parade in Toronto in more than a decade.

An interesting and important side note: When George Armstrong declared, "For once the Indians came out on top!" into the microphone at the Stanley Cup parade, he did so in a climate in which Indigenous Canadians still weren't viewed as equal citizens in Canada. It wasn't until a month later, on May 22, 1962—with Canada nearly a century old—that Indigenous Canadians were finally given the right to vote in the federal election for the first time.

Chapter 12: Big Fish

A photograph of Gordie and Johnny fishing together in the fall of 1962 was distributed in newspapers across Canada. Howe told the story of how he scored his first goal in a Red Wings sweater in the foreword to *The China Wall*. He also told stories of their time together in Waskesiu in the same passage. Local tales of the two hockey stars in Waskesiu were found in the book *Memories of Waskesiu*, a copy of which is kept at the Prince Albert Historical Society. Mark Howe, Nancy Bower and John Bower Jr. shared stories of family antics at Waskesiu. Concerns that Johnny was washed up were written by the Associated Press, *The Hockey News* and the *Globe and Mail*.

Dick Beddoes of the *Globe and Mail* captured the friendly exchange between Gordie and Johnny on the ice after a key collision as the Leafs faced off against the Red Wings in a heated series. Various newspaper articles filled in the colourful details of the remainder of the Red Wings and Leafs series. The interview with Gordie and Johnny after the Leafs victory came from footage from *Hockey Night in Canada*. Milt Dunnell of the *Toronto Star* captured Johnny's appreciative gesture to the crowd at Maple Leaf Gardens and the scene in the locker room afterwards.

Chapter 13: "Everybody Welcome"

The story of Johnny's 1,000th game was told by Jim Proudfoot in the *Toronto Star*, a couple of weeks after the fact—when Johnny had turned 39 years old, becoming the oldest player in NHL history. The scene outside the Bower home on Halloween was captured by a television crew, likely *Hockey Night in Canada*, although the clip is uncredited.

Stephen Brunt described the fear that Imlach instilled in players when it came to negotiating their salaries, throwing them out at the slightest hint of an agent. Imlach discussed his negotiations with Johnny in his autobiography, and his apparent wish that Bower had asked for more. Imlach also told the story of telling Johnny he still didn't believe his age even after he presented his birth certificate.

Johnny's collision with Ferguson—and the subsequent fallout with Imlach, was recorded in *The China Wall*. The incident was captured by Gord Walker of the *Globe and Mail*. At the time, several newspaper columnists, like Dick Beddoes, took aim at Imlach for how he handled the situation. A CP story from January 1964 captured Milt Schmidt's fun with his "Everybody Welcome" sign at the expense of Imlach, who had banned reporters because of Walker's story on his blow-up with Johnny. It was Walker who first wrote about Imlach's giving his players a copy of *The Power of Positive Thinking* a short time later. Johnny shared the impact the book had on him in *The China Wall*. In his autobiography, Johnny also told the story of his goalie stick striking him on the head for stiches after the Leafs won the Cup. John Jr. shared his memories of his father coming out from the locker room and seeing him on the ice while the Cup celebrations were going on.

Chapter 14: The Odd Couple

Nancy Bower spoke about the decision to finally make Toronto their permanent home and moving away from Saskatoon, as well as the details about Johnny's infrequent contact with his parents. Margot Duncan described her joy at receiving tickets to the Beatles concert through Johnny. David Dupuis's biography of Terry Sawchuk provided details of how Sawchuk came to be a Maple Leaf. Johnny shared his own reaction in *The China Wall*. Sawchuk and Johnny's interactions are a composite of recollections from *The China Wall* and Dupuis's Sawchuk biography. Johnny himself told the story of asking Eddie Shack to injure Sawchuk in practice, as shared in his autobiography. Eric Zweig's oral history of the Maple Leafs provides excellent insight and detail into the race for the Vezina Trophy, shared by Sawchuk and Johnny.

Chapter 15: What's Good for the Goose . . .

Nancy Bower described the process of looking for a new cottage paradise to replace what the family had left behind in Waskesiu. Further details were provided by John Jr., Cindy and Barbara. The conflict between Carl Brewer and Johnny was discussed in Imlach's autobiography as well as *The Power of Two*, by Sue Foster, about Brewer. The tensions in the Leafs' training camp in the fall of 1965 were also discussed in great detail by Stephen Brunt in *Leafs '65*. Brunt also shared the detail of Bing Crosby being in attendance at Maple Leaf Gardens that fall.

Johnny's affinity for singing was described by his children. He told the story of how he came to be involved in "Honky the Christmas Goose" in *The China Wall*. The recording process was described by John Jr. and Nancy Bower. Various newspaper reports told the story of Johnny's success as a star of children's Christmas songs.

The terse exchange between Johnny and Imlach later that season was captured and reported by Dick Beddoes in the *Globe and Mail*. Paul Rimstead wrote about Johnny's turn at coaching in the *Globe and Mail*. Johnny also shared his humorous account in *The China Wall*. Red Burnett reported on Johnny's uncertainty about his future in the *Toronto Star* after the Leafs had been knocked out of the playoffs by Montreal. The awkward negotiations between Johnny and Imlach for his salary were shared in *The China Wall*.

Chapter 16: The Old Fellows Athletic Club

The opening scene of this chapter on the Leafs' 1967 season, with Johnny forgetting to take out his teeth, was captured by Louis Cauz of the *Globe and Mail*. Cauz also reported on Johnny's taking a shot in the hand and breaking his finger in late December. Johnny shared his thoughts on what the sentiment among players on the Leafs roster was like that winter, knowing it was likely their end, in an interview with Roland Harris, obtained through the Hockey Hall of Fame.

Dick Beddoes's columns through the spring of 1967 proved incredibly helpful in bringing colour and detail to this often discussed and written about season. He captured the scene of Johnny once again injuring his finger in practice, threatening his season. Beddoes also wrote about the exchange between Imlach and his goaltender, in which Johnny decides he is not well enough to risk the team's chances at winning with him in net. It was Beddoes who, on April 19, described Johnny's play against the Habs as though he was playing in the "last game for the championship of the universe," as well as the exchange between Johnny and Sawchuk about getting hit in the nose.

Jim Proudfoot of the *Toronto Star* recorded Imlach's awe at Johnny's play and the relaxed atmosphere at practice the next day. Beddoes captured Terry Sawchuk's quiet reaction in the locker room to winning the Stanley Cup. Johnny told the story of stealing the champagne bottles. David Dupuis wrote about Johnny and Sawchuk sitting side by side smoking in the locker room after the win.

Chapter 17: The Last Parade

Details of the '67 parade were collected from a *Globe and Mail* report on the event. Johnny expressed his displeasure at being given only one Stanley Cup ring in *The China Wall*. Further details of Johnny's return for the 1968 season were gleaned from reports in the *Toronto Star* and the *Globe and Mail*. The story of Mahovlich learning he'd been traded from a reporter was told in Eric Zweig's oral history of the Toronto Maple Leafs. Johnny's displeasure at the Mahovlich trade was shared in *The China Wall*. Johnny told Louis Cauz of the *Globe and Mail* that he didn't mind the Leafs fans booing him because they had paid their money and had the right to express their displeasure.

Chapter 18: Time

Johnny discussed his salary in his final seasons with the Leafs in *The China Wall*. He spoke about his hope to play enough to stay sharp, and his new mask saving him from being in Honolulu, with the *Globe and Mail*. Johnny told the story of his final game with the Leafs and his painful decision to finally retire in *The China Wall*. News reports helped fill in the details of the press conference announcing Johnny's retirement. The report that Johnny was back on the ice with the Leafs the next day was taken from a *Globe and Mail* article.

To close out part 3 of this biography, I sat with Bob Baun in his kitchen in Ajax to discuss his memories of Johnny. Baun shared stories of his old friend that made him laugh and stories that made him cry. He provided valuable insight into how Johnny was viewed as a teammate and friend.

Chapter 19: The Extraordinary Ordinary

My interview with Cindy and Barbara in a Tim Hortons west of Toronto opens up this chapter. Their memories carry us through much of the subsequent action, as they recalled what Johnny was like as a father through their adolescence, with his playing days behind him. Johnny recounted his efforts with the Leafs as a scout and goalie coach in *The China Wall*, including his brief firing by Harold Ballard. John Jr. shared stories of his father attending his junior hockey games. Cindy talked about her father attending her skating competitions. Nancy, John Jr., Cindy and Barbara shared stories of the family's time up at the cottage in Bobcaygeon.

Newspaper obituaries provided details about Johnny's parents' later years. A relative who asked not to be mentioned told the story of James Kiszkan's last days. Bambi Lafferty, another relative, shared her extensive research on the family—including the search for Michael Kiszkan. That was backed up and discussed by Anne Batting, the last remaining sibling of the Kiszkan family. Nancy Bower described the distant relationship Johnny had with his younger brother.

Chapter 20: Dusk

The stories in this chapter rely entirely on interviews with Johnny's immediate family. John Jr. provided details of his father's tireless efforts to help out charities he believed in. Barb and Cindy described their father as he moved into the later stages of his life. Interviews with Johnny's grandchildren helped shape the narrative of the iconic hockey player as he became a granddad. In particular, interviews with Staci Sudeyko-Switch and Bruce Bower provided details about family trips to Bobcaygeon to spend time with their grandfather. Nancy Bower told me the story of their last day at the cottage before it was time to go.

Chapter 21: "It Was a Privilege"

Johnny's journey to say goodbye to his old friend Gordie Howe was told to me by Pat Boutette, who made the trip to the funeral in Detroit with him. Johnny's participation with the Maple Leafs—his constant commitment to bringing joy to the fans—was shared by Drew Rogers. Johnny's last game at Air Canada Centre was also described by Rogers. Footage of Johnny's 93rd birthday was provided by Jim Amodeo.

Bob Baun described his last meeting with Johnny. Ron Ellis also shared his recollections of his final interactions with his friend, as well as the "it was a privilege" anecdote, at Johnny's memorial. Father Mark Curtis shared touching stories of his close friendship with Johnny. And the final days of Johnny's life were described to me by his family—Nancy, Cindy, Barbara and John Jr.

The final scene, Johnny's memorial, was recreated through news articles noting the game's dignitaries who came to pay tribute, as well as footage of the pregame ceremony. Nancy Bower described her emotion of feeling empty as the ovation rose but of hearing the "go Leafs go" chant—and clapping hard, one more time, for him.

Epilogue: No Beginning, No End

This chapter is based on the last of several visits with Nancy Bower at the home she and Johnny shared in Mississauga, Ontario. The artifacts described were carefully placed—with love and care—by Johnny and Nancy. They remain in place.